# DIONYSUS

# DIONYSUS

## A SOCIAL HISTORY OF THE
## WINE VINE

EDWARD HYAMS

*with 128 illustrations*
*8 in colour*

THE MACMILLAN COMPANY
NEW YORK

*Dedicated, with love, to*
*Mary and Edward Bacon*

LIBRARY OF CONGRESS CATALOG CARD NO. 65-15581

© THAMES AND HUDSON 1965
FIRST PUBLISHED IN THE USA BY THE MACMILLAN COMPANY 1965
PRINTED IN GREAT BRITAIN

# CONTENTS

# PROLOGUE

PLANTS HAVE BEEN THE MOST IMPORTANT OBJECTS which peoples have borrowed from their neighbours in their business of advancing civilization. All the high civilizations have been built upon cereal grasses, barley, wheat, rice and maize; from three to a score of people can be fed by one man's work in the cultivation of these plants. When first brought from the Andes into the Old World, the potato wrought a series of major economic and social revolutions, and examples of the same kind could be multiplied.

But the case of the grape-vine, *Vitis vinifera*, is a special and peculiar one. Its wine is not a necessity of any people's diet yet it has colonized the greater part of those climatic zones which are congenial to it, and it has done so, very often, to the detriment of the people's essential food supplies. There have been three principal reasons for this.

First, the human condition being what it is, only a very small number of very primitive tribes at the very lowest economic level have failed to develop some intoxicant to help them face the facts of life. Poppy juice, toxic fungi, the dried flowers of a cactus, the leaves of the coca bush are among the most important sources of intoxication. But neither poppy nor mushroom, peyotl or cocaine can compare in economic and social importance with alcohol, which is the most nearly universal as it is the pleasantest and least deleterious of the benign poisons we use to justify God's ways to man. And the wine of the grape has long been the least coarsening medium in which alcohol can be taken and the least liable to dangerous abuse.

Secondly, the strange power of intoxicants to release the human spirit from the control of mind led to their being regarded with superstitious awe and, seized upon by shamans, witchdoctors and priests, they became early and everywhere instruments of religious experience. Their use became a religious rite, and this was the case of wine as of others. In the sixth century B.C., Orphism gave a new, long, and civilized lease of power to the formerly savage and barbarous religion of Dionysus; the use of wine in the rites entered into the later religions of the Mediterranean peoples; and Christianity, by the eucharistic use of wine, borrowed from older cults, carried the religious significance of wine-drinking forward into the two Christian civilizations, the Greek and the Latin. The massive conservatism of these two branches of Christianity accomplished what no other social force could have done—maintained the religious attribute of an intoxicant into a sophisticated technological epoch. This is unique. And the religious necessity for Mass-wine, accompanying the expanding Christian cultures, has been the second powerful force promoting the prosperity of the vine.

Thirdly, the fruitfulness and adaptability of the plant itself, *Vitis vinifera*, the wine-vine, and the two great needs mentioned above, have made the planting of vineyards very apt to enrich the planter. In suitable, and sometimes even rather unsuitable climates, and excepting in certain economic conditions which have been rather rare, the cash yield per acre-man-hour of viticulture has nearly always been from three to ten times as great as that from any other kind of farming or gardening.

But if these three forces, spleen, religion, and profit, have succeeded in covering so considerable an area of the planet's surface with vineyards, why have they not carried the vine even further? The spread of the vineyards is clearly limited. There are, in fact, two forces working against the vine, one natural, the other social.

Although, as explained in Chapter I, the vine is a plant adaptable past comparison with any other, and by its adaptability now diversified into literally thousands of varieties, yet there are climatic limits to its successful cultivation. It is hardy against cold, but not beyond a certain low limit; it will stand great heat, yet it is a deciduous plant and therefore cannot be grown properly in the tropics, and it could not cross them to reach its second home in the south temperate zone, until man helped it to do so. The typical tropical fruit-tree is an evergreen, and the typical tropical process of flowering and setting fruit is continuous, not seasonal, as anyone knows who has grown oranges. But the temperate-zone fruit-tree—apple, pear, peach, grape-vine—is deciduous; it burgeons, flowers and matures its fruit between spring and autumn; and, at the same time, it forms those buds in the leaf-axils which bear, *in potentia*, the following year's crop. Since plants of this kind evolved to cope with winter conditions, these buds have to be held back and not allowed to burgeon until winter is over: the phenomenon is called 'bud dormancy' and it is ensured by another phenomenon called 'apical dominance'—growth of the plant is concentrated in the apices and while these grow, the axillary buds will not. The apices do not stop growing until the whole plant enters dormancy at leaf-fall. What the plant then 'expects' is a period of rest, of cold more or less prolonged, say not less than six weeks at not more than 45 degrees Fahrenheit. Unless this dose of cold is received the plants may not 'break dormancy' properly. In the course of the last World War many English vineries had their glass broken by bombs and were neglected; for the first time in their lives, hot-house vines all over the country received a fair dose of cold, with prolonged freezing. As a result, post-war crops of grapes in such houses as were repaired were extraordinarily fine. Another difficulty with deciduous plants in hot climates is that they may never enter dormancy properly; they make an effort to turn into ever-greens, and fail to bear any fruit at all. When the French grew grapes at Pondicherry they had to remove the leaves by hand every year.

All plants respond, moreover, in various ways to length-of-day: as an example, strawberry plants are so very sensitive to this influence that a difference of 2 degrees of latitude will turn a variety fruitful at A, fruitless at B and producing, instead of flower-bud, an excess of stolon-bud. Although grape-vines are less sensitive, nevertheless their correct behaviour depends upon day-length differences from one season to the next, differences which do not exist at the equator and which are very small in low latitudes: a species native to about 40 degrees will be upset and fail to function properly if transplanted to 20 degrees, even though the climatic change be compensated by much higher altitude. Flower-bud formation is much more dependent upon these factors of seasonal change of temperature and day-length than is growth-bud, so that a vine shifted through many degrees of latitude may continue to grow quite well, but may become unfruitful.

The natural habitat of *Vitis vinifera* is in highlands between 40 degrees and 45 degrees latitude North. Lines delimiting the habitats of species are, of course, iso-lines, if there is such a word, that is they are the averages of figures varying in both space and time; and like the words 'genus' and 'species' they represent formal, imaginary, not real categories. But still they are valuable in representing norms of behaviour or of morphology. Now clearly, to transplant a species from 45 degrees to, say, 51 degrees latitude North involves much less of a change for it than to transplant it from 40 degrees to 25 degrees. And consequently the southward expansion of viticulture within the northern hemisphere (or the northward expansion within the southern hemisphere) is more difficult than the reverse process: the vine can be grown in sub-arctic conditions, for example in parts of Canada and Siberia. In the tropics, it is hopeless.

In the northern hemisphere, the southernmost of the very ancient vineyards was at Meroë in Egypt (perhaps, rather, Ethiopia). At a later date, the Phocaean colonists of present-day Morocco planted vines as far south as Cape Spartel, which, indeed, became known as the Vine Cape (Ampelusia). Not even the Carthaginians were ever able to plant further south. In the fifteenth century Prince Henry the Navigator, of Portugal, caused vineyards to be planted in Madeira, thus becoming the originator of one of the world's great wines; somewhat later vines were transplanted thence to the Canary Islands, and the vineyards of Hierro at about 27 degrees 45 minutes North are the most southerly in the northern hemisphere. Probably some of the ancient vineyards of the Punjab and of Kashmir were about the same latitude, more or less, but in them great altitude did something to help the vines. If we had to state a line south of which it was useless to plant the vine in the northern hemisphere, then we should call it 30 degrees North. That, then, is one of the geographical limits to viticulture.

There is no known northern limit to viticulture. The breeding of more and more *hâtif* varieties of the vine, varieties able to get very quickly through the whole process from burgeoning to vintage, makes possible very northerly planting; wherever, indeed, there is a short, hot summer. The only other limiting influence is cold; where temperature falls regularly and for prolonged spells below minus 20 degrees Centigrade, many vines will be killed unless protected, for example by being completely buried before the cold sets in. But there is another factor: at a certain latitude it becomes uneconomic to grow vines, whose vintage must compete with that of more southerly vineyards. The practical limit is, therefore, about 51 degrees North.

Now it is self-evident that there are very large tracts of the world between 30 degrees and 51 degrees North and between 30 degrees and 51 degrees South where there are no vineyards. There are indeed, particularly in Asia, many thousands of square miles of perfect vineyard land in perfect vineyard climates, where grapes are hardly grown at all, and then only for dessert fruit or dried fruit. It seems that the wine-vine is excluded from some parts of the world which would be congenial to it by influences other than climatic or geographical. These influences are subtler: they are social, almost religious. There are those who are people of the vine; and others, simply, are not; and the curious facts touching the repeated introduction of the vine into China, described in Chapter VIII, bear out this contention. The wine-vine is very much a plant of Mediterranean man: it is a part of the Mediterranean cultures; it is deeply involved in their religions, both ancient and modern; for even the positive, the conscious rejection of wine by ancient peoples of the vine under the influence of Islam is a negative involvement very different from the total indifference of the Chinese or the merely commercial interest of the Japanese. There are, in short, peoples whose culture has never included the vine and which have rejected it when offered; and this is the other limit set to the expansion of the vineyards.

European man overran the whole planet; he has now withdrawn or is withdrawing from parts of it, leaving them again to the older cultures which already possessed them and were fossilized, or to any new ones which may arise. Curiously, the places he has withdrawn from are those where the vine, too, was hopelessly alien; and the places he has made permanently his own are places where the vineyards have flourished. One might almost regard *Vitis vinifera* as his peculiar hallmark; and in his new absence one would expect to find it lingering only among those people who have taken something fundamental from Mediterranean culture, the Christian religion for example. For, Lord Snow notwithstanding, the Western type of tool-making, called 'Science' and now oecumenical, while a part of a culture in the archaeological sense of the word, is not fundamental to culture in our sense here: a Chinese may accept our nuclear physics; he rejects our poetry, our music and our wine-vine. There is a curious sentimental illusion, fostered by liberals, that though the minds of men may differ, the heart is the same everywhere; the curious history of the association between men and grape-vines is part of the evidence that the converse may be true.

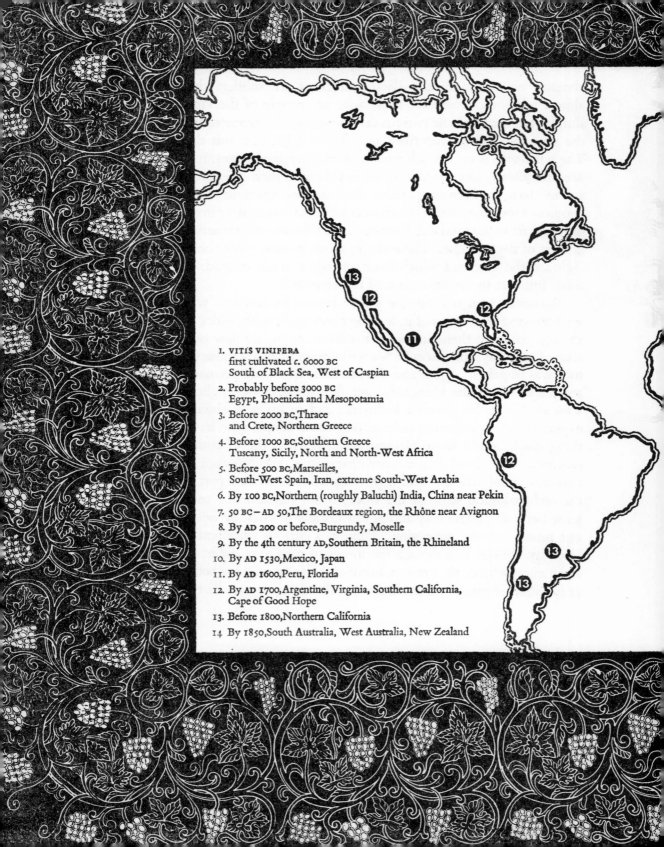

1. **VITIS VINIFERA**
   first cultivated *c.* 6000 BC
   South of Black Sea, West of Caspian

2. Probably before 3000 BC
   Egypt, Phoenicia and Mesopotamia

3. Before 2000 BC, Thrace
   and Crete, Northern Greece

4. Before 1000 BC, Southern Greece
   Tuscany, Sicily, North and North-West Africa

5. Before 500 BC, Marseilles,
   South-West Spain, Iran, extreme South-West Arabia

6. By 100 BC, Northern (roughly Baluchi) India, China near Pekin

7. 50 BC – AD 50, The Bordeaux region, the Rhône near Avignon

8. By AD 200 or before, Burgundy, Moselle

9. By the 4th century AD, Southern Britain, the Rhineland

10. By AD 1530, Mexico, Japan

11. By AD 1600, Peru, Florida

12. By AD 1700, Argentine, Virginia, Southern California,
    Cape of Good Hope

13. Before 1800, Northern California

14. By 1850, South Australia, West Australia, New Zealand

# CHAPTER I

# *Origins and Early Practice of Viticulture*

THE ORIGINS OF VITICULTURE are so remote in time that nothing certain can be known concerning them: the Russian authorities on the subject believe that the craft began in about 8000 B.C., which seems improbably early. The earliest evidence of any sort of agriculture consists of remains of reaping-hooks dug up at Wadi el Natuf in Palestine, which had, as is known by the kind of polishing received by the microlithic cutting edges in the course of use, been employed to cut some sort of ripe grain. Whether this grain was cultivated or wild is not certain. There is, however, some reason to think that horticulture is older than cericulture: both in the New and in the Old World, farming probably began with fruits and roots, rather than with grass seeds.

During the Palaeolithic epoch man had subsisted by hunting and gathering wild food, and in some places had done so well out of this business that it was possible to create a high aesthetic culture, manifest not only in the perfection reached by stone tools and weapons, but in such cave drawings as those of Lascaux and La Madeleine. A change in climate, followed by the spread of forests which clothed the tundras and drove out the great herds of game animals, entailed first a change in hunting and gathering patterns, the large Palaeolithic communities giving way to the smaller and less civilized Mesolithic ones: and, later, the Neolithic revolution, with man stepping outside the order of nature, ceasing to be a hunting animal, and becoming, slowly but steadily, a cultivator. This revolution must have begun in regions where wild vegetable foods were plentiful, for example where the date-palm flourished along the banks of the River Euphrates, or at those points in Breasted's 'fertile crescent' which extended from west North Africa, along the shores of the Mediterranean, by way of Palestine and Phoenicia to northern Syria and east to the lower valley of the Tigris–Euphrates system. At various places in this fertile crescent occurred the wild ancestors of the principal cereal grasses and many of the fruit-trees.

The vine of history, *Vitis vinifera sativa* (*plate I*), is a cultivated version, or, as it is technically called, a *cultivar*, of *Vitis vinifera silvestris*. The genus *Vitis* belongs to the natural order *Vitaceae* of which four genera bear edible fruits.[1] The genus is divided into two subgenera: the *Euvites*, including the greater number of species; and the *Muscadiniae*, with only three species.[2]

There are in all between forty and fifty species of true grape-vines, native to Europe (one only), Asia (about twelve) and North America (about thirty-five).

The genus *Vitis* has a much longer history than man. The earliest representative yet discovered is the fossil species *V. sezannensis*, which flourished in the sub-tropical forests of what is now eastern France during the Lower Eocene epoch. At that time mankind had not, of course, been heard of: the greater mammals were still engaged in imposing themselves as the dominant animal type. As the northern hemisphere became even warmer, the vines retreated northward, to populate regions still covered, in our own time, with ice, but of these no remains have yet been discovered. It seems, however, that one or more species of this vine were to be found in the region of north-east Asia/north-west America when the gulf of the Atlantic was opening to divide that land-mass into two continents nearly joined by the natural bridge of the now Bering Strait. This split the *Vites* into two races, an American race and a Eurasian race. Since, as will appear, these two races faced different conditions of geography and climate, they began to evolve along slightly different lines; and this evolution may have been quite well advanced by the beginning of the Holocene, or recent, epoch, when it again becomes possible to study species.

The fossil remains of vines of the earlier millennia of this epoch all belong to a morphological class which botanists, or some botanists, call *Labruscoidae*. At the reappearance of vines sufficiently far south to be found today in places clear of ice and so subject to examination by palaeobotanists, species[3] still favoured this ancient Labruscoid form.[4]

It is interesting that the Lower Miocene species probably belonged to the subgenus *Muscadinia*, or rather were apparently morphologically indistinguishable from the species which are now so classified. The fact may, and perhaps must, mean that the climatic conditions in which they flourished were the same as that of the Gulf of Mexico countries in our own time; the vines that had reached as far south as those countries, in America, were apparently not required to evolve any further in order to survive. This movement towards the south occurred in both continents as the climate provoked it by changing. But whereas in America the geological folding of the earth's crust was mainly along a north-to-south line, so that the vines encountered no mountain obstacle in their slow spread southward, in Eurasia the case was different: geological folding was mainly from east-to-west, so that high mountains barred the southern migration of the vines. These different conditions had important effects.

Labruscoid forms could not survive in the increasingly harsh conditions of the north; only those which had reached far to the south found an environment to which they were adapted. It is for this reason that the three *Muscadina* species of our time most closely resemble the ancient Labruscoid vines. But vines did not become extinct in the north of America; they evolved, adapted themselves, and in due course gave rise to those species of northern habitat which are classified as *Viniferae* as distinct from *Labruscoidae*. These northern American species more closely resemble the Eurasian ones, for the good reason that they were forced to evolve along similar lines in order to survive.

In Eurasia it was much more difficult for vine populations to spread southward because of the mountain barriers. Probably many more individuals of the vine population perished. Fewer species evolved, but the evolution went further. All Eurasian species now living are Euvites. But not all are the most advanced, *Viniferae*. There are, in northern India and China, species which remain Labruscoid in form.

The process of change, away from the primitive Labruscoid forms towards the modern *Viniferae*, can be traced in a series of intermediate species occurring towards the end of the Miocene epoch. Found as a fossil on the warm southern slopes of the Massif Central in France, *Vitis proevinifera* is near-Labruscoid in form; morphologically further removed from the primitive is *V. takayensis*: next in the series is *V. salyorum*. And at last, by the end of the Pliocene, came *V. vinifera*, by which time man, too, was in being as *Homo pekinensis*.[5]

The genus *Vitis*, then, as it emerged into the settled condition of the recent epoch, comprised two subgenera including about fifty species distributed from California eastward to Japan, and between the 30th and 50th parallels of latitude North. Originating in the northern hemisphere, and unable to cross the torrid zone, the genus remained confined to the northern side of the equator until carried across it by man. A botanical description of this genus and a list of its species will be found in the Appendix. Of that list only one, *Vitis vinifera*, will occupy us in the first chapters of this book, for no other species became of any economic importance until the seventeenth century, or of great importance until the nineteenth.


As one of the first plants to be domesticated by man, the grape-vine[6] is of particular interest. It has, as it were, been in partnership with mankind for many thousands of years in the task of imposing order upon chaos, the garden upon the wilderness. Whether civilization, culture, is, indeed, anything more than a fortuitous by-product of horticulture might be an interesting question; but I will not discuss it here. What we have to establish is, where and when did man and vine come together in conditions favourable to the development of a partnership between them for the forwarding of civilization? Having done that to the best of our ability, we can then glance at the earliest viticultural techniques in ancient Babylonia, and, more thoroughly, in ancient Egypt.

The happy union in question antecedes the rise of urban civilizations in Mesopotamia and Egypt, India and China, and by so much that no documents of any sort are available and we are forced back on speculative reasoning which hostile critics might characterize as guesswork: it is, we hope, a good deal more than that.

The Neolithic revolution was taking place between eight and ten thousand years ago: it expressed itself in several ways: by the rise of a new stone-chipping industry and style, for instance; and by the invention of the first arts of husbandry, horticulture, later followed by agriculture and stock-raising. With the latter we are not here concerned, but the beginning of horticulture was, in some places, probably the beginning of viticulture, and the vine, like the date-palm, is one of the oldest garden plants.

It is probable, in fact more or less certain, that in Palaeolithic and Mesolithic communities, while the men hunted, the women gathered such foods as fruit, grass seeds, esculent leaves and roots, and perhaps grubs. And it was the women who dressed the food, of whatever kind. It was therefore a woman who first came to the help of some favourite fruit shrub, clearing the other plants away from its roots, thus making the first distinction between weeds and economic plants, and doing the first act which can properly be called gardening. There can be very little doubt that it was a woman who, having carelessly thrown away a few grains of wild barley or wheat at the bottom of some vessel, on to a patch of ground trodden into mud by her tribesmen and women, saw seedlings spring up, and conceived the immensely important idea of planting and cultivating such grasses, instead of merely collecting them in the wild: the fundamental inventions of mankind are equally shared between the sexes: to women probably belong agriculture and pottery and weaving; to men stock-raising, stone-chipping and metallurgy.

Reaping is an older craft than ploughing and sowing. The people of Wadi el Natuf had sickles but no hoes.[7] Tools for gathering the wild harvest thus come before tools for cultivating, but it may be assumed that the possession even of reaping tools marked an advance, and that among people who had such tools there would have been curious and enterprising spirits capable of the notion of planting a garden, a farm.

Among many species of essentially carnivorous animals the eating of a certain amount of vegetable food is common: everyone has watched a cat eat grass, and some carnivorous bears are fond of fruit, and go out in late summer to gorge themselves on wild berries. No doubt several kinds of nourishment are thus absorbed into their systems, but what attracts them is sugar. Ripe cereal grains are sweet, but not only is ripe fruit much sweeter, it is much more striking, much more obviously attractive from its size, colour and fragrance. Food-collecting Palaeolithic women, and indeed food-collecting sub-humans or super-apes of an epoch prior to man's first attempt at making tools, must surely have been attracted to fruits long before they discovered the food value of grass seeds.

Fruit then, both berries and drupes, would have been food for proto-mankind before the first stone tool had been chipped or the first fire lit by *Homo pekinensis*. It is entirely possible that wine, a spontaneous product of ripe fruit, and especially of ripe grapes, is older than Neolithic culture. As soon as women had some sort of vessel, first of wicker and later of earthenware or clay, they would surely have stored or tried to store surplus gatherings of fruit. It is, I feel, virtually certain that when the first notion of cultivating food plants occurred to some or to several primitive females, grapes, in certain localities, had long been eaten, long been kept at least for some days.

The great majority of edible fruits grow in singles or small clusters which are, in the wild state, relatively insignificant. But wild grapes, though the bunches are small by cultivated standards, hang down in thyrsus clusters of great beauty; they are striking and tempting, so that they would have received particular attention from food gatherers among communities fortunate enough to be living where vines could grow. Moreover the power of the vine to accumulate sugar is very remarkable; grapes are among the sweetest fruits and wild grapes may contain as much as twenty-five per cent of their substance as sugar. Finally they are juicier than most fruits, and therefore attractive to the thirsty in the thirst-provoking climate which they favour.

If a gatherer of wild grapes found herself with more than her family could at once consume, she would either hang the surplus clusters up, out of reach of children and animals, in which case, in a sub-tropical climate, they would dry and become raisins; or she would put them into a vessel, and if the vessel happened to be of clay rather than wicker, so that the juice of any crushed or bruised fruit could accumulate, the grapes would begin to ferment, since yeasts are present in the bloom on the skins of all wild grapes. As any housewife in a warm country knows, you cannot leave a bowl of fruit-juice twenty-four hours but it ferments. The tumultuous fermentation of ripe grapes breaks down the solid structure of the fruit even if crushing and bruising has been only partial, and all the juice is liberated. Sooner or later some thirsty member of a food-gathering community, not long after the first invention of pottery, would have taken a drink from a vessel which, two or three days earlier, had contained grapes, but which *now* contained —wine.

The behaviour of the drinker, of this primal inebriate, might first have been taken for some kind of demonic possession; it would have been supposed that some divine afflatus had entered into him. And, as every wine-lover knows, this supposition would have been correct. Cause and effect would, in due course and rather laboriously, have been connected; and wine, thereafter, deliberately made from the wild vintage.

It was, I believe, in some such manner that wine came to be discovered and the grape, long valued as a refreshing food, appreciated at its true and incalculable worth.

There are a number of places in the world where this could have happened, and where it could have been followed by the cultivation of the vine, first by assisting it in its natural habitat, later by transplanting it. It will be as well to begin by eliminating the places where it could not have happened, and then those where it could have happened but did not. Since no vines grew south of the equator until men took them there, we can discount the southern hemisphere. The cultivation of the vine was unknown in the Far East until the second century B.C. (see Chapter VIII) and in the Americas until the sixteenth century A.D., in both cases introduced from Eurasia. We are left with approximately the world as it was known to the third-century Greeks. We can eliminate one habitat of the wild vines—northern India, since we know that the native vines were never brought into cultivation. The Fertile Crescent, at least from Tunis to the Persian Gulf and north to the latitude of about Aleppo, apparently had no wild vines in association with relatively advanced human communities. We are left, excluding climatically unsuitable regions, with Transcaucasia, the region south of the Black Sea, Turkey, the Balkans, France and Italy, in all of which countries *V. vinifera silvestris* was represented.

The introduction of viticulture to Greece is prehistoric and conjectural, but sufficiently capable of being recalled to make it certain that it *was* introduced and was not native. As to the Western European countries, the introduction of viticulture is so much later that it falls in historical times. These countries definitely received wine and vine from the east. Turkey, Thrace, Macedonia cannot be eliminated in this manner, but their inhabitants, at the time in question, were almost certainly not in a condition to devise and carry out a settled form of husbandry, although, as will appear hereafter, they were capable of learning viticulture at a rather later date. There remain Transcaucasia and the southern littoral of the Black Sea.

The next part of the evidence concerns the vine itself. The cultivated vine of the Old World can have derived only from the sub-species *silvestris*, which has been established in the countries indicated, that is the Balkans, Transcaucasia and most of Western Europe, since Tertiary times. The earliest urban civilizations were those of Mesopotamia and the Nile valley because these regions, by favouring agriculture and stock-raising in primitive conditions and with primitive tools, enabled their inhabitants to pile up surplus wealth more rapidly than the peoples of other parts. Both ancient Babylonia

and ancient Egypt had an advanced viticulture by, and probably considerably before, 3000 B.C. As neither of them had any wild vines, they must have
acquired both plants and the art of cultivating them elsewhere. Or they
may have had wine and vines from beyond their frontiers, but devised for
themselves ways of cultivating vineyards.

If we suppose that the peoples who had taken possession of the Tigris–
Euphrates plain and delta, the proto-Sumerians coming from the north-east
and the Semites from the south and west, were most forward in agriculture,
as they must have been since they were certainly most forward in civilization, then Mesopotamia was a centre of diffusion of the agricultural and
horticultural arts. To the north of Mesopotamia were less advanced peoples,
perhaps kindred of the Sumerians, inhabiting, like the wild vines, the hilly
country of ancient Armenia, Georgia and Azerbaijan. Great cities such as
Ur of the Chaldees and Kish of the Sumerians were already flourishing in
Mesopotamia by about the middle of the fourth millennium B.C. We must
allow a very long period of tribal, village life before this, to give time for
the accumulation of wealth, techniques and social systems able to support an
advanced civic life, an expensive religion and military forces, and wide mercantile enterprise. Agriculture and stock-raising must have been well advanced and a civilized village life like that of pre-Moghul India well established by, say, 5500 B.C. and probably a good deal earlier. In that case it is
not unreasonable to suppose that by 4000 B.C. at latest the hill people to the
north of Mesopotamia had learnt a good deal from their southern neighbours,
enough perhaps to be practising a settled agriculture in their fertile valleys,
and to be bringing the wild vine, which had long been a source of wine, into
cultivation.

This relationship between a hill people to the north and a more advanced
people in a river system of alluvial flood soil to their south is repeated in
India, and that by people akin to the Sumerians. The civilized village or
township communities of Baluchistan, according to what has been revealed
concerning them by Sir Aurel Stein and later scholars and archaeologists, may
actually have been ahead of their neighbours in Sindh and the Punjab who
created, in the Indus valley, the great urban civilization of Mohenjo-daro
and Harappā. If that had been the case, however, with Mesopotamia and
Armenia, then the people who came down and took possession of Mesopotamia after the rivers had made it out of mud would have been relatively

advanced, whereas archaeology has revealed in various parts of that country the whole process of the evolution of agriculture and settled living, from the most elementary beginnings. It is probable that the ancient Armenians, Georgians and Azerbaijanis learnt cultivation from the south.

It is well known that man triumphs over his fellow species on this planet by failing to specialize; by, as it were, specializing in not specializing, and thereby remaining immensely flexible. Among vegetables, and certainly among woody, fruit-bearing plants, the vine has, within the limits of its vegetable nature, this attribute of flexibility to a marked degree. If a true clone of any variety of the vine be established, so that each individual originating in a cutting from a single parent vine is virtually a fragment of a single plant, and if, thereafter, individuals of that clone be taken away and planted in a great number and variety of soils and microclimates, then each individual will, at least to some extent, adapt itself to its new environment, and acquire new habits more suited to its new habitat. There are, of course, strict limits beyond which the vine is not adaptable; but for a plant its flexibility of character is remarkable.

It should be made clear, lest the author be suspected of excessive 'Lysenkism', that this power of the vine to respond to local conditions by changing its habits does not entail any fundamental change, any permanent alteration in its nature. The matter is expressed by biologists in the following way: the differences observed in diverse individuals of a single clone are no more than fluctuations about an average type: the vine can modify the *phenotype* by responding to local conditions, but it cannot modify the *genotype* in this way, it cannot change the hereditary potentialities of the clone.[8]

'*La vigne est une plante qui réagit d'une façon remarquable à l'action du milieu. L'étude de ces réactions est en quelque sorte le fondement de la viticulture traditionelle. On sait, par exemple, que la seule modification de la taille peut faire varier dans d'importantes proportions la quantité et la qualité de la vendange, et des relations de nature mathématique ont pu être mises en evidence entre plusieurs des modifications apportées à la culture de la vigne, et le résultat de ces modifications sur la production; aussi a-t-on pu parler d'un véritable déterminisme de la qualité ou de la quantité de la production chez la vigne.*'[9]

From this passage it will be obvious that primitive man, as a gardener, when he came to lift the vine from its woodland habitat and plant it on hillsides or in the fertile valleys, had fortunately chosen an object for his work eminently capable of surviving his novice attempts at domesticating the plant.[10]

Not only, however, does the vine respond rapidly to environment, adapting itself, within wide limits, to new conditions, and yielding a superior crop to the clever vine-dresser. It is more than usually prone, by comparison with other fruit plants, to spontaneous changes in its nature, to the phenomenon known as the bud sport or bud mutation, from which derive new clones, or rather new varieties; new, this time, in the fundamental sense, since in this case there is a modification of the genotype, and not merely a fluctuation among individuals about a genotypical norm.[11]

The cause of bud mutations is unknown although it can now be provoked in certain plants. Certain points about this problem do, however, seem to be tolerably well established: varieties or clones which are stable in country where they have been long established, become prone to bud mutations when planted in new soils and new climates; such mutations occur more frequently when the change in climate and nourishment and methods of cultivation is considerable, even extreme; a mutation-prone variety will repeat the same sport over and over again, as if the change it can make in itself is of one order only, limited, no doubt, by the permutations and combinations of characters possible to its particular genetic organization.

That bud mutation in vines is relatively commonplace is very well established.[12] Cazalis-Allut in his *Œuvres* (page 353) records: '*J'ai greffé, il y a plusieurs années, un cep*[13] *de "Terret" en "Epiran gris". Ce cep, taillé en chaine, a aujourd'hui 12 mètres de longueur. Les six premiers mètres font constamment des raisins gris, et le restant du cep, jusqu'à son extrémité, des raisins blancs.*' From a cutting taken anywhere beyond the sixth metre of this vine, Cazalis-Allut could, of course, have built up a clone of *Epiran blanc*, for the new attributes of such mutants are stable unless and until a new mutation occurs. M. Levadoux notices a case of Gamay vines, several individuals, normally bearing black grapes, which produced branches bearing white grapes. That several individuals were involved strengthens the hypothesis that soil or climate or both factors common to all the affected vines were the cause of the mutation. L. Ravaz has given an account[14] of the appearance, in Australia, of a Super-Gros Colman, doubtless a polyploid. The most spectacular of fairly recent mutations of this kind, however, was perhaps that which was responsible for the variety *Sultanina gigas*. This giant Sultanine, says Levadoux, was noticed by Bioletti in 1918, but its origin as a bud sport was not established until 1920, when L. F. Arnold of Mercedes, California, discovered, on a plant of ordinary Sultanine, a single branch with the character of Giant Sultanine.[15] Subsequently this polyploidal mutation was repeated elsewhere in California, this time by a number of individuals of the variety.

In my own small vineyard a single plant of fifty Seibel 13,053, which bears black grapes, once produced a branch which bore white grapes. They were of inferior quality—and in this connection it should be noted that most mutations of this kind are either economically useless or even retrogressive: the valuable mutation is very rare.

Examples could be multiplied: seedless varieties have produced themselves in this way, and mutations affecting every organ of the vine, although absolutely rare, are relatively common. The point as it affects our argument here is that this proneness to mutation, which the vine must have shown quite as frequently in prehistoric times as today, was another quality making the plant peculiarly suitable as an object of cultivation for men who were making beginnings in horticulture; a quality, moreover, which made the vine very easy to transplant and which, therefore, was of use in the diffusion of new crafts from some centre of origin outwards to the rising agricultural communities within a wide geological and climatic range.

Finally, might not this attribute, this tendency for sudden and spontaneous if rare production of different and often superior fruit, have appeared to the primitive horticulturist to be extremely strange? Far stranger, surely, even than the production, by seedling vines, of new and better kinds of fruit which would have followed the inbreeding of vines transplanted to the fertile oases of early agrarian settlements, remote from the habitat of wild vines. This inbreeding, a result of the isolation of clones, would, by the accumulation of recessive characters, have also produced new varieties, but in a fashion less 'miraculous' than bud mutation which the primitive cultivator, an animist, must have attributed to the active goodwill of the plant. The vine had doubtless been a god long before that; or at least conceived of as animated by a demon, and here was confirmation of this theory, here was the earth mother, or her son, visibly at work in the service of mankind. Where the women of the tribe had yesterday, or last season, dressed a vine which bore small, black grapes, they found themselves today, or this season, dressing that same vine which now however bore larger grapes, sweeter grapes, grapes of a different colour. Such a plant was clearly animated by spirit, was divine.

Of the very great antiquity of the cultivated vine we shall treat hereafter, but one aspect of that story belongs here, in the natural history of the vine.

Vines being dioecious, the flowers are unisexual. Nevertheless, individuals occur with hermaphrodite flowers, although they are rare in the wild populations. On the other hand the overwhelming majority of cultivated varieties bear only hermaphrodite flowers, and that form is, indeed, almost a condition of cultivation, since the crop would otherwise be very unreliable. The female vine flowers are equipped with short and deformed stamens bearing infertile pollen. The male flowers bear a short and deformed pistil normally incapable of being fertilized. But it sometimes happens in nature that these stamenate flowers possess a well-constituted pistil capable of fecundation; such are the original hermaphrodites among vines, and the origin of the hermaphroditism of cultivated varieties.

A perfect flower of this order consists of a calyx formed of five sepals joined together throughout their length, and a corolla of five petals also joined together, either completely or at the top, separating from each other where they join the calyx. The corolla thus forms a cap completely enclosing the other organs of the flower until, at the maturity of the blossom, the cap falls in the shape of a minute star of withered petals, a *capuchon* as the French call it, leaving the vital organs exposed. These consist of five stamens opposed to the petals and five nectaries about the ovary, pistil and stigma being in the form of a minute urn. When the cap of petals has fallen the stamens reach out away from the ovary in the form of a star or fringe (*plate I*).

The flowers do not depend upon insects for pollination. If the pollen becomes ripe in hot, dry weather, the pollen sacs burst, and the pollen hovers as a small cloud of particles about the cluster, so that every stigma receives some grains. In damp, cool weather this does not happen, and fecundation depends on the fall of pollen through the cluster as it separates from the stamens.[16]

Such are the hermaphrodite flowers of the vine, very rare among wild populations, overwhelmingly the rule among cultivated vines. How has this change come about? The genetic conditions are such that it could not have happened in nature that a population of wild vines should have been predominantly hermaphrodite;[17] it follows that the hermaphroditism of cultivated vines is a product of artificial selection.

If a population of wild vines, or cuttings from them, had been planted by some prehistoric gardener, he would have noticed that some vines bore no fruit at all (males), some bore much or little, unreliably and uncontrollably (females), and that a third class—the vines with a proportion of hermaphrodite flowers—always bore some fruit and could be regarded as reliable. The gardener, if a sensible man, would have chosen the first class for destruction, the third for propagation. But the male vines being grubbed and destroyed, the females would have received less pollen than before, and the crop from them would have fallen, showing up the hermaphrodite vines even more clearly as the most useful class. Thus, in subsequent rogueing of the vineyard, the female vines would have been eliminated and the hermaphrodite propagated until only this last class was left. Seedling vines of a uniquely hermaphrodite population would be about 87·5 per cent hermaphrodite (see note 17); moreover the degree of hermaphroditism, the proportion of hermaphrodite to unisexual flowers, would have been constantly increased.

From experience of my own with certain imperfectly hermaphrodite cultivated varieties (such as Muscat Hamburgh) I do not believe that viticulture on any considerable scale would have been possible, or rather profitable, even for subsistence crops until the vast majority of vineyard subjects was hermaphrodite. Moreover, in the earliest records of viticulture from Mesopotamia, Egypt and Palestine, we hear nothing of barren vines, nor do any of the classical writers refer to such vines, nor to what would have been a necessity, the planting of a proportion of male plants in every vineyard. It seems at least highly probable that by the time of our earliest records of viticulture, the transformation of the wild dioecious vine into the cultivated hermaphrodite vine had been achieved, and perhaps for a long time. Yet even the earliest records seem to imply a large-scale and expert viticulture possessed of craft traditions: by 2400 B.C. the planting of vineyards had become an advanced trade. It seems to follow that the origins of viticulture are very remote indeed.

I come now to what is only partly a digression, a scheme of classification of the cultivated vines of the Old World, devised by A. M. Negrul of the Leningrad Institute of Applied Botany, in the course of establishing which he revealed a good deal concerning the evolution and places of origin of the varieties in question.[18] Negrul believes that the cultivated ssp. *sativa* DC is more than ten thousand years old, in which case it has been in existence since 8000 B.C. This is, apparently, rather improbably early, but it is based partly on archaeological evidence for the antiquity of agriculture in general, partly on an estimate of the time required for the vines to develop the characters which distinguish them. He first examined the wild vines of the Black Sea coast, in the neighbourhood of ancient Kolkhidia, and concluded that at some time these vines had acquired some of their characters from cultivated vines. In this region he found vines at every stage of evolution from true wild vines, *V. vinifera silvestris*, to ancient and local cultivated varieties of the wine type. Next, in Kopet-Dagh, were found wild vines which turned out to be hybrids between the wild vine, ssp. *silvestris*, and the advanced, cultivated grapes of the East. These cultivated grapes of the East, all varieties of which have characters in common, were classified by Negrul in an ecologico-taxonomic group called *orientalis subprol. caspica* Negr. Growing alongside ancient escapes of this group, in Kopet-Dagh, were the true wild vines, which accounted for the other characters found in the hybrid population.

The wild grapes of western Tian-Shan and Tadzhikistan were found to be escapes of wine varieties introduced in remote times from the Caucasus and widely cultivated there before the destruction of the agrarian communities by Turkish nomadic horse-herding tribes. But these vines have nothing in common with the large-fruited, firm-fleshed varieties now cultivated in Central Asia.

'Historical data indicate that the grape was first introduced into cultivation at the time of the development of wine-making in regions of ancient eastern civilization. Inasmuch as the habitats of the wild grape ssp. *silvestris* Gmel. nearest to these regions are Asia Minor and Transcaucasia, there is full justification for considering that precisely here is the homeland of the cultivated grape. The local origin of a large number of ancient varieties of Western Georgia, Kakhetia and other regions of the Caucasus we now consider an indisputable fact.'[19]

The statement is rather generalized, but when we consider that we can trace the arrival of the vines and of wine into the West from an Eastern source, it may be accepted.

All the wine varieties—that is, varieties with small, juicy fruits, small seeds and densely pubescent leaves, close in form to the wild vine, and found

growing in Georgia, Asia Minor, Greece, Bulgaria, Hungary, Rumania—
are grouped ecologico-taxonomically as *prol. pontica* Negr.

The varieties cultivated in Italy, Spain, France and even, anciently, the
British Isles, reveal their origin as partly oriental, that is coming from Asia
Minor and the Caucasus, and partly wild and local. It is supposed that at the
time of the introduction of viticulture to the West, not only were varieties
of the group *prol. pontica* Negr. crossed with native wild vines, but these
wild vines were brought into cultivation thereafter, and improved by the
selection of good clones and the propagation of bud mutants.[20] There is a
recent historical analogue: the European colonists of North America began
their viticulture by introducing vines from Europe, and only subsequently
took the native American vines into cultivation. The typical European vines
with archaic characters are grouped as *prol. occidentalis* Negr.

'With the extension of viticulture to the south [that is, into Mesopotamia
and Egypt], under conditions of the intensive irrigated agriculture of the
ancient oases there were created for the grape conditions of isolation which,
combined with the repeated sowings of seeds and the selection of bud mutations facilitated the accumulation of recessive characters. The first stage of
such selection gave, in regions bordering on the Caspian Sea, wine and table
varieties (with smooth leaves, fairly large often branched clusters and medium
sized juicy fruit) which are found to this day in Daghestan, Azerbaizhan and
Turkmenistan.'[21]

This group of varieties, regarded as transitional to the large-fruited,
firm-fleshed varieties of the East, Negrul classifies as *prol. orientalis subprol.
caspica* Negr. Thereafter comes a period of vine-breeding coinciding with
the Moslem dominion in the regions concerned, resulting in large-fruited,
firm-fleshed varieties for eating, and seedless varieties, selected and propagated
bud mutants, for raisins: these are grouped as *prol. orientalis subprol. antasiatica*
Negr.

Negrul's investigation and ordering of the cultivated vines does reveal
a number of facts bearing upon the origin of viticulture. Everything seems
to point to a Transcaucasian centre of diffusion. First there was the collection
of wild grapes by Palaeolithic and antecedent communities; then the making
of wine with wild grapes, just as English housewives, even today, make
wine from wild elderberries and other fruits and flowers: then the first
cultivation of wild vines for wine grapes; then the diffusion outwards,

south and west and east, of the primitive cultivated forms, and their improvement in isolation from both wild vines and cultivated vines of other
varieties. Very early the social peculiarities of man began to bear upon the
vine and change it: we can only guess at this process in those remote times,
at how local taste and custom selected one character rather than another, but
we can be guided by the typical case of the effect of Islam on the grape-vines:
the Moslems were forbidden wine, although this rule was, later, often more
honoured in the breach than in the observance. But they might enjoy grapes
and raisins. Accordingly they selected and bred for varieties unsuitable for
wine by reason of their want of juice, but very suitable, by the excellence of
their flesh and flavour, for eating, and by seedlessness, for raisins. The superb
Muscat flavour is one of the products of this process, and the fact that
Mahomet shared a common Semitic, rabbinical distrust of wine, which
found expression in scores of Hebrew texts as well as in the Code of Hammurabi, has given us the luxury hot-house grapes of today.

It is not, of course, possible to arrive at any definite date for the origins of
viticulture: we can place it fairly safely between 8000 and 6000 B.C. Although
later the Transcaucasian prehistoric peoples were notable metallurgists and
potters, at the period in question they cannot have arrived at a high cultural
level. Presumably they were kinship groups developing into matrilineal,
exogamous tribal communities dominated by the mothers.[22] They would
have cultivated emmer wheat and barley and stored it in straw-lined pits.
They still hunted, of course, game being their principal food, but their
cereals must have been cultivated; moreover they must have passed the stage
of nomadic agriculture, of repeated assartage, and been able to settle more or
less permanently on one site, for, if they cultivated the vine, which will not
bear a worth-while crop for three or four years, and which is hardly worth
planting unless one can foresee many years of settlement, they could not have
been forever shifting their cultivated patches in search of new soil.

Obviously, there is a good deal of improbability in the idea of a barbarous, Early Neolithic people such as this cultivating the vine at all. The
occupation is a civilized, relatively sophisticated one. Yet we have to
account for the fact that Mesopotamia and Egypt, far from any habitat of
the wild vines, apparently practised viticulture long before 3000 B.C. and
probably as early as 4000 B.C. or even before that. One of the conditions for
a settled as against a nomadic agriculture is that the soil of the settlement be

annually renewed in some way to make up for the consumption of fertility by cultivation: this condition was only fulfilled in most parts of the world after deep ploughing and manuring had been invented, but in favoured places there was a natural soil renewal due to annual flooding by waters heavily laden with soil nutrients. There were such soils in the mountain and foothill valleys on or about the 40th parallel of latitude between Batum in the west and Baku in the east. Moreover, it should be realized that whereas crops dependent on a few inches of top-soil, such as cereals, must be manured or shifted to new sites, the grape-vine will flourish on eroded and exhausted soils by reason of its power to exploit the sub-soil. Despite these facts, one would feel a good deal more comfortable if, while recognizing that the collection of wild grapes and the making of wine originated in Transcaucasia, it were possible to attribute the actual cultivation of the vine to a people more advanced in the arts of settled, village living than any Transcaucasian folk seem likely to have been at a period sufficiently early to account for the advanced state of viticulture in the cities of the Tigris–Euphrates system in 4000 B.C. or thereabouts.

Such an attribution is not impossible: between a line from Batum to Baku, and another from Antioch drawn due east, lies a region to the northern parts of which *V. vinifera silvestris* is, and was, native. In ancient Armenia, to the south, are the sources of the Tigris and Euphrates. Quite possibly a people intermediate in cultural advancement between the savages to the north, with their wild vines and their wine, and the civilized villagers, soon to become the citizens of Kish and Ur, to the south-east, may have been the first actual cultivators of the vine. It is even quite possible that the Sumerians themselves may have brought wild vines from the country of their origin, not in their first migrations, but by means of adventures up towards the sources of the Two Rivers which gave them life and wealth. The adventurers may have had a tradition of the marvellous plant from their ancestors; or they may have tasted wine when visiting their savage neighbours for trade. Is there, perhaps, an echo of some such adventure in the Gilgamesh Epos? Before examining this possibility it will be as well to recall some Mesopotamian prehistory.

Mesopotamia, as a land peculiarly suitable to be a forcing house of the civilized crafts, was made by the silt carried down by the Two Rivers, a flat, marshy, alluvial plain. It was first occupied by two distinct peoples, the Semites who came from Arabia and Southern Syria to occupy the delta north of the Persian Gulf, and other Semites, more advanced in culture, who came from the upper reaches of the Euphrates valley and filled the northern half of the plain; and the Sumerians, a non-Semitic people from somewhere in Central Asia, apparently related to the pre-Aryan people of the Indus valley system who built the ancient city cultures of Harappā and Mohenjo-daro, and the semi-urban communities of prehistoric Baluchistan. The Sumerians were evidently a hill people, but how and when and exactly whence they came into Mesopotamia is conjectural. They competed with the southern Semites in occupying the torrid delta at the head of the Persian Gulf, taking the lead, since their culture was by a good deal the more advanced, until the climate, or some other cause, so debilitated them that they gave way before the hardier Semites.

The earliest glimpse of the Sumerians which archaeology has yet given us, at Tell Al 'Ubaid near Ur, shows them already in possession of copper tools, though these were rare and precious since even reaping-hooks were, very inconveniently one would have supposed, made of baked clay. Aesthetically these folk were very gifted: they made, without the potter's wheel, pottery so regular, and decorated in such excellent taste, that it was not thereafter surpassed, even with increasing technical skill and facility. Probably, between the Tell Al 'Ubaid culture and the next to be revealed, intervened the 'Babylonian' flood. Thereafter come the wealth and sophistication of Ur (c. 3500 B.C.), with its silver and gold, copper and shell work, all evidence of an advanced culture antecedent to that of Egypt, a point of great importance when we come to consider the diffusion of viticulture. The approximate dates for the founding of the 'First' Dynasties in Mesopotamia and in Egypt are perhaps about the same; that of Egypt is said to be c. 3400 B.C. But as the late Dr Henri Frankfort pointed out and demonstrated, since the shape and nature of the Nile country called for an integral social system throughout the whole region, and therefore a centralized government, whereas the shape and nature of the Two River soils called for a large number of independent and autonomous city states, it seems likely that the foundation of a wide-ruling Dynasty in Mesopotamia was a relatively late and—in Spengler's sense—declining phase in the civilized history of that country, whereas in Egypt such a foundation would rise naturally out of the very geology of the place, as it were. Consequently, this comparison of

Dynasty-founding dates has no meaning in the context of considering the relative advancement of the two regions. And if the products of industry from the Nile valley civilizations be compared with those from Ur dated by Woolley *c.* 3500 B.C., there can surely be no doubt which civilization was the more mature, and which, therefore, the older.

The earliest tablets containing pictographic writing came from Kish. This city was considered by the Babylonians to be the first to establish an Imperium in Mesopotamia, antedating that of Ur by several centuries, perhaps by as much as a thousand years. The temple built by A-anne-padda at Ur is dated with some certainty 3100 B.C. We may be justified in guessing that civilization had advanced to the stage of some sort of writing, at Kish, by 4000 B.C. Among the pictograms used in the earliest inscriptions we have yet been able to examine is a stylized vine-leaf. This figure, further stylized almost out of recognition, is carried over into the cuneiform script. It is true that pictograms were often derived from wild, natural objects and not always from artefacts, but as we know that the vine was not native to the country about Kish, nor indeed to any part of Mesopotamia, it is obvious that the pictogram in question is derived from a cultivated vine. We can therefore probably place the origin of viticulture back beyond 4000 B.C., and perhaps by a good many centuries.

To sum up:

i. The most advanced peoples anywhere near the habitat of the wild vines were those of the Tigris–Euphrates valleys, since they were the first to create an urban civilization.

ii. Viticulture was almost certainly established in Tigris–Euphrates soils before 4000 B.C., and perhaps much before.

iii. The vine was, and is, native to Transcaucasia. This region was inhabited, between 6000 and 4000 B.C., by people in a late Palaeolithic or Early Neolithic stage of culture, who later must have come under the influence of cultural energy radiating from the south, and who had probably long collected wild grapes and made wine from this wild harvest.

iv. Between this northern savagery and the civilization of the south there may have intervened people in an intermediate phase of civilization, settled, and capable of viticulture.

v. The source of life for the Mesopotamian peoples was the flood-water of the Tigris and Euphrates rivers. The sources of these rivers must have been of interest to them, and all the land to the north and west through which the rivers flowed. The floods may even have been intensified by the deforestation of Armenia by herdsmen, in which case the two economies were linked.

vi. From a time before their city-building phase the Mesopotamians must have been used to trading abroad, timber and other primary materials being scarce or wanting in their country. Bitumen and copper had to come from beyond their frontiers. Some of these materials were most nearly available in the hill country to the north and east—habitats of the vine.

It is not impossible that we may be able to find an echo of the introduction of viticulture, vine and wine, to civilization, in literature.

# CHAPTER II

## *The Drunken Gods*

THE EARLIEST REFERENCE TO THE VINEYARD in literature is in the earliest work of literature that we have. I suggest that this poem, the Epic of Gilgamesh, may contain an echo of a remote adventure by some citizen of Kish or Akkad to the vine-rich source of Mesopotamia's life-giving waters. The poem is in a Semitic language, but if it refers to a remote past in the history of the poet's country its hero might be a Sumerian of non-Semitic speech. No mythical tale, no epic is without foundation in actual adventure: Gilgamesh had his model in history as surely as Odysseus did; and since his story was not written upon paper which lasts only a few years, but upon earthenware which lasts for ever, his ancient tale has been preserved to us.

The story of Gilgamesh appears to have been written about the time of Hammurabi, that is, the eighteenth century B.C., but refers to a much earlier epoch, a commonplace of epic poetry. Gilgamesh was tyrant of Erech. His adventures, most of which would be out of place here, included fighting, taming and befriending the wild man Enkidu, killing a divine bull, and-rousing a dangerous passion of love in the bosom of the goddess Ishtar, her-self a wine-goddess in one of her avatars, who, however, was contemplating no such *mésalliance* as the Greek divinities frequently stooped to, since Gilgamesh was the son of gods himself.[1]

According to Babylonian beliefs an enormous number of the dead were forced to lead an excessively tiresome existence as wandering ghosts: this was, for example, the fate of such as starved to death in prison, or were drowned, or died in childbed, or died unwed. The obvious way to avoid a fate which was the consequence of the sort of misfortune that could happen to anyone, was to live for ever. Gilgamesh accordingly set out in search of the way to eternal life, moved by the terror and grief which he experienced when he had to witness the death of his erstwhile enemy and later bosom friend, Enkidu.

Shall I, after roaming the desert the way of a wanderer,
Lay my head in the bowels of the earth and throughout the years slumber?
Oh, let mine eyes see the sun, that I may be filled with sunlight,
For the darkness is banished afar if the light be widespreading,
When will the dead see the blaze of the sun?[2]

Gilgamesh is reluctantly allowed to enter the domain of the sun by the giant scorpion men who guard the gate, and after travelling on for another twenty-four hours, he comes to a miraculous vineyard.

If this epic, like so much Semitic poetry, was written to be sung to the accompaniment of instrumental music it must have been very impressive: it is not necessary to understand a language in order to feel something of the power of its sound. Of the vineyard the poet wrote:

> *samtu nasat inibsa*
> *ishunnatum ullulat anadagate tabat*
> *uknu nasi hashalta*
> *inba nasi-ma ana smari sa'ah . . .*

A language so rich in vowels is a great boon to the poet. The verse means:

> Amethyst it bore as its fruit,
> Grape vine was trellised, good to behold,
> Lapis lazuli it bore as grape clusters,
> Fruit it bore, magnificent to look upon.[3]

This vineyard belonged to the maid Siduri, a goddess, or at least an immortal, the divine Tavern-keeper. (The taverners of Babylonia were, according to the Code of Hammurabi, frequently and perhaps usually women.) The vine-stock stands for the tree of life, and the 'noble and precious' fluid which Siduri prepared was the means of imparting eternal life. Not that Gilgamesh was allowed to partake of it. The maid Siduri did not hold with mortals living for ever. He continued his travels and ultimately found the life-conferring plant at the bottom of the sea, only, however, to lose it to a serpent on his way home.

Without insisting that the poetic image of Siduri's vineyard is the reflection of an historic event, it is, I think, not impossible. That the poem does refer to historical events is clear from at least one case: at a later stage in his adventures Gilgamesh meets Utnapishtim, the Babylonian Noah, who tells him the Flood story from which that of Genesis derives, and whose basic historicity has been established by archaeology. It is a commonplace that the epic poets wove together history, legend and myth in making their magic: it was so, for instance, with the Homeric account of the Trojan war; with the Saga account of Leif Ericsson's discovery of America in *c*. A.D. 1000; and even the last of the epics, *The Lusiads* of Camoens, is written in the same immensely ancient tradition.

That the Sumerians, and the people of Kish and Erech, Lagash and Ur, had their viticulture from a hill country might be deduced from the fact that they planted their vineyards on artificial mounds or platforms; but the object of this was probably practical; for it was with difficulty that vines could be cultivated in this climate at all—so much so that there is a myth to explain it. Dionysus, or at all events that god under an earlier name, in an earlier avatar, was said to have turned away from the land of the Two Rivers in anger because the inhabitants preferred to drink beer.

The earliest written record of a vineyard in this part of the world is that of the scribe of Gudea, *Patesi* of Lagash, and it is dated *c*. 2400 B.C.: 'The Ne-sag was like a mountain with vines.'[4] At the same time it seems that vineyards were already being named as they were in Egypt from almost the beginnings of viticulture. Thus, for example, in the inscription 'The garden *anqullu* which was planted by the Temple was like a mountain with vines',[5] I take it that *anqullu* can only be the name of the garden, planted by Gudea to embellish his city.

The use of the artificial hills called *ziggurats* for the planting of vines and other fruit-trees[6] may, in the southern half of the country, have been of practical origin; but that does not seem to have been the whole story, for the *ziggurats* were temple sites, and the association of vine and wine with the temples, repeated in Egypt, and even in the Europe of the Middle Ages and the California of the eighteenth century, seems to have been so strict in Babylonia, perhaps in earlier Sumeria, and certainly much later at the time of the codification of the laws by Hammurabi, that quite possibly the ordinary people never tasted wine at all.

We know nothing whatever about viticulture in northern 'Babylonia' in very early times, although if my guesses about the origins of the art are right, it was here that the whole thing began. All we can say is that much later, and in strong contrast to the southern part of the country, it was celebrated for its wines. By the time that Assyria was established as a kingdom and later an empire, official interest in promoting viticulture was keen: vineyards were numerous during the first millennium B.C. Assurnasirpal caused vineyards to be planted in Calah (Nimrud), and Sennacherib caused vines to be brought from all over the Near East so that they might be tried and the best of them propagated. The fact that the best wines come from mountain or at least from hilly situations was already established, for the best wine[7] is called 'mountain wine', and came from a mountain called Arzabia, or from another hill called Hi-hi. The really great vintages, however, came from the city of Ninua (Nineveh) in the Hamrin mountains, a region sacred to the wine-goddess Siris (*plates 5–8*). Still later, the country about Bakuba, north-east of Baghdad, was renowned wine country.[8]

All that this, and very much more evidence of the same kind, serves to establish is that at a time much later than the one we are considering, viticulture was very well established, but I believe that this can be taken as evidence that it did have a very early start in that country. And this theory receives some support from two myths of very great antiquity. One of the oldest of the Sumerian divinities was a wine-goddess called either Geštin or Ama-Geštin, which apparently means 'Mother Vine-stock'; there was a temple to her at Lagash which is mentioned in an inscription of King Urukagina. Later in her career she ceases to patronize wine and patronizes, instead, water. As we shall see, wine and beer were no more 'respectable' in ancient Babylon than in Victorian England, excepting when they were drunk with ceremony by the upper classes. But I do not suggest that the transference of this goddess from wine to water had anything to do with a total abstinence movement. I think that she must have been a northern goddess whose dominion extended into the south; in the north, wine was all-important; in the south the vine could only be grown with difficulty, and was perhaps grown only for the provision of sacramental wine; much more important, in the south, was water; and so Ama-Geštin took over that department. Her name changes to Geštin-Anna, which is translated as 'Vinestock of Heaven', which may mean that water was regarded as a heavenly wine. Her career is upon a familiar pattern: she begins as all-powerful and independent; but as feminine values decline and yield to dominion by the male, the goddess is degraded, becomes the mere consort of a god, who is occasionally her own son.

The Urukagina inscription is dated 2700 B.C. At that time Geštin-Anna is still a vine and wine goddess. Less than a thousand years later she is Nina, goddess of the waters. Whether the change reflects her own migration from the wine land of the north to a region dependent on the flood-waters of the Two Rivers, or whether it reflected a decline in southern viticulture, or neither, one cannot, of course, say with any assurance.

The second of these old Sumerian myths is I think rather clearer, for our purpose, in its implications. It concerns a vine-god, an ancestor of Dionysus perhaps, whose name is Pa-geštin-dug, which apparently means 'the good vine-stock'. His wife was a goddess with two different names, according to her function at the moment: Nin-kasi, 'the lady of the inebriating fruit', and also Sa-bil, 'she who causes burning'. We may safely take this pair as wine-deities. A third name by which the consort of Pa-geštin-dug is sometimes known is Kastin-nam, 'the intoxicating drink which decreed life'. In that epiphany the goddess' mother is, it seems, always Nin-til, 'Lady of Life'—presumably our old friend the earth mother, the great goddess.

Pa-geštin-dug and Sa-bil had nine children, one of them Siris, wine-goddess of the Hamrin mountain vineyards; but in her later epiphany she seems, or so her name implies, to have been more concerned with beer, or perhaps with intoxicating drinks in general. Her siblings were Sin-kas, which competent persons say means 'spiced barley beer'; Sim-kas-gig, another beer-name; M-hus, 'he of frightening speech' (it is suggested that this may imply 'the drunken brawler'); Me-azag, 'he of clear speech' (which could imply the *in vino veritas* stage of drunkenness); Eme-te, 'eloquent of tongue' (yet another stage of drunkenness); Ki-dur-ka-zal, the meaning of which is 'one who abides in mirth', which is, again, a reference to one of the effects of alcohol; Nu-silig-ga, 'the braggart'; Nin-ma-da, 'lord of the land' (perhaps the implication here is to drunken *hubris*). Also interesting is the place where Nin-kasi or Sa-bil, the mother of these archetypes, dwelt: it is Mount Sabu, and Lutz[8] says that this was not a geographical designation but means 'the mount of the taverner', where 'taverner' means one who sells beer and wine.

When we come to consider Babylon itself, for many centuries the greatest city in the world under its several different masters, it seems unlikely that wine was ever grown in the region dominated by that city. We know, in fact, that in the fifth century B.C. the people of the city had no vineyards, for Herodotus tells us so in so many words. With the help of irrigation the Babylonians obtained an immense yield of wheat, and they also grew the date-palm in great numbers; Herodotus has an interesting note on the method of ensuring pollination of the date flowers by bending the heads of the male trees into the females; and he confuses this, to some extent, with the pollination of the fig, for what he calls (or his translators call) 'gall flies' are probably the fig-wasp (*Blastophyga psenes*). He says, too, that the dates were used to make wine. But the Babylonians in their day had no vines and no olive trees and it is not likely that they had any in earlier ages nearer than the Zagros mountains, where the vine may have been planted before the site became an olive grove, enabling the citizens to replace their oil of sesame with olive oil.

But, as will appear, the Babylonians did drink wine; and it is again Herodotus who tells us how they got it. It was, he says, imported from the north; and for several reasons the passage is so interesting that I shall quote it in full:

'But that which surprises me most in the land, after the city itself, I will now proceed to mention. The boats which come down the river to Babylon [the River Euphrates] are circular and made of skins. The frames which are of willow are cut in the country of the Armenians above Assyria, and on these which serve for hulls, a covering of skins is stretched outside, and thus the boats are made, without either stem or stern, quite round like a shield. They are then entirely filled with straw, and their cargo is put on board, after which they are suffered to float down the stream. Their chief freight is wine stored in casks made of the wood of the palm-tree. They are managed by two men who stand upright in them, each plying an oar, one pulling and the other pushing. The boats are of various sizes, some larger, some smaller; the biggest reach as high as five thousand talents burthen. Each vessel has a live ass on board; those of larger size have more than one. When they reach Babylon, the cargo is landed and offered for sale; after which the men break up their boats, sell the straw and the frames, and loading their asses with the skins, set off on their way back to Armenia. The current is too strong to allow a boat to return upstream, for which reason they make their boats of skins rather than wood. On their return to Armenia they build fresh boats for the next voyage.'

There are three points of interest here, especially if we suppose that the traffic was already an ancient one: first, Babylon was importing her wine not

I

From the earliest times the vine has been sacred to gods of death and rebirth, and one of the most extraordinary instances of this special feeling for the vine is to be found in the words of Christ: 'I am the True Vine'.

On the silver chalice from Antioch (2) Christ and the Holy Lamb are surrounded by the vine of life, while on the marble plaque from Ravenna (1) a vine and peacocks symbolize the resurrection and eternal life, and the monogram of Christ rises above an urn.

2

3

4

Some of the earliest representations of drinking come from southern Mesopotamia, though we cannot be sure what was in the king's cup (3) or the god's libation vase (4) on plaques from Lagash of the third millennium B.C. But the city of Nineveh to the north was the centre of a great vine country, where the plants were grown on irrigated hills (5) and trained on trees (6). In the seventh century B.C. at the Palace of Nineveh the Assyrian king Assurbanipal feasts with his Queen under a vine pergola (7), and pours an offering of wine over four dead lions, the bag of a hunt (8).

5

6

7

8

9

In Palestine the raiding Assyrian king
Sennacherib receives the surrender of the city
of Lachish on a hillside covered with vines
(9). Canaan was legendary as a vineland;
Joshua's spies returned with a bunch of grapes
so large that it had to be carried on a staff
between the shoulders of two men (10).

10

11

*Vintaging in an arbour in Thebes in the fifteenth century* B.C. *(11). It is curious that no knives are being used to gather the grapes. In Egypt wine was pressed in a linen cloth and below, athletic workmen stretch one between two poles to the accompaniment of music, (12).*

12

13

A wine funnel from Tuna near El Amarna is decorated in turquoise and brown glaze, with a lotus bud at the base (13).

Below (15) the whole process of wine-making is depicted in a Theban tomb-painting: picking the grapes in an arbour, treading in a vat, filling the jars, topping them up and sealing them with wax, and finally, transporting them to the tomb as an offering for the dead man.

15

## 14

Wine was stored in large pottery jars. The royal wine jars from El Amarna (14) have decorated stoppers and bear the overseer's descriptions of the quality of the wine they contain. The inscription on the right-hand jar reads: 'Wine of the Delta, fit for Horus to offer to his father Osiris'—that is to say, fit for the gods.

At a banquet a servant offers wine to one of the guests, while below right, two girls dance beside wine-jars garlanded with flowers and vines (16).

16

The vine accompanied men even after death. Painters of the tomb of Sennufer, a Keeper of the Vineyard, at Deir-el-Medineh took advantage of the rough surface of the ceiling to paint bunches of grapes in relief (17), so that the deceased might sit for all eternity in a vine bower.

17

from the vineyards of Assyria but from the very source, Armenia; second, we have here the first instance of what, as will be described in Chapter V, was one of the most important influences on the development of commerce in wine: an easy means of transport by river; this consideration was to remain important in the geographical placing of the greatest viticultural undertakings for the next couple of thousand years or more. Third, it would seem that the Armenians were the first coopers, or they may have bought their wine-casks in Assyria. The point, and this again is discussed in Chapter V, is that Europe did not begin to use wooden casks until about the first century B.C. and perhaps rather later than that; and that Pliny attributes the invention of the wooden wine-cask to the Allobroges or some such Celtic people. It seems perfectly clear from Herodotus' account, however, that wooden casks were in use in the fifth century B.C.; how long before his time this had been the case there is no means of knowing, since wood, unlike earthenware. rarely leaves traces for the archaeologist.

A study of the available inscriptions and of the Code of Hammurabi reveals quite clearly that the important drink in Babylon was beer; important, that is, from the economic point of view. How much wine was drunk by ordinary people, or even by the aristocracy and the theocracy, it is not possible to say. But that wine was a requisite of religious ceremonies, and therefore essential, is clear; and it may be that all the peoples who successively occupied and built empires from the land between the Two Rivers had this same need. The cup-bearer has his place beside the king in ancient images of life in Lagash (*plate 3*), even in the time of the founder of the great dynasty, Ur-Nina. But we cannot say what was in the cup. Inscriptions dating from the time of the last king of that dynasty, the reformer Urukagina, repeatedly mention beer, but rarely wine. Part of the fee for priests officiating at funerals had been seven jars of beer: Urukagina cut this down to three, which may not have been a fee, but may have been intended for burial with the dead. To find wine referred to as frequently as beer one has to go back to much older documents, which again supports my view that wine comes first, from the north, and is superseded by beer owing to the difficulties of cultivating the vine in the south. But at all periods wine as well as beer was used for libations to the gods (*plate 4*); there may have been a kind of class-distinction here: Gudea orders his donkey-keeper Ensignun (donkeys were the important beasts of draft and burden) 'to make plenty of beer for the god Ningirsu',[9] but the much more important Bel-Marduk gets six large measures of wine from huge golden chalices. A relief (*plate 8*) shows King Assurbanipal pouring a libation over four dead lions, the bag of some hunt; the inscription reads: 'An offering I offered up over them. Wine I libated over them.' Moreover, from another inscription of the same king, it is clear that wine was poured as a libation over the foundation stones of new buildings: 'With strong wine and wine I sprinkled its cellar. I poured it on the foundations.'

It is curious that in the earliest times of which we have any record, two kinds of people who have since made themselves persistently troublesome to the producers and drinkers of wine, were already active: I mean social moralists and excisemen. Just how early taxation of wine was levied in some form or other one cannot say: but although it is not clear to me, from the very confusing documents relating to the official control of wine prices in the kingdom of Assyria in the first millennium B.C., that home-grown wine was taxed, it is clear that imported wine had to pay customs duty. This must have made it dearer than the home-grown product, unless of course production costs were very high at home which, given the climatic difficulties, may have been the case. There are two very odd and ingenious aspects of this wine-taxation which have never, as far as I know, been repeated by any fiscal authority since. First, although money could be used in certain circumstances, the duty was paid at the frontier in kind, that is, a proportion of the wine imported had to be handed over to the fisc; secondly, once an exporter of wine to Assyria had accepted an order from a merchant inside Assyria, he was committed to pay the duty; and if something happened to prevent him from making the delivery as contracted for (for example, perhaps a ship-wreck, a raid on a caravan, a failure of the vintage), then he was obliged to buy within Assyria an equivalent amount of Assyrian wine to meet his tax obligation. It is not clear how this could be enforced on foreign exporters; but the bloodthirsty Assyrian governments were not people to quarrel with; and in any case, I presume that the right to export wine into Assyria, which could of course be withdrawn, was valuable. As we shall see in the proper place, wine was also taxed in Egypt, at least from the XX Dynasty.

As to the anti-alcohol moralists, they too have been at work since the memory of mankind runneth not to the contrary. It is clear enough from the many texts available that ritual and upper-class social drinking were perfectly in order, but that taverns, to which the common people resorted, were as frowned upon among the respectable as gin palaces in Victorian London or the saloons of pre-Prohibition America. Babylonia had many taverns; in the Code of Hammurabi these are called 'wine-shops', but from the texts of that Code it seems that wine was rarely, perhaps never, sold in them; what they sold was barley-beer. This inconsistency between the name of the pubs and what they sold may be further evidence in support of my case that wine was the older drink of the country and that it had given way to beer for mass consumption simply because the country could not produce enough wine in that difficult climate, so far from suitable for viticulture. At all events, although in much earlier times the taverns had a kind of sacred attribute, being associated with a special goddess and cult, by more sophisticated times, and in any case by 2000 B.C., they had evidently become dens of vice. In a text quoted by S. A. Smith in *Miscellaneous Texts*, one moral precept is 'O lord, thou shalt not enter a beerhouse' (cf. the case of Athens fifteen centuries later, where a single visit to a public tavern was sufficient to have one expelled from the Areopagus). Lutz thinks that all taverns in Babylonia were without exception also brothels. Even this could have been of religious origin: religious prostitution and religious drunkenness may have stemmed from a single source, despite a much later (and physiologically questionable) view that whole-hearted drinking to the point of drunkenness and whole-hearted fornication are incompatible. It is significant, in my opinion, that if we take the Code of Hammurabi as a reliable guide, then the trade of tavern-keeping was confined to women. Lutz suggests that this is either a mistake, or that the taverns legislated for were only those which were also brothels and therefore, I suppose, run by a bawd. These explanations seem to me improbable; the trade may well have been confined to women, and a rough time they had of it with the licensing laws; apparently it was illegal to accept coin for drinks, the liquor had to be paid for in barley grain, the raw material of the taverner's brew-house. I feel sure that there is something wrong here; perhaps, rather, the price of beer was forced to follow the ruling price of barley, which might be sensible enough. Yet it does read as if the taverner had to take only a measure of grain against a measure of beer. If she gave short measure, the punishment was savage: 'If a taverner [beer merchant] do not receive barley as the price of drink, but if she receive money by the great stone, or make the measure for liquor smaller than the measure for barley, they shall call her to account and throw her into the water.'

Whether to drown, or merely as a ducking, is not clear. Moreover, the police held the taverner responsible for riotous behaviour at her wine-shop, as they do in Britain today. But in Babylon the punishment was more serious: 'If outlaws collect in the house of the beer dealer, and she does not arrest these outlaws and bring them to the palace, she shall be put to death.'

If a priestess (female votary, vestal) left her cloister and set up as a taverner, the punishment was to be burnt alive.

Enough has been said about this part of the world. There can be no proof, but on the whole it seems to me clear that the highly-civilized city-states and later empires of Mesopotamia were the channels through which wine, the vine, and the art of viticulture reached the other civilized centres of the most ancient Near East.

The link between these places and ancient Egypt was the land of Phoenicia, Syria, Palestine (*plate 9*), and if my argument is sound then viticulture must have been established there before it was to be found in the Nile delta. An examination of the map on pages 12–13 will remind the reader that the Nile delta is much further from the country which appears to have given rise to viticulture than is the deltaic region of the Two Rivers, and that the northern half of Mesopotamia is much nearer than any centre of ancient Egyptian civilization to the highlands where the vine was first cultivated. But Egypt had very early connections with Phoenicia: the first of which we have a record belongs to the reign of Sneferu, about 2600 B.C. At that time Byblos, which, as we shall see, was of enormous importance in the history of viticulture, was apparently a prosperous and ancient colonial centre of Egyptian culture. It lay about halfway between modern Beirut and Tripoli. So ancient was the connection between Byblos and the Egyptian culture that the city has an important part in at least one chapter of the complex and confused religion of the Egyptians. It was at Byblos that the body of Osiris was washed ashore and coffined. Greek writers identified Osiris with Dionysus; and in fact Osiris was the patron of vine and wine in Egypt. We know nothing of the very early history of the vine in Byblos, but in later times it was so celebrated for its vineyards and wines that it is safe to say that these arts were established there at a time so remote that no records of them survive. As an Egyptian colony it probably began its career about the middle of the fourth millennium B.C., as a factory for the cutting and shipping of timber, principally the Lebanon cedar, a commodity which Egypt was forced to seek beyond her frontiers. Viticulture may have been established in the region by then, and the Egyptians may have brought it home from there. Indeed it is perfectly possible that both the ancient oasis civilizations, or riparian flood civilizations, may have had the vine from some semi-barbarous but settled north Syrian people. It is here that philological clues should be helpful, but they are not; they tend to rest upon assertions that such and such words are, or are not, Semitic. If the roots from which such words as vine, wine, vineyard derive *are* Semitic, not directly, as in the case of these words in the European languages, which is certain (see Chapter IV), but also indirectly, in the case of the ancient Babylonian and Egyptian languages, then it is very probable that both Egypt and Mesopotamia did, in fact, get the vine, wine and the arts of viticulture and vinting by way of north Syria. Hommel, in *Aufsätz und Abhandlungen*, asserts that such words as vine and wine and vineyards were not, in these languages or any ancient language of the centres of culture, Semitic; or that, if they are, their sense is not specific to viticulture and kindred matters, but general—vineyards, for example, being really fruit-orchards—and therefore useless as a guide to the origin of viticulture, or to its route of diffusion. He says that the root of 'vineyard'—*karanu*, that is, καρα, and a word of like sound in Hebrew—is non-Semitic. As it is almost a rule that when a people receives a new plant, a new food or a new thing of any kind from an alien source, it also receives the name for that plant, food or thing, if the ancient Egyptian and Babylonian words for vine, wine and viticultural matters were *not* of Semitic origin, then probably there was no north Syrian intermediary between Egypt and Mesopotamia and the non-Semitic peoples of Transcaucasia, whence came wine, the vine and viticulture.

Be that as it may, certainly north Syria, Phoenicia, Canaan, and all that country were famous for vineyards and for wine. 'The wine in the presses of Daha is as copious as running water', records an inscription of Thutmose III. Daha was either Phoenicia or Canaan. Joshua's spies, although this is rather late (*c.* 1200 B.C.), brought back from the land of Canaan a bunch of grapes so large that it had to be carried on a staff between the shoulders of two men (*plate* 10). This is not mere romancing. Such bunches have been grown in California and in English hot-houses. In the tale of Sinhue it is said of Yaa, in Syria: 'more plentiful than water is its wine'. Tyre of the Phoenicians had wine, but water had to be brought to that fortress-city in ships.

All these accounts and many more belong, it is true, to an epoch much later than that which we are considering, but they imply a long establishment of wine-making in this country which formed a link between Egypt and Mesopotamia. Hesychius believed that Pangenu in Syria was the birthplace of Dionysus: that lexicographer was, it is true, writing comparatively recently, in the fourth century A.D., but perhaps he was drawing on an ancient tradition. There was the legend that Osiris was washed ashore and coffined at Byblos, mentioned earlier, and Phoenicia was one of the places said to have given birth to Dionysus; his birthplace was, it seems, Nysa.

Unfortunately there are no really early records for Phoenicia or for Syria; the earliest accounts we have from that part of the world are biblical and Talmudic, and to these we turn below. Of Phoenicia itself, we can only claim that her later oinological fame probably argues the antiquity of her vineyards. Of that fame there is no question. Byblian, Syrian and Palestinian wines were shipped out to Arabia, to Spain and even to India in later times; this trade was so ancient that its early history is lost. For century after century it was a source of wealth to the wine-growers, or at least—and more probably—to the wine-merchants.

> . . . *dives ut aureis*
> *mercator exsiccet culullis*
> *vina Syra reparata merce*
> *Dis carus ipsis, quippe ter et quater*
> *anno revisens aequor Atlanticum*
> *impune.*

('. . . that the wealthy trader may draw from golden cups wine for which he has exchanged goods from Syria, dear to the gods themselves because three or four times a year he returns safe and sound from the Atlantic Sea.') Thus Horace (Ode 1, 31, 10). But it could have been written a thousand, and maybe two thousand years before that poet flourished. We know, too, that at least two wines of this region became world-famous: Tyrian; and the Chalybonium grown first at Beroea and later about Damascus.

One of the amenities which the ancient Hebrews complained of leaving behind when their prophet Moses insisted upon leading them out of the land of Egypt, were the Egyptian wines (Numbers xx, 5). They need not have worried: Palestine had been producing a variety of wines of quality long before the Israelites went to Egypt, let alone left it. Of the phrase 'a land flowing with milk and honey' (Exodus iii, 8) Lutz has this of interest to say: 'It is probable that the proper rendering should be "A land flowing with *leben* and *dibs*." '

Leben was sour milk (? cheese or curds) and dibs is grape-syrup; thus the claim made is that the promised land is rich in flocks and vineyards. Many very ancient Palestinian place-names are vine or viticulture derivatives, for example, Nahal Eshkol (Numbers and Deuteronomy), near Hebron, is 'Valley of Grapes'. The plain of Sharon was great wine-country and so was Shiloh. During the building of the first Temple, the people of Tyre and Sidon were provided with wine from Judaea, perhaps in connection with a contract for importing materials; and the vineyards of Palestine are noticed in the records, such as they are, of invading powers: a relief (*plate 9*) shows King Sennacherib before the city of Lachish, during one of the Assyrian invasions, with a vine-clad hill in the background. There is an inscription (Una) which records: 'This army returned in safety [from Herusha] after it had cut down the vines and fig-trees.' Making war on the enemy's plantations was an old custom, later followed by the Greeks during the Peloponnesian War. Egyptian inscriptions include references to the wines of Haru and of northern Palestine.

What were these wines like? It seems certain that all the wines of Palestine and of Syria were very sweet and syrupy and that they were often, and perhaps usually, diluted with water and mixed with spices. Apparently the wine of the Sharon plain was notably strong, as well it might be: in that climate and with suitable varieties, the grapes at the time of the vintage would contain perhaps thirty-five per cent by volume of sugar: even if we suppose very efficient fermentation, the finished wine would be about sixteen per cent alcohol and a lot of sugar would probably be left unconverted into alcohol. But in fact there is even more reason to suppose them strong and sweet, for the technique now used only in the case of *vin de paille* was used: the grapes, that is to say, were half-dried, as if for raisins, before vinification, so that the proportion of sugar was even higher, perhaps fifty per cent. The wine would have been virtually a syrup. In some parts of the country new wine was drunk; the *hiliston* wine mentioned in the Babylonian Talmud (*Baba Bathra*) was very sweet and very weak; this means that either it was drunk still fermenting; or that grape-sugar produced by reduction of the must was added in sufficient amount to the fermenting wine to check fermentation altogether. Wines were made from raisins; special distinction was given to wine made from the first crop of young plants, for the so-called 'three-leaf' wine can only, I think, be wine made from vines in their third leaf, that is, third season. A point of the greatest viticultural interest is that there was a wine mentioned in Isaiah v, 2, 4 which, it is suggested (by Lutz *et al.*), was made from the grapes of a wild vine. Lutz calls this vine *Vitis labrusca*, which is, of course, botanically incorrect: any wild vines in Palestine, whether genuinely indigenous or vineyard escapes, would have been *V. vinifera*. The wine of this wild vintage is said to have been used only for medicinal purposes.

'My beloved is like a cluster of camphire in the vineyards of Engedi', wrote the poet-king Solomon. This vineyard was famous for centuries, not only for its wine but for its balsam: according to Josephus, quoting the *Speculum Historiale*, when the Queen of Sheba came to visit Solomon she brought with her, among many other gifts, one beyond price, a root of balsam, and this was planted in the vineyard on Mount Engedi. Felix Fabri, writing late in the fifteenth century, records a tradition that the wine of Engedi was the one with which Lot's daughters made their father drunk.

The Rabbinical shrinking from the Samaritans is expressed in some curious Talmudic prohibitions of certain wines at certain holy periods of the year: 'The wine of Ogdor is forbidden to be drunk on account of the neighbourhood of Kefar Pagesh; that of Borgatha on account of the neighbourhood of Birath Sariquah; that of 'Ain-Kushith on account of the neighbourhood of Kefar Shalem.'

In Palestine, as in Babylonia and doubtless in Sumeria much earlier, there was in the earliest ages no objection raised by anyone to intoxicating drinks in general; wine is praised by all, condemned by none; and drunkenness is tolerated if not approved. Later, however, in the cases of all these countries, a temperance movement develops, usually of clerical origin. There may be a

I. The *vine of history*, Vitis vinifera Linn, *showing leaves, inflorescence, hermaphrodite flowers, seed, and three varieties of grape: blue, white and red (this last of 'cornichon' variety, resembling the 'mare's nipple grapes' of Central Asia, which was first described in Roman Republican Italy). Coloured engraving by Plenck from 'Icones Plantarum Medicinalium', 1784.*

*Die weintragende Weinrebe.*

rather special reason for this, at least among the Jews. The rabbis looked back with yearning to the good old days of the simple Bedouin herdsman's life: *that* was the right way for good Jews to live, not building cities, cultivating vineyards and generally conducting themselves as if they were no better, no more God's favourites, than those shocking Babylonians. The stories of Noah's drunkenness and Lot's are awful warnings. According to Deuteronomy the father of a son who has become a drunkard is entitled to hail him before the judges to be tried for his life; and Leviticus forbids the clergy to drink any wine at all during their turn of service. It seems always to be assumed by the rabbis that a man could not drink without getting drunk; there is no question of simply drinking a glass or two of wine for refreshment and the quenching of thirst; but then, Palestinian wines were not thirst-quenching, any more than, say, a modern muscatel wine. Here is a Hebrew song, supposedly sung by a royal mother to her princely son:

> It is not for kings to drink wine
> Nor for rulers to mix strong drink,
> Lest, drinking, they forget the Law,
> And disregard the rights of the suffering.

> Give strong drink to him who is perishing,
> Wine to him who is in bitter distress;
> That, drinking, he may forget his poverty,
> And think of his misery no more.[10]

But one has only to look through the Book of Proverbs to see the strength of the ancient Hebrew temperance movement.

Long after the famous vineyards of Bordeaux, Burgundy and the Rhine have been nuclear-bombed, bacteria-sprayed or otherwise served to demonstrate the triumphant advance of science, it is possible that their names and memories will survive in the vintages of Californian 'burgundy', Australian 'sauternes' and South African 'hock'. Palestinian, Syrian and Byblean wines were similarly imitated in the fourth century B.C.

*II. Treading grapes and collecting the juice in ancient Egypt. Large storage bottles appear on the wall above. From a wallpainting in the tomb of Nakht, a Theban official. Fifteenth century B.C.*

Byblean vines were brought into Sicily by Pollis of Sikyon (Syracuse), and into other countries, including Thrace.[11] Moreover the wine made from these Byblean vines, although actually Sicilian or Thracian, was called Byblean wine, as today we talk of Chilean Riesling, or Caucasian Pinot.

All things considered, we may guess that Egypt had her viticulture from Phoenicia early in the fourth millennium B.C., and that Phoenicia had it either from Mesopotamia to her east or from the source, in the north.

Needless to say, vines and viticulture had reached Egypt long before the stage of oinological sophistication which we have been discussing. Vineyards were first planted in the Delta region in pre-Dynastic times, and during the times of the Thinitic rulers. They were, as usual at the beginning, for the purpose of providing funerary wines for the princes and prelates, and not for daily consumption by the people. But there is a difficulty here: it may simply be that whereas we know of the royal and religious vineyards because their names and purpose had to be recorded, if only on the stoppers of wine-jars, privately-owned vineyards, if they existed, would have left no record. I base the statement that there were no such vineyards until later on an estimate of the economic and social conditions of that time and place, and this may be quite wrong.

The source of our knowledge of the early Egyptian vineyards is the sealing-inscriptions of amphora-stoppers; it is almost as if we were trying to estimate the nature and extent of the Gironde vineyards from the printing on the bottle labels and the wax seals of the corks. These early vineyards were outside what was called the White Wall of Memphis; there were others equally ancient at Nebesheh, Sajn and probably other places. They were oval in shape, surrounded by a wall with some kind of *cheval-de-frise*, presumably to exclude thieves. That the vineyards were religious, were temple property, is apparent from their names: typical are 'Praised-be-Horus-first-of-heaven', of King Zoser; Khasekhemui's 'Praised-be-the-souls-of-Horus'. Earlier still, in pre-Dynastic times, the names are 'Beverage-of-Horus' or 'Enclosure-of-the-beverage-of-Horus' (or '. . . of-the-body-of-Horus').

From such evidence as we have, it would seem that the Egyptian vineyards, first these ecclesiastical properties and later the private and commercial vineyards, were not at all like those we know now, but were, rather, vine-gardens. The vines were trained on trellis supported by rafters fixed to columns of brick or stone often finely carved, and forming many colon-

nades. The vines thus shaded the soil and minimized loss of water by evapo-
ration (*plate 11*). Every garden had a water-tank, for irrigation was of course
necessary, in fact the gardener or vine-dresser watered the vines every
evening. But such vineyards were also pleasances of the princes, high
officials and priests. The simpler vineyards which probably came later are
more like those of southern Italy (see Chapter IV) in that ordinary poles or
perhaps even papyrus reeds were used as stakes; forked sticks were also used,
set upright in the soil and with a cross-stick to carry the extension of the vine.
Finally, the device of planting vines close and pruning them hard to form,
virtually, rows of bushy hedges, is an Egyptian invention which has been
copied for the last four or five thousand years. Another Egyptian invention,
unless they had it from the north, was deep mulching with top-soil to preserve water about the roots, as is apparent from the tomb-painting of Paheri
at el-Kab. From coloured representations of the vine it appears that the
Egyptians had several *cépages*, for in some the grapes are deep blue, while in
others (from the XVII Dynasty onwards) they are white, pale green, even
red or pink.

As the grapes ripened, birds became troublesome and scaring them off
was a chore for women and children. As soon as the grapes were gathered
it seems—if one mural at Beni-Hasan is a reliable document—that the farmyard animals (in this case goats) were turned into the enclosure to browse on
the foliage. Since the Egyptians understood pruning, an art they probably
learned from the Syrians or Phoenicians but may have devised for themselves, doubtless this browsing was checked before any harm was done to
the vines.

The vintage was carried directly from the vineyard to the treading vats,
enormous vessels of acacia wood, roofed, and large enough to enable six
men to move about in them more or less at their ease. The quantity of grapes
put into the vats at one time was sufficient only to cover the ankles of the
treaders, who were provided with ropes dependent from the roof in order to
steady themselves as they trod out the vintage (*plate II*). Alternatively, the
treaders arranged themselves in single file, held each other by the hips, and
trod rhythmically round the vat, singing or chanting to time kept by men
and women who stood by watching, and clapping out the rhythm.

If the Egyptians were as intelligent in their vinting as in their other crafts,
red wine would not have been pressed. From the treading vats the must

would have been run into the fermenting vats, solids and liquids together. But the must for white wine was pressed. With the exception of very few varieties of grapes, known to the French as *teinturiers*, the juice of black grapes is white or colourless, the colour of red wine being derived from the skins. This colour is extracted from the skins during and by means of fermentation, and since the Egyptians had red wines, it follows that they did not press and filter all their wines.

The wine-press for white wine was an effective device: it consisted of a massive timber framework of two uprights, set in the ground about six feet apart or rather less, and held apart at the top by a cross-beam. The two uprights were each drilled with a hole about three or four feet from the ground. The trodden must was put into a large linen cloth provided at its ends with cords, which were passed through the holes in the beams and tied there, the bag full of must being thus slung like a hammock between the uprights. A stout stick was passed through a loop of the cord at one side, a tub or earthen vessel was placed on the ground beneath the bag, and four burly vintners then twisted the bag by turning the stick. The juice was thus *wrung* from the must, and, in fact, in ancient Egyptian the verb to press means, literally, to wring. A simpler version of this wringing-out process appears in a relief from the tomb of Mereruka of the fourth millenium B.C. (*plate* 12).

In some murals it is possible to see the Egyptian vintners applying heat to the must, that is to say, boiling it. The object of this was to reduce it to a grape-sugar syrup, which might be used for its own sake or to sweeten and colour the wine, a practice still to be met with in Jérez and in parts of Rumania.

After fermentation, the new wine was filtered through linen into stone or earthen vessels, thereafter stoppered and sealed (*plates 13–15*). The jars were first smeared internally with pitch or bitumen, as a preservative, a practice later copied in Greece, in Italy and in France (*plate 48*), and still common in some Balkan vineyards; it is ruin to good wine but improves some ordinary wines. Wine was also kept and transported in goat-skins.

The Egyptians very early discovered a nice taste in wine, distinguishing various qualities, vintages, age and colour. Valuing old wine, they kept careful records of each vintage, noting the vineyard, the year and even the name of the vintner. A typical wine-jar label reads: 'In the year I. Good wine of the large irrigated terrain of the Temple of Rameses II in Per-Amon. The chief of the vintners, Tutmes.'[12]

'Good wine' seems rather vague, but no doubt a definite meaning was attached to it, and the words not uncommonly appeared on wine labels.[13] What 'good' and 'very good' meant we cannot know, but probably body would have been appreciated, for the Egyptians liked to get drunk. Moreover, since 'sweet' wine is also distinguished, perhaps the good and very good wines were, on the contrary, dry. But I doubt it.

Once made, the wine was tried and inspected by a public official, the Inspector of the Wine Test, and then stored according to an ingenious cellarage plan whereby new wine went to the back of the cellar as old wine was brought forward.

How many centuries passed from the first, accidental vinting of wild grapes to the establishment of such routine practices of cultivation, vinting and cellarage as I have described? We do not know. Not less than ten and not more than fifty is about as near as we can get to an answer. But it is certain that the time was very much shorter between the first rustic vintage and the growth of that state of mind succinctly expressed in an ancient Egyptian inscription in a wine-cellar at Esna:

> This is the wine-cellar,
> the place for the produce of the vine is in it.
> One is merry in it.
> And the heart of him who goes forth from it rejoices.

In historical times the vineyards of Egypt, other than those owned by temples or the State, were taxed, the tax being payable not in kind as in the Assyrian case, but in money. How early this began we do not know; the earliest documents relating to this excise are of the third century B.C., which is of course very late. We have earlier documents to show that the Egyptians understood that where possible vines should be planted on hillsides and in stony ground; having few hills, they built raised platforms or mounds for their vineyards, after the Mesopotamian model but nothing like so elaborate.

In the Prologue, discussing the limits imposed on viticulture by climatic and other considerations, I have tried to show that the Egyptian delta was about as far south as vines could be grown; there may have been some vineyards further south, in fact it is almost certain that there were. But it was recognized that the best were those of the delta, and in historical times the wines of what is now the Faiyum were famous far beyond Egypt. This Arsinoitic wine was still famous in Strabo's time; and the wine of the Mareotic nome also had a great name in the second and first centuries B.C. The wine of Tenia (again this is very late in the day, but it demonstrated the expansion of viticulture into an important commercial undertaking, and its geographical extension) was praised by Athenaeus:

'Its colour is pale and white and there is such a measure of richness in it that when mixed with water it seems only gradually to be diluted, much the same way as Attic honey when liquid is poured into it; and besides the agreeable flavour of the wine, its fragrance is so delightful as to render it perfectly aromatic and it has the property of being slightly astringent.'

Astringent or no, this wine was clearly a syrupy one. Sebennyticum wine, anciently famous in Pliny's time, was another Egyptian vintage. Three different grapes were used in making it, the Thasian, outstanding for sweetness; the 'Smoky' (possibly 'grizzled'), and the 'Pitchy', whatever that may mean. The southernmost vineyards of which we hear are those of Meroë, but only one commentator has anything good to say about their wines.

The general conclusion from the whole body of the evidence must be that by 3000 B.C. at the latest and probably much earlier, viticulture, having come down from ancient Armenia, had reached an advanced stage of sophistication in the states of Mesopotamia, in all the lands of Syria and Phoenicia, and in the Egyptian delta; that its extreme southern point in prehistoric times was Meroë; and that its very great antiquity even by the year 3000 B.C. is vouched for by the diversification of the species *Vitis vinifera*, for such diversification is a work of much time.

# CHAPTER III

## *Bacchae in Greece*

THE GRAPE-VINES HAD, THEN, BEEN TAKEN FROM THE WILD, domesticated, and their diversity and yield had been greatly improved well before 3000 B.C.—in other words, at a time when the peoples of Europe were as yet unready to become cultivators or gardeners. Vines closely related to those which had given rise to the cultivated varieties of the East grew in the woods of Greece, Italy and France. But the peoples of those countries were never to be called upon to go through the long, slow process of taming these wildings, for both the vineyard vines and the art of making wine were to be introduced from Asia. Both were preceded by wine itself: traders from the civilized East brought it, if only as a means of taming the natives. We do not know how early the gentry among the barbarous peoples of Europe imported wine from the cities of Tyre and Sidon and from the Nile delta. The pattern of this trade was repeated later in history, when civilized southern Europe was exporting wine to Northern France and south Britain for the Belgic aristocracy, and across the Rhine to the Germans, at least three centuries before the vine was planted in Britain, and probably much more.

By the time Homer was writing the *Iliad*, or the poems which he used as his material were composed, wine was not only the ordinary drink of the Greeks, but was clearly regarded as one of the country's natural products. Although we believe that the poet was working-up traditional history into a poem centuries after the events described occurred, it is certain that wine had long been 'natural' in Greece and was as necessary to the Homeric Greeks as bread and meat. Thus the shield of Achilles depicts, among other rural scenes, a vineyard in which the vintage is proceeding.[1] More to the point, not only do young maidens drink wine, but children seem to have been brought up on it, at least if they were intended to be heroes; for the infant Achilles was given wine with his meals by Phoenix the son of Amyntor, though it is true that it seems to have made the poor child vomit.[2]

The Troy of Homer fell about 1200 B.C., and about the same time or a little earlier or later the Israelites were beginning their conquest of Canaan. rich in vines. Canaanite viticulture had doubtless been learned from the Sidonians, Byblians and Tyrians, their neighbours and kinsfolk; in fact it is not really possible to separate Phoenicians and Canaanites. And there can be no doubt that it was from the same source that the peoples of Asia Minor, of what is now Anatolia, the Phrygians, the Lydians, the people of the Troad, Mycia and the Pontus, obtained their first wine and their first vine-cuttings. From these countries it is but a step into Thrace (indeed half the Thracians were Asiatics), and so into Greece proper. But very ancient Greece had other connections. Wine and vine could easily have come from Cnossos to Mycenae. In fact it may come to very much the same thing, for the Cretan culture spread to the shores of south-west Asia Minor as well as to those of Greece. The Cretans were among the very ancient peoples of the vine, and they, again, could have had it from either or both of two sources: from the cities of Phoenicia, with their alphabet which we now know to have been used to write Greek, so that the language of the Hellenes was the tongue of the later Minoans, perhaps through the rising influence of Argos; or from Egypt, with which country Crete seems to have had far closer relations, for the fashion of Minoan things is doubtless more Egyptian than Phoenician (*plate 24*), and we know that commerce between Crete and Egypt was brisk, even in the period called Early Minoan.

The Minoan civilization, with its centre in Crete and its colonies in the Aegean islands, in south-west Asia Minor and in Argos, apparently had its dawn in the third millennium B.C. The colonies do not belong to the earliest epoch, and Early Mycenaean is dated from 1800 B.C. The Early Mycenaeans could have had wine from Crete and could probably also have cultivated their own vineyards. The historic Greeks, or some of them, knew, indeed, that wine and the art of cultivating the vine came to them from Crete. Thus when Diodorus Siculus says, 'As for Dionysus, the myths say that he discovered the vine and its cultivation and also how to make wine . . .', he is writing of Crete and of one divine generation later than Demeter's, of

*III. Dionysus at sea after he had miraculously caused a vine to grow up the mast of his ship. The dolphins swimming around it are metamorphosed sailors. The scene illustrates the Homeric hymn to Dionysus, II. 34–53. From a cup by the potter Exekias, c. 535 B.C.*

whom he says that she discovered and gave wheat to mankind, 'probably in Sicily'. The Cretans told Diodorus that the discovery of vine and wine happened 'many generations' before the time of Minos. One myth makes Oinopion the wine-man himself a grandson of Minos. But 'some writers of myths say that Oinopion was a son of Dionysus and learned from his father the art of making wine'.[3]

Later Diodorus has a fit of rational scepticism and says: 'but there are those who state that there was never any birth of him in human form whatever, and think that the word Dionysus means only "the gift of wine". Those authors, then, who use the phenomena of nature to explain this god and call the fruit of the vine "Dionysus" speak thus: "The earth brought forth of itself the vine at the same time with other plants and it was not originally planted by some man who discovered it. And they allege as proof of this the fact that to this day vines grow wild in many regions and bear fruit quite similar to that of many plants which are tended by the experienced hand of man ..."'

The myth of the thrice-born Dionysus is then explained as a symbol of natural phenomena:

'... For he is considered to be the son of Zeus and Demeter, they hold, by reason of the fact that the vine gets its growth both from the earth and from rains—and the statement that he was torn to pieces, while yet a youth, by the "earth-born" signifies the harvesting of the fruit by the labourers ... And with these stories agree the teachings which are set forth in the Orphic poems and are introduced into their rites ...'[4]

In the last sentence Diodorus is describing the typical 'platonization' as well as rationalization of a savage and primitive religion by a civilized and sophisticated teaching. But the art of viticulture would not, at that early date, have spread into the interior, for at that stage Mycenae seems to have been an enclave of civilization in a wilderness of barbarians: beyond the fortress walls of Tiryns and Mycenae lay a land of game and hunters; people, perhaps, of the same race as the men of Mycenae and Tiryns and with the same language, but not yet impressed by the new culture from Crete.

*IV Bacchus standing in front of Vesuvius, dressed as a bunch of grapes, spilling wine from a cup and attended by the traditional leopard. Wallpainting from a villa in Pompeii. Mid first century A.D. The Pompeiian vintages were famous.*

Yet it seems fairly sure that by the time the Achaeans descended upon Greece to conquer and enslave the indigenes, and to be conquered and enslaved by the language, religion and arts of those indigenes, the aborigines, the so-called 'Pelasgians', were a settled, farming people cultivating, among other things, the vine. This gives us two limit dates: by 1200 B.C. wine and vine were commonplaces of the daily life of Greece, and were supposed by the Achaeans to have been so since the beginning of the world; and by, let us say, 1600 B.C., the people these Achaeans were to conquer had reached a stage in their culture which would have made viticulture possible. It would be foolish and impertinent to insist upon this reasoning or these dates. But it does at least seem rather likely that the Asiatic grape-vine cultivars, the art of growing them, and the art of making wine, reached and was established in Greece in the second, rather than in the third or first millennium B.C.

Now as to the other, and in my view equally probable, route of vine and wine into Greece, I shall have recourse to an ancient myth embodied in the deathless and sublime poetry of a much less ancient poet:

> Behold, God's son is come into this land
> Of Thebes, even I Dionysus, whom the brand
> Of Heaven's hot splendour lit to life, when she
> Who bore me, Cadmus' daughter, Semele,
> Died here. So, changed in shape from God to man,
> I walk again by Dirce's streams and scan
> Ismenus' shore. There by the castle side
> I see her place, the Tomb of the Lightning's Bride.
> The wreck of smouldering chambers, and the great
> Faint wreaths of fire undying—as the Hate
> Dies not, that Hera held for Semele.
> Aye, Cadmus hath done well; in purity
> He keeps this place apart, inviolate,
> His daughter's sanctuary; and I have set
> My green and clustered vines to robe it round.
> Far now behind me lies the golden ground
> Of Lydian and Phrygian; far away
> The wide hot plain where Persian sunbeams play,

The Bactrian war-holds, and the storm-oppressed
Clime of the Mede, and Araby the Blest,
And Asia all that by the salt-sea lies
In proud, embattled cities, motley-wise
Of Hellene and Barbarians interwrought;[5]
And now I come to Hellas—having taught
All the world else my dances and my rite
Of mysteries, to show me in men's sight
Manifest God.

Thus, in Gilbert Murray's beautiful translation, the hero of Euripides' *The Bacchae* introduces himself and the play. Now, as will appear, Dionysus is not only the wine-god; he is the Vine, and his later name is Oineus, the Vine. He is much more than that too: but relevant here is his statement that he has conquered all Asia (Anatolia), Arabia, Media, Phrygia and Lydia. The order of mention of these place-names—if we suppose that he mentions the last halt first and works back, as one does—is very likely that of the order in which, in fact, viticulture came to those places. I do not of course go the length of saying that this is significant: it is, at most, curious.

Dionysus' grandfather, the Cadmus he refers to and to whose great city he has come, was a Tyrian or Sidonian, that is, a Phoenician, who had migrated to Greece and founded Thebes. Semele, one of Cadmus' daughters and the mother of Dionysus, was in another context the Phrygian goddess of the underworld, that is, the Phrygian Persephone. But Cadmus' Semele was not the god's first mother, for he had at least two epiphanies, and in the first his mother was Persephone (*plates 19, 21*). Her father was Zeus, who begat her on Rhea who is often called Demeter. Demeter took the young goddess to Sicily and hid her in a cave where her father Zeus found and, in the form of a serpent, possessed her. As a result of this incest she bore Dionysus, the god who was to succeed Zeus as fifth ruler of the universe. That, at all events, is what much later, Orphic, prophets made of it. The goddess Hera, however, held Persephone (or Demeter, or both; in any case they are sometimes one) in hate. She sent certain 'earth-born beings' called Kouretes to destroy the baby god. Two points here: in Euripides' play, Pentheus the antagonist of Dionysus is said to be 'earth-born'; and we find the Kouretes again, later, in Thrace, but as a fighting tribe, or so it seems to me, at war with the

Aetolian guardians of Dionysus' first European shrine. Diodorus Siculus says that these Kouretes were Cretans; they succeeded to those proto-deities the 'Idaean Dactyli', and (again), 'earth-born', invented sheep-herding, beekeeping, the bow and arrow, swords, helmets and the war-dance. At all events, in the myth these Kouretes tear the child Dionysus in pieces,[6] and (sparing one limb; I don't know why) boil and then burn his parts, and scatter the ashes. From the scattered ashes spring grape-vines.

I have simplified as best I can a complex of myths so involved that there is no sorting them out; but the 'story-line' has not been falsified. In the second birth either Zeus came to Semele in the form of a human lover and behaved as such; or he sent to her, by Hera, a pomegranate seed, most potent nucleus of fertility, or an infusion of the heart of the first Dionysus, taking which she conceived, so that she was to be a virgin mother. Unhappily for her she asked that her lover visit her, if only once, in the divine form that he wore with the goddesses, notably with Hera. The wish was granted and he came to her as a flash of lightning by which, being mortal, she was blasted. (Hence Dionysus in the play says of himself: 'Whom the brand of Heaven's hot splendour lit to life.') The child in Semele's womb, being an Immortal, was not hurt by his father's lightning; Zeus took him from the mother's womb and, tearing open his thigh, sewed him into it to grow there until the time came to be born. When that time came Zeus went to Mount Nysa and there gave birth to the Vine. Dionysus was reared by nurses, his aunts, and educated by a tutor, Silenus. In another context his aunts deny his divinity and rites. One of his reasons for coming to Thebes is to chastise them.

Summing up at this point: Dionysus was the Vine; they are one and the same. He was an Asiatic. He conquered the (Minoan) coast-lands of Asia Minor. And he invaded Greece.

I do not want to retell the whole story of Euripides' play: but I must refer to it in so far as it yields us some insights. The antagonist is Pentheus, son of Cadmus, to whom the old Tyrian king has, for reasons of age and infirmity, resigned the Theban throne. Pentheus is shocked and infuriated by the way in which the matrons and maids of Thebes, including his sisters and his mother, converted or rather possessed by Dionysus (a thoroughly undesirable, because new, Asiatic, and probably spurious, god), have rushed off dancing and singing in a most unseemly way to dwell on the mountains and in the woods.

# Bacchae in Greece

18  *Maenad dancing, early fifth century* B.C.

The Greek god Dionysus was the son of Zeus, and had at least two epiphanies. An archaic votive tablet (19) shows him with his first mother, Persephone. In the second epiphany his mother was a mortal, Semele (21), daughter of the Phoenician who founded Thebes—a geneology which suggests the origin of the Greek vines themselves.

Dionysus came to the Greeks from Asia, and his 'foreignness' is apparent in his elaborate costume and long dark curls (20). The meeting of Apollo (left) and Dionysus is a meeting of opposites: Apollo represents the rule of order and the intellect, and Dionysus the power of the instincts and the vine's gift of inspiration.

Dionysus and Ariadne with the bacchic rout (22). While Ariadne was taking part in the revels on Naxos she was stealthily abandoned by Theseus, whose life she had saved, and Dionysus came to her rescue.

21

22

*A libation vase of the second millennium B.C. from the island of Crete (23) is decorated with marine plants and animals. Below (25), a fine goblet.*

23

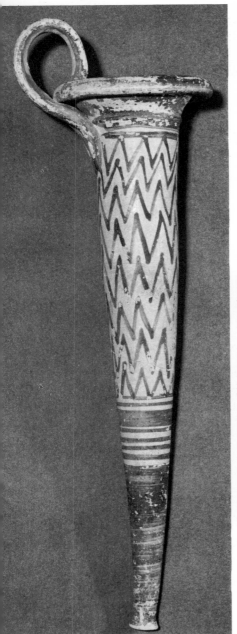

24

25

26

*The design of the tall libation vase (24) is a reminder of Crete's contacts with Egypt (cf. plate 13), and indeed it may have been from Egypt that the vine came to Crete and passed to the Mycenaeans of southern Greece. The Mycenaean gold cup (26) has two small birds on the handles.*

27　*A servant carries wine for a feast, on a sixth-century vase.*

28

29

*A wine cooler of the fifth century* B.C. *is decorated with satyrs playing with a wine skin (29). When the cooler was in use the outer bowl (28) was filled with cold water or snow and the decorated inner vase placed within it.*

A Greek child's toys: a wine jug two inches high (30) and a horse-cart with six miniature amphorae (31).

30

31

32

The vine's social and economic importance in Greece led to its frequent use as decoration on coins and medals (32). Towns and regions famous for their vineyards celebrated the fact in coinage bearing grapes, satyrs and Dionysus. The extent of the Greek viticulture is suggested by such coins, which range from Trapezus on the Black Sea in the east, (top left) to Soli near Tarsus (top centre), and Sicily in the west (top right).

The greatest viticultural areas of Greece proper were islands like Naxos (above left) and Tenos (above right), and on the mainland Mende (above centre and lower right).

A locust sits on a vine-leaf, on a pottery lamp (33) from the Greek colony of Massilia. Locusts were a scourge of the vineyards of Greece, and in certain parts of the country every citizen was compelled by law to collect annually a certain measure of locusts or locust eggs for destruction. Birds, too, are redoubtable enemies of the vinegrower. On the sixth-century cup from eastern Greece (34) a man frightens a bird from the vines, while a locust perches on a branch at the lower left.

33

34

As is usual in Greek drama, the unfortunate Pentheus is never told that his opponent is a god in person; he knows he is fighting one who claims godhead, but the fellow is his own brother, and as to the dark, effeminate-looking stranger who has appeared at Thebes and is causing all this trouble, Pentheus takes him for what he claims to be, a missionary of the god, not the god in person. Like Oedipus, like every Greek protagonist, Pentheus is in fact doomed in advance whatever he may do; for in this play as in others of the Greek canon, the Greek knowledge of the ultimate frightfulness of the human condition is displayed in a way our own great drama never displays it. Pentheus stands for man's law, man's good order, woman in her 'proper' place; for commonsense, if you like, intellect without imagination: ultimately then, for the rational, formal Establishment anywhere, any time. Naturally, nothing he can do to bind and restrain either the Theban women turned maenads, or the god, is any use. Finally, the god, instead of allowing Pentheus to go on behaving after his own mind and character, 'possesses' him and thereby persuades him to attire himself as a maenad (pure comedy this scene), in order to go to the hills and woods and spy on the bacchae and see what they are really up to. The bacchae are led by Pentheus' own mother, and neither she nor her companions see Pentheus, whom the god exposes to them, as himself. They see him as a lion, and they set upon it in the bacchic mania, the Dionysiac 'raging', and tear the creature to pieces, Pentheus' mother getting the head. (This sacrifice appears in every Dionysiac rite: it is notable that in the legend of Rome's founding the men of the Senate tear Romulus to pieces; the Witches' Sabbath, with only one male wearing an animal mask to a coven of women, is clearly derived from the thriambus of the maenads.) Not until the maenads, rejoicing at their victory over the lion, return to Thebes, does old Cadmus make his daughter see what she has really done. And the whole human cast are condemned to go raging in the bacchic dance through Hellas, missionaries of vinous disorder.[7]

Very significant in the context of this study of the vine in its social influence is the nature of the bacchic mania. Nothing in the character of the god and his rites could be more utterly remote from our conception of vinous jollity, of the good-natured frivolity and the jovial good time, of the drinking-song type of cheerful humour; or more utterly remote from the spirit of the poetry of Horace, Hafiz or the prose of Saintsbury or, for that matter, Mr Cyril Ray. The terror and madness of a really bad drunk-in-charge-of-car case are much nearer. The bacchic 'rage' is full of laughter, but what a terrible sound it is; of wild play, but how destructive. The god himself is a very peculiar person indeed: not only deeply alien to the Achaean spirit, and to the Achaean idea of a man, he is effeminate in his clothes, in his long, dark curls, in his pink and white complexion, his soft skin and softer manner (*plate 20*). Overwhelmingly attractive to women, he also draws to him men; in him normal sexuality is confounded, but, and this is important, it is also lost: the bacchic raging is not an 'orgy'; it is utterly chaste. It is destructive of both social order and of property—the maenads are apt to wreck the premises. But it is not sexual. Nor is it in any way a worship of youth. When, for example, the very old priest Tiresias and the even more ancient Cadmus put on the livery of the god, the fawn-skin and the ivy-wreath, and make the first, highly formal, motions of the manic dance, they feel their youth and strength restored to them, and they justify their conduct.

> Aye, men will rail that I forget my years
> To dance and wreathe with ivy these white hairs;
> What recks it? Seeing the God no line hath told
> To mark what men shall dance, or young or old.

In the same spirit women of all ages cast off their 'inhibitions', those rules which make the social order of all civilizations, and gain a tremendous, an explosive release;[8] are 'possessed' but by a happiness, or rather joy, which is, literally, bestial. Their feeling is not merriness; it is not human at all; it is the joy one observes in a cat or a fox at the kind of wild play which ends not in an embrace but in a killing. That is the price.

What came into Greece from Asia was the power to release, or rather to unleash, in ourselves the carefully suppressed creature of immediate apprehensions (whose stylized and regulated representative is the great artist), capable of enjoying experiences and having knowledge which man, as man and not either beast or god, has been obliged to suppress in himself. It is amusing to find, in innumerable classicists, a certain head-shaking over the conduct of the Olympian gods in general; how could men worship such monsters of vice? Easily, of course, recognizing in them the creature with the mind of man and the free instincts of the beast, which man can himself be—at the cost of sacrificing social order and therefore civilization. The

Man-Plant-God, the True Vine which came into Greece from Asia by way
of the Thracian mountains, was no vintage for Nausicaa to drink with her
*al fresco* washing-day luncheon; no urbane Falernian or Caecuban for a
Horace or a Martial, those Sunday newspaper wine-correspondents *avant la
lettre*, to praise in verse; no great claret to rejoice the palate of some well-bred
don. The Dionysian wine was dark and sweet and aromatic and thick; was
powerful, pernicious, terrifying.

But the civilizing of this appalling power began very soon. In Euripides'
play, one of the greatest poems in the world's literature, a marvellous work
of partly covering the hard bones of the old myth with the soft flesh of Orphism's gentleness has been accomplished by the poet. Thus Dionysus is a dual
creature: capable of attacking the very seat of reason and humiliating men as
he releases them from their self-control, yet that he does only to chastise. It
is not his only aim: he abjures Pentheus:

> Dream not that force is power
> Nor, if thou hast a thought and that thought sour,
> And sick, O dream not thought is wisdom.

To force men to cease worshipping the intellect instead of using it, that seems
to be the idea. And again the Orphic reform of the cult is apparent in the
sweetness of many of the choral passages, in which the noble, the sublime,
gentleness of Dionysus is propagated:

> Is it so hard a thing to see,
> That the spirit of God whate'er it be
> The Law that abides and changes not, age long
> The Eternal and Nature-born—these things be strong?

> What else is Wisdom? What of man's endeavour
> Or God's high grace so lovely and so great?
> To stand from fear set free, to breathe and wait;
> To hold a hand uplifted over Hate;
> And shall not loveliness be loved for ever?

The movement of reform of the bacchic cult which produced the gentler
Dionysus, which civilized the use of the Vine, occurred in the sixth century
B.C. But the material it used, the God of Intoxication from the mountains of
Asia Minor and from Thrace, was very much older; was, if I am near right,

perhaps a thousand years old when the Orphists set about it. Why turn to Dionysus? For just that emotional element which was needed to offset the inevitable consequence of intellect-worship, the hardening of the heart.

We can find, once again in myth, traces of the movement through Thrace. The *thriambos* (whence our word *triumph*), the Dionysian hymn, sounded there before it was ever heard in Greece, unless it was coming to a meeting and union of voices by the Mycenaean route also. That is likely enough, for the god had been in Crete too, becoming involved with Ariadne (plate 22), daughter of Minos and Pasiphae. Typical of the Thracian epiphany is the story of Orestheus and his dog (or should it be bitch?) Sirius, which comes from southern Aetolia. This remarkable animal, whose name apparently stands for midsummer heat, gave birth to a piece of living branch—in fact to what gardeners call a 'cutting'. Orestheus, who was the son of Deucalion the Hellenic Noah, buried this piece of wood and from it there grew a grape-vine. (The first thing that Noah did after the flood was to plant a vineyard and get blind drunk on the product, and who shall blame him?) It may be to the point that Orestheus means 'man of the mountain'; his grandson was named Oineus, the Vine. Hehn says that Locria also had this legend.[9] Oineus and the Kouretes turn up in the *Iliad* with Oineus refusing to sacrifice to Artemis, which, again, may just possibly have social and economic significance. The Aetolians are described by ancient Greek authorities as having the earliest shrine sacred to Dionysus; their enemies, in Homer, are the Kouretes.

In other and again numerous legends, the grape-vine is given to man by the Lydian-Thracian Dionysus: the Icarian legend of Erigone and the dog Maira (Sirius again) is typical of many. But for geographical and several other reasons, it is only the Thracian legends, and facts, which need interest us, for not only was Thrace the country by way of which the cultivated vine and the art of vinting could have entered Greece, it was almost certainly the focus of both the introductions, from the two sources I have suggested. Because of its geographical position, it was in touch, through trade and war, with the civilized countries of western Asia. Herodotus, for example (and he is far from unreliable as to principal events, however credulous in details), says that, before the Trojan war, there was a major invasion of Thrace by Mysians and Teucrians. If this be true they would certainly have had wine with them, and it is possible that they introduced both the cultivated vine and the making of wine to the barbarous but teachable worshippers of Ares.

For, says Hehn,[10] Mysia '. . . was celebrated for its wealth of grapes. The representations of a suffering and then triumphant god of the sun or Year [that is, in Thracian religious ceremonies] . . . the heart-breaking laments and furious mirth with which the Thyiades celebrated his death and resurrection; the double character in which Dionysus and Apollo, or Ares and Dionysus melt into one; this . . . smacks of Phrygia and western Asia in general.'

If this method of tracing the diffusion of vine-planting and wine-making —that is, by trying to follow the rise and growth of the new Apollo-Dionysus cult through Greece—be sound (and we have no other method), then it would seem that from Thrace these arts spread throughout Macedonia, native heath of the raving Bacchanals, to Parnassus, to Delphi, Thebes, Boiotia, Attica, perhaps in that order. And if the new cult met with fairly rapid success, despite fierce opposition from conservative elements like Pentheus and from clerical vested interests, it may well be because the cult was indeed entering Greece by another route, but still by way of Thrace, so that two mutually supporting 'movements' met and merged. The Phoenicians, it seems, established first trading-posts and later colonies on the Thracian coast. It is suggested that they may have been, rather, Cretans, of the Early Minoan culture. Whoever these adventurers may have been, they would have used wine, long since established in Crete, to tempt the natives to trade; and later, when firmly established as colonists, would have persuaded or obliged the natives to plant vines. It seems likely enough: our own nineteenth-century traders made a like use of spirits.

'From Crete . . . this culture and legends attached to it made their way to the islands of the Aegeans, to Naxos, Chios and farther still. Fr. Osnann's "Oinopion and his Kin" shows that the diffusion of viticulture through the world was personified in the story of a Cretan family travelling by way of Naxos to Chios, which then became a centre of an improved culture and of numerous colonies which propagated the vine. Now according to a tradition as old as Hesiod even the Thracian Maron of the Odyssey was the son or grandson of this Oinopion; and thus the two branches or outlets of Greek wine-cultivation meet in one.'[11]

Hesiod's *Biblios oinos*, Byblian wine, may perhaps be a clue to the diffusion story, a clue in nomenclature[12] (see Chapter II). Byblian wine reappears at intervals later as, no doubt, 'sauternes' will reappear in the coming centuries wherever wine can be made and the maker wants to exploit a great and ancient name. The name was used in Calabria and in Sicily (see, for example, Theocritus 14, 15). There is an historian (I have not read him), Hippys of Rhegium, who tells how the vines capable of yielding 'Byblian wine' were first planted in Sicily, from a southern Italian vineyard. But there is more and other significance in this Byblian wine which the poet's husbandman seeks to quench his thirst—or rather to restore his strength, for these sugary wines made, as Hesiod elsewhere indicates, from half-dried grapes, can never have quenched a man's thirst: it is not very likely that the eighth-century Greek peasant was drinking imported Phoenician wine; Byblian wine, then, becomes in all probability wine of the Byblian vine; Hesiod is speaking of Byblian wine in the spirit of a Chilean poet praising the Riesling—of the Andean foothills, not the Rhine. If this be so, it might be considered as good evidence that not only the art of viticulture but, as I believe and others deny, the cultivated plants, were introduced into Hellas.

A study of the names of the principal objects involved, and of the word *wine* itself, reveals an immediately Semitic source of Hellenic viticulture. The Greek word οινος, (v)*oinos*, Latin *vinum*, Italian *vino*, French *vin*, English wine, etc., is the same as the Hebrew word *yain* and the Arabic word *wain*. Not, of course, that we all had this word from the Jews, still less from the Arabs. Both the Hellenes and the Jews had it from a Semitic origin in some part of Asia Minor, very probably Phoenicia.

'The true home of the vine, which is the luxuriant country south of the Caspian sea, was also, as far as can be historically determined, close to the cradle of the Semitic race or of one of its chief branches. There, in the woods, the vine, thick as a man's arm, still climbs into the loftiest trees, hanging in wreaths from summit to summit, and temptingly displaying its heavy bunches of grapes. There, or in Colchis on the Phasis, in the countries lying between the Caucasus, Ararat, and Taurus, the primitive methods of cultivation we read of in the works of the Greeks and Romans are still practised . . . the pitching or chalking of the amphorae, the burying of them in the ground, etc. There grow the spicy, orange-yellow wines of penetrating odour, and the precious Cachetian grape yields a juice so intensely dark red that ladies write their letters with it. From these regions the vine accompanied the teeming race of Shem to the lower Euphrates in the south-east, and to the deserts and paradises of the south-west . . . To the Semites then, who even invented the distillation of alcohol, who accomplished the gigantic abstractions of monotheism, measurement, money and alphabetic writing . . . belongs also the dubious fame of having arrested the juice of the grape at the stage of fermentation, and so produced an exhilarating or stupefying beverage . . .'[13]

This passage was first published in 1888 and needs revision in its details. But it is still, no doubt, substantially true; moreover it is worth noting that Hehn, who believed that already, even in 1880, the scientist was having things too much his own way and that it was time that historical and philologic methods came into play, did arrive at certain conclusions by those methods which genetical and other sciences have since confirmed: Vavilov and Negrul have not really added anything new to Hehn's findings; nor have the archaeologists.

It is, however, only fair to point out that the philological arguments for a Semitic origin of viticulture are far from conclusive. In all the scholars in whose writings I have sought enlightenment, I have found only opinion and confusion; nor has later criticism by men of science done anything to make a choice between the opinions of men of letters any easier: modern phyto-genetics has done nothing to enable us to say that this or that nineteenth-century philologist was right. To me it seems that the arguments in favour of a Semitic origin for the art we are discussing are sound. But there is a theory that some sort of very primitive viticulture was practised, or at least that wine was made from wild grapes, by the ancient people who spoke the proto-language called Indo-European, which as far as I know is hypothetical. The Semitic peoples, according to this theory, borrowed the words for wine and other, cognate, terms from this language, with the idea and the art themselves. Billiard,[14] for example, cites the Sanskrit word *draksa* as evidence that the ancient 'Aryans' must have been wine-growers, but his argument collapses when one discovers, after much labour, that the best Sanskrit scholars consider this to be a loan-word and not of ancient Indo-European origin at all. Billiard is not to blame; he is imply following Hommel and other learned Germans.[15]

Touching the spread of viticulture through first barbarous and later civilized Greece we have little information. Mycenaean sites yield to the spade not only amphorae or pithoi, but also, and this is true for the earliest, lumps of densely compressed grape-pips which appear to be the vestiges of *marc.* And it is true, too, that Columella (see Chapter IV), the greatest of ancient agronomists, writes: '*Et ut agricolationem romana tandem civitate donemus (nam ad hunc istis auctoribus graecae fuit . . .)*' 'and so that we may confer Roman citizenship upon agriculture (because those who have written about it were all Greeks . . .)'. It is also the case that this author, as likewise Varro, another agronomist of merit, quote no less than ninety authors who have written on agriculture and horticulture, including viticulture, and imply that for the most part the Latins among them simply copy from the Greeks. Yet the anthology of such writings made (probably) by Cassianus Bassus, the so-called *Geoponica*, in the tenth century is drawn chiefly from Latin writers. One can find odds and ends about Greek viticulture in Theophrastus,[16] but that their usefulness is limited is suggested by a remark, surely directed at books of that kind, which Varro put into the mouth of Stolo, one of the dialoguists in his agronomical writings:[17] 'In my view such books are less suitable for men who till the soil than for those who attend schools of philosophy.'

Whatever can be gathered from fragments of textbooks tends, however, to confirm the men of letters and their mythical sources; if myth and poetry point to Thrace as the first wine country of Greece, so does the immense antiquity of that Maronean wine which Ulysses used to make Polyphemus blind-drunk; Maro, eponymous ancestor of the Maroneans, is said to have been a great-grandson of Dionysus, and the agronomists are so impressed with the antiquity of the Maronean vineyards of Thrace that they accept this as true. Thracian wines were still in good repute in Pliny's time. And it is certain that if Thrace was the first, then Macedonia must have been the second of the Hellenic vineyard countries. The *grands crus* of Macedonia were those of Acanthus and Mende,[18] but from what date their reputation was established we cannot determine. Other parts of the northern and least-civilized of the Hellenic states were well known for their wines. Both the Heraclean of Thessaly and the Ambraciot of the Epirus were recommended by Appollodorus for their medicinal if not for their aesthetic qualities, as was also the Œniat of Illyria. These growths, still in repute in Roman times, were doubtless among the oldest of 'Greek' vintages.

Despite the commercial importance of subsistence viticulture in Attica, and of the commercial, especially export dealing in the small farmers' surpluses, Athens had no great vintages, no wine ever to become famous by name excepting an artificial wine, some kind of vermouth, called Chrisatti-kos. Viticulture was an ordinary part of farming in Attica from about 1000 B.C., but so far did Athens remain from being a producer of fine wines that the wealthy imported something better than they could grow, from the Aegean islands. The Peloponnese was not quite so poor; it is true that in the seventh century B.C. only a single Laconian deme was known for its wine; but later the wines of Corinth and Arcadia were reputed fine. As early as the sixth century B.C. the wine of Argos which, if I am right in my speculations, was in the making as early as, and perhaps earlier than, the wines of Thrace, had become a legend of past excellence, like Falernian in the fourth century A.D. when Ausonius was writing about Moselle, or like Constantia today when one considers the wines of South Africa.

Boeotia, if we may follow Homer, was famous for its vineyards and its growths as early as the eighth century B.C. According to Alcman, Spartan wine of the Seven Hills was remarkable for the delicacy of its bouquet. And Athenaeus praises the wines of Tanagra and Anthedon which may have come, by his time, from vineyards centuries old.

It is safe to assume that vineyards were most ancient about those towns and places which have the radicle (*v*)*oinos* in their name. Such were the Thessalian and the Acarnanian *Oeniades*; the Laconian *Oenus*; the ancient name, *Oenopia*, for Aegina; *Oenoe*, an Attican deme and also an Aegean island; the Boiotian *Oenophyta*. Doubtless I have missed many examples which those better acquainted with the Greek literature than I am will recall. And even where no such nominal guide is provided, it is clear that many of the islands were very anciently provided with vineyards; the fame of their wines endured for many centuries, and in some cases special qualities were attributed to them. The black wine, as it is called, of Cos was heady but medicinal (I do not know what it cured); the white of the same island was mixed with, of all things, sea-water, apparently to preserve it. Not only must it have been very nasty, but it was said to cause headaches; yet it was in such great demand in the Rome of the second century B.C. that Cato[19] (see Chapter IV) found a way to exploit the demand by faking the wine with an Italian one; whether that stern moralist sold the stuff as genuine Cos does not appear.

The greatest growths among the island wines were the two Chian: Virgil wrote of one, the Phanaean, '*rex ipse Phanaeus!*'; the other was the Methymnaean of Lesbos; and the six-year-old wine of the islet Peparethe which Appollodorus preferred to both the others but of which only a minute quantity ever reached the market.[20]

The only reason for naming these growths is that their fame is evidence of the antiquity of their vineyards; it usually takes some centuries to produce a fine wine; and among the places named above are certainly the most ancient sites of European viticulture. By Roman times Greece had become to the whole Mediterranean world what France is to us, *the* land of wine. And her vineyards held this place from about the fifth to about the later first century B.C. (see Chapter IV). The Italians of the second century B.C. drank domestic wines in the ordinary way, but they imported Greek wines as superior; Greek wine was, however, an article of luxury, for it was relatively scarce, and it was dear, even very dear. Lucullus said that at his father's table no guest was ever given more than one cup of Greek wine. But, as will appear, by the end of the first century B.C. the Italian *grands crus* were driving the Greek ones out of fashion, and it was not long before they had driven them quite off the Roman market. By A.D. 300 Greek wine was no longer heard of at all; in the list of controlled maximum prices for wine issued by Diocletian's government in 301 to check profiteering in wine, the only Greek wine which appears is the Attican 'vermouth', Chrisattikos.

The principal cause of this decline, the rise of Italian viticulture, belongs in the next chapter. But another important cause was the failure of the Greek wine-growers to change the pattern of their industry. They could not produce in quantity. In an increasingly egalitarian, vulgar, commercial oligarchy of the Roman imperial type, fashion and conformity are very important. In Trimalchio's day he could have made no impression on his guests by serving them Greek wine of Lesbos or Chios, even by the bucketful, and even though it was still better than Falernian; for Falernian was the fashion, as whisky is the fashion today in France. It has nothing to do with quality, everything to do with vogue. Probably if Chios and Lesbos had been able to increase the quantity they produced so that all the rich of Rome could buy their wines, these wines might have retained their place. But what was wanted was a wine which was reputed very good, was dear, but was also plentiful.

The conservatism of Greek viticulture was a product of the farming situation generally in that country. In the fifth century B.C., and in the democracies, taking Athens as a model, seventy-five per cent of the citizens were small landowners; small, freehold farms were the rule, large commercial farming undertakings the exception. The majority of small freeholders farmed their own land; they cultivated their vines with their own hands and their vineyards were very small. They might employ one, or perhaps even two, slaves, no more. In the tyrannies the case was different: large estates worked by slaves predominated; it was from the vineyards of such estates that the wine came that was exported in bulk and without a name to such markets as the Crimea and the coast ports of the Red (Erythraean) Sea. Much earlier, in the seventh and early sixth centuries B.C., many vineyards were worked on a share-cropping basis, but this system did not last long and in the democracies there is no evidence for it after the first decades of the sixth century. It lasted much longer in Sparta and similar polities, until, in Sparta at least, it was replaced by serfdom—the working of the vineyards by helots for masters of large properties. In Attica, after the abandonment of share-cropping leases, vineyards not worked by their owners were let to tenants on a money-rent basis. Tenant vinearoons were given, under law, long leases, security of tenure on condition of good maintenance of the vineyard; owners reserved the right, in typical leases, to send in their own expert vine-pruners during the last five years of the lease. This right is, as far as I can discover, peculiar to Athenian agricultural law; it would, of course, have ensured that when the time came to renew the lease the vines were in the best condition to attract a tenant.

The Greeks had been pruning vines for as long as they had had any, and the origin of the practice is clearly much older than Greek civilization—is therefore Asiatic. There were, of course, legends and myths about it: Pausanias says that it was invented by the Nauplians who got the idea after observing the fruitfulness of a vine which had been eaten down by a donkey. The very great importance of pruning to the quality of wine was recognized so early that it seems always to have been known: in the earliest codes of which we have any knowledge it was enforced on the farmer by law, though I cannot discover that this law was given religious sanction in Greece, as it was in Italy. In Italy—or rather in Rome, for this does not seem to have applied to Magna Graecia—the wine of unpruned vines could not be used at the altar.

Among the causes of the decline of Greek commerce in wine was the rise of the Greek vineyards of Magna Graecia. From the eighth to the sixth century colonies were being established in Sicily, in southern Italy as far north as Naples, and in southern France (Massilia, 600 B.C.) and northern Africa (Cyrenæica). In every case vineyards were planted, and the Sicilian vineyards in particular became deadly rivals of those of Greece, and among the most dangerous rivals of the Campanian wine-growers of later times. Cumae and Sybaris produced immense quantities of wine and, as we shall see in Chapter IV, so closely was Magna Graecia associated with the vine that Herodotus knows the whole of this territory simply as Oenotria, Vineland.

The Greek wine-grower lost not only his trade, but his wine-varieties, his *cépages*, to Italy, and I prefer to deal with these in the next chapter, as also with the pests and diseases which did their best to check the expansion of viticulture, for they too were the same in Greece and in Italy, with one exception: Italian vineyards were very rarely troubled with locusts. In Greece these were a serious pest, especially in the vineyards of Cyrenæica and Lemnos, and in both these States every citizen was compelled by law to produce annually to the authorities a certain measure of young locusts or of locust eggs, for destruction.

The Greek period in the history of *Vitis vinifera* as a cultivated plant is, then, important for the European evolution of the plant and the art of growing it, from the primitive to the small commercial phase; but also for failure, in the end, to carry this process to the most profitable conclusion by industrializing viticulture. That step, a triumph for the vine and the ruin of the real farmer, was left to the Italians.

# CHAPTER IV

## *Italy: jam vinctae vites . . .*

THIS CHAPTER ON THE VINE IN ITALY and, ultimately, under Roman discipline, is central to the whole history of the diffusion of the plant and its cultivation: to it lead the chapters, in that history, of primitive viticulture, of essentially religious viticulture, and of that kind of commercial wine-growing which was based, for the most part, on the surpluses available from subsistence holdings. And from it stems modern, scientific, industrialized wine-growing on a mass-production scale.

There are two recognized opinions touching the origins of viticulture in Italy; and I find it possible to entertain a third. The Greeks appear from their writings to have believed that vineyards were already to be found in Italy when they first knew that country; at least, they called the southern half—especially Calabria—Oenotria, that is, Vineland. But this might refer to an abundance of wild vines. It was widely held until about 1900 that the Italian peoples, arriving from across the Alps from that mysterious reservoir of the 'Aryan race' which German scholars were so fond of invoking, came with a knowledge of wine-making, even of viticulture, and set about domesticating the wild *vites* of Italy. Doubtless, said the advocates of this theory, the Italians later learned from the Greeks, but only the refinements of the art.

Those who held this view explained the Greek derivation of the word *vinum* as merely apparent; in fact, they said, both the Greek *oinos* and the Latin *vinum* derived from a word in the proto-Indo-European language; and they could point to the fact that Latin *wine*-words, as distinct from *vine*-words, are not Greek derivatives. To these arguments we can add one more: it is possible that there were Mycenaean trading-posts, and even, perhaps, small colonies, in Italy long before the epoch of Greek settlement in that country, and it is conceivable that the Mycenaeans set the example of growing the vine in southern Italy.

But it is difficult to hold this opinion in view of what is now known of the state of Italian social and economic development between 800 and 700 B.C., when the Greek colonies in southern Italy and Sicily were founded. A folk of primitive Bronze Age or Iron Age shepherds making only a beginning in agriculture is not generally ready to plant the vine. A little wine may, indeed, have been made from wild grapes, but the business can hardly have gone beyond that stage.

It is now held that viticulture, including at least some cultivars of the vine, was introduced by the Greek colonists who created Magna Graecia in Sicily and southern Italy as far north as Naples between 800 and 600 B.C. The picture which most writers on wine and the vine draw for us is that of viticulture spreading steadily northward as one of the arts of civilization which the Latins were learning from the Greeks, and perhaps from the Carthaginians, and which they were passing on to the other Italian peoples as they extended their dominion. This, however, will not do at all. For it seems quite clear that the Etruscans arrived in what is now Tuscany quite as early as, and probably rather earlier than, the Greeks arrived in Sicily. And it seems now to be more or less accepted, for example by Raymond Bloch,[1] that Herodotus' account of the origin of the Tyrrhenian people, that is the Etruscans, is, after all, substantially correct. I am aware of the theory that they were, on the contrary, indigenous, but find it unconvincing. In short, I take it that the Etruscans did indeed come from Asia Minor and were probably Lydians. Now in that case there can be no doubt at all that even if their migration occurred before 1000 B.C., which is apparently not likely, they were perfectly familiar with viticulture and wine-making and it is inconceivable that they should have failed to practise these arts in their new country. It is surely significant that the very earliest poems written in Latin in praise of wine are concerned with Etruscan, not with Greek wine. At all events, I believe the following to be as near to the truth as we can get.

Taking, not quite arbitrarily, the year 900 B.C. as a point of departure, southern Italy was populated by an Indo-European-speaking people, one of whose languages was Latin and who are known to archaeologists as 'Villanovans'; they were newcomers to Italy and they had brought with them iron tools and weapons, whereas the people they had found there, men of their own stock from an earlier wave of immigration, were still using bronze. These people were shepherds and perhaps cattle-raisers, and if they also practised agriculture to the extent of growing bread-grains, they were still in a primitive phase of farming. It is on the whole improbable that they planted the vine. But they had some contact with the Greek traders who had been landing in Italy from about 1000 B.C., and had perhaps begun to learn from them. They were not ignorant of wine, for among the refuse found by archaeologists on their sites of settlement were densely packed masses of grape-pips, such as would have been formed in some kind of wine-press, the vestiges of *marc*.

In about the year 900 then—but an error of date as great as a century either way is perfectly possible—the Etruscans were colonizing Tuscany and the country to the north of Rome down as far as the Tiber; they must have brought with them a culture more advanced than the Latin, one including that of the vine. Slightly later the Greeks also started colonizing to the south of Rome and in Sicily. And at about the same time the Carthaginians were forming their first colonies in Sicily, and they too brought with them viticulture and vines from the oldest wine-culture in the world, that of Phoenicia. In short at least three introductions of viticulture must have occurred within a short time of each other and at different parts of Italian-Sicilian territory.

Rome began in the late eighth century as a group of villages belonging to a people of shepherds. Lumps of pressed grape-pips are found on the sites of this early Iron Age people; they are almost certainly wine-press rubbish. All the authorities save one agree that the pips in question are those of wild grapes; the one exception claims to have found the pips of cultivated grapes among them.[2]

Pliny says that 'Romulus made the libation with milk and not with wine.' Romulus is thought to have been a legendary character, but that does not matter: for 'Romulus' read 'the earliest Roman government'; and the libation was made with the chief crop of the primitive Romans, milk, as it is always among pastoral peoples. It cannot be assumed, as it is by Hehn,[3] that they knew not wine; only that wine was a scarce and unimportant commodity with them. The use of it was forbidden to women by the earliest code of laws; and even, according to one authority,[4] to men under thirty; and when a Roman named Egnatius Mecenius knocked down and killed his wife because, sent to draw wine, she had drunk some herself, 'Romulus' acquitted him as justified.

The Postumia Law of King Numa, who came somewhere between Romulus and Tarquin and was certainly an historical not a legendary person, forbids the use of wine in the asperging of the funeral pyre. Pliny makes the ridiculous suggestion that this was a measure of economy, but no people ever economize on religious rites, they will ruin themselves rather. Numa was clearly trying to get back to the good old days of primitive virtue. The conclusion must be that wine became a commonplace though not a plentiful one to the Romans between the 'founding' of the city and the 'founding' of the Republic.

We know, as real history, nothing whatever about the period before 510 B.C. when Tarquin was driven from Rome and the Republic founded. But it is probable that Tarquin was not a solitary case of an Etruscan king of Rome, but the last of an Etruscan dynasty; that, in short, Rome was transformed from a congeries of villages into a city, and given the first arts of civilization, by the more civilized Etruscans whose empire lay to the north of the city; though perhaps 'empire' is the wrong word for what seems to have been a sort of loose federation of Etruscan autonomous states on the Greek model. Far from carrying the civilized arts, including the art of viticulture, to the north, Rome seems more likely to have received them *from* the north, and I hold it to be not only possible but probable that Roman viticulture was started not by the Greeks of Cumae or Sybaris or Neapolis, but by the Etruscans of Veii.

We can also dismiss the theory that the vineyards of northern Italy postdate and derive from Roman viticulture. The highly-civilized Etruscans conquered or colonized the Po valley in the sixth century. Felsina (now Bologna) was one of their cities; Ravenna and Rimini were developed from villages into cities, as Rome had been, by the same people; Spina was founded. Trade from these centres was carried on with Celtic Europe, and Etruscan as well as Greek influences are discernible in the exquisite arts of Late Hallstatt and Early La Tène. There can be almost no doubt, then, that vineyards were planted in the Po valley in the sixth century. But the Romans may later have had to reintroduce the vine; for in 350 B.C., at the battle of Circumpadana, Etruscan civilization was flung back towards the Tiber and the Tuscan coast by the Celts, and the early vineyards probably perished.

A little evidence which can be interpreted in favour of a Greek origin even of Etruscan viticulture is to be found in some Etruscanists. Bloch[5] points out that the Etruscan god Flufluns is identifiable with the Greek Dionysus; he carries the thyrsus and he is associated with both Semele and Ariadne. But I do not know what evidence Bloch has for saying that this god had 'come north from Magna Graecia with his mysteries and his dishevelled retinue of Bacchantes'. For Dionysus was no more a native Greek than he was a native Tuscan: as we have seen, he was a Lydian, or a Mycian; at all events he was born in Asia Minor. And if it be accepted that the Etruscans came from Asia Minor, then clearly they brought this Flufluns with them, as the colonizing Greeks brought him, but under the name of Dionysus, from Thrace and metropolitan Greece. Finally, there is a piece of evidence which could be interpreted to show that the Etruscans grew no wine: in Livy's list of the contribution made by the Etruscan cities to the commissariat for Scipio's campaign against Carthage in the year 205 B.C., there is no mention of wine. But there would be no sense in bringing wine from Tuscany for ships loading in the neighbourhood of the Greek vineyards in the south.

Viticulture may have begun earlier in Sicily than in Italy. The island was a rather late outpost of the Anatolian copper culture, later bronze culture; its potters were making amphorae long before the first Greek colonists settled there.[6] But we do not know what went into them; perhaps only water.

In the historical and well-documented epoch of the vine in Italy, and in the course of its complete conquest of the country, the plant obtained an astonishing and unprecedented importance in the economy, the mind and the spirit of the Italians, enjoying a peculiar status: '*La vigne jouissait dans l'esprit des anciens comme d'une sorte de noblesse ou prééminence sur les autres végétaux cultivés. Dans l'armée romaine une tige de vigne était l'insigne de commandement des centurions; c'était l'instrument de châtiment réservé aux seuls soldats romains, tandis qu'on se servait d'un bâton de bois vulgaire pour frapper les auxilliaires.*'[7] In this account by Billiard of the singular privilege enjoyed by the Roman soldier of being flogged with a vine stick whereas the foreign auxilliaries had to put up with being beaten with any old wood (*plate 37*), the authority is Pliny. It is not, of course, all that our assertion rests on: vine-leaves, stems and fruit appear as motifs at all levels of art.

But perhaps the most extraordinary instance of this special feeling for the vine in the Hellenistic–Roman culture is to be found in the claim made by

Jesus (in which he shows the measure of his Hellenism), that he was the True Vine. From the Greek or (by then) Roman point of view, he might as well have said that he was the True Dionysus. Maurice Besnier points out[8] that the important place held by the vine (*plate 38*) and vintage scenes in catacomb paintings recalls Christ's comparison of himself with a vine whose branches are his disciples; this figure is far more Graeco-Latin than Jewish, and again, it is Dionysian.[9]

It is possible to distinguish five epochs in Italian viticulture:

(i) the primitive, which we have discussed;

(ii) from about 350 B.C. to about 150 B.C. when viticulture becomes a commonplace part of Italian farming, but the reputation of Greek wines remains dominant and Greek wines dominate the market;

(iii) from about 130 B.C. to about 30 B.C., the golden age of vineyard expansion and of the rise of the Italian *grands crus*;

(iv) a century of decline, beginning with huge expansion of quantity production, collapse of the reputation of the *grands crus*, falling profits and over-production, ending in contraction of the area under vines and rising prices;

(v) restoration, with some improvement in quality of the *grands crus*, and rising profits from vineyards. This period can be said to conclude in the edict of Domitian (see below) which attempted to stabilize the industry.

For the second of these epochs we shall be obliged to leave the early part in obscurity, for we have no documents at all. For the later part of it we have two excellent and fairly complete documents, the *De re rustica* of M. P. Cato, the Censor; and the *De re rustica* of Varro. The latter was a professional writer who, in his eighties, wrote an agricultural treatise to help his wife run a farm she had bought. Cato, politician, publicist, moralist and farmer, was born at Tusculum in 233 B.C. He is best known for his implacable determination, as a Senator, to see Carthage totally destroyed. By our standards he was a detestable man; his advice on the sound, economic treatment of slaves, for example, is revolting in its inhumanity; to him slaves were not human, they were simply cattle. (Cato's readers would not, of course, have been shocked. In Roman law the slave was considered to be *pro nullis, pro mortuis, pro quadrupedibus.*) His *De re rustica* is one of the best farming manuals ever written, and pays close and detailed attention to viticulture, wine-making, and the correct marketing of the vintage.

In this second epoch of Italian viticulture the vineyards were at first small, and they were part of innumerable subsistence farms worked by yeomen-burgesses who sold their surplus crops to the small urban populations. Not until the second century B.C. was there such a thing as a viticultural industry, or farms composed solely of vineyards. A typical holding was of about one hundred jugera, that is, about fifty acres; by mid-second century B.C. two hundred jugera was held to be a more viable size. On a two-hundred jugera farm not more than half, at most, would be planted to vines even where the owner specialized in wine-growing. But the economic pressure on the farmer to plant his whole farm to vines was constantly growing: as the policy of the government increasingly favoured cheap imports of wheat the price of wheat fell, whereas the price of wine, still scarce, was rising. In mid-second century the cash return from vineyard was far higher than from any other kind of farm. But this was not the case until the Punic wars were over, the demand for home-grown wheat from a country whose farmers were all in the army fell off, and Rome controlled Sicily with her immense production of wheat. Writing of the year 154 B.C. Cato places the profit from vines at the top of his list, that from wheat only sixth. Market-garden crops were the second most profitable where irrigation was possible and practised.

Vineyards were more expensive to run than any other kind of farming: on a fifty-acre farm where vines were the principal plant, the owner had to have thirteen or fourteen slaves, that is, a ploughman, eleven general labourers and one, occasionally two, cattle-hands. But the price of wine was so high and the demand so strong that it was worth it.

After the Second Punic War there began a process which was to ruin the social life of the ordinary Roman, wipe the yeoman-burgess out of existence, create an idle and dangerous urban proletariat, and involve Rome in that long series of civil wars which killed the Republic and created the Empire in its place. This was the take-over of the Italian countryside by big capital. The small, free-holding Roman citizen-farmer with his large family, one or two slaves decently treated, and the duty to fight for his country, became a victim first of the Senate's policy of importing cheap wheat, second of the Equites class of financiers' (which we may think of with reservations as the class of big businessmen) discovery that land, worked as cattle-ranch, coppice-wood fuel source, or vineyard, could be made to pay very well indeed. In the second century B.C., as in the twentieth century A.D., politicans had a sure instinct for their own advancement; a man who is master of an urban, pro-letarian mob whom he can buy, whether with doles of corn or family allowances, has far more power than the elected leaders of a class of free-holding farmers who can feed themselves off their own land. Crops like wine, meat, timber require long-term financing and heavy capital investment. The Roman farmers had been able to finance such cropping out of the cash received for bread-grain. When their barley and wheat crops became per-fectly worthless, quite unsaleable, they had no source of cash income, and the growing of wine or the production of meat became very difficult for them, and in the end impossible.[10] They borrowed money and could never repay it, for the situation which had led them to borrowing did not improve, but got worse. Their land was seized by the bankers and they and their families became part of the growing city mob.

The small vineyard as part of the family farm (*plate 39*) disappeared; in its place came the big—sometimes very big—vineyard belonging to one or a company of financiers, managed by a steward and worked by slaves treated exactly as we now treat machines: with reasonable care while they were valuable; with an annual writing down of their value in the farm accounts; and finally with scrapping and replacement.

These first industrial vineyards were very intensively cultivated. Where the vines were trained and pruned low and bushy, fodder crops were raised between the rows; where they were grown high, or trained between fruit-trees, a crop of wheat was grown to feed the slaves. By 200 B.C. probably half the wine in Italy was grown on such farms. The rest came from the properties of gentlemen-farmers who managed their own, smaller but similar undertakings on just the same lines, and from farms rented by tenants—formerly themselves smallholders—from city men who liked to keep a country-house and home-farm outside Rome.

One of the most powerful influences in promoting the overwhelming suc-cess of the vine in Italy, to the ruin of the small farmer and the enrichment of relatively few great capitalists, was a book: the treatise on agriculture, in-cluding viticulture, of a Carthaginian gentleman-farmer named Mago. At the final destruction of Carthage this book alone was chosen from the city's many libraries (see Chapter V) as worth saving, and to be translated into

Latin and Greek. If the use of this work made by the Italian writers on farming is a fair guide, Mago had upon Italian farming much the same effect as, for example, that of Jethro Tull or Arthur Young upon English, and ultimately European, farming sixteen or seventeen centuries later. It was from Mago that the Romans learned the best methods and rules for the planting, manuring, irrigation and pruning of a vineyard; the rational and economic (but, of course, heartless) use of slaves to get the most value out of them; and it may also have been the suggestions of this Punic specialist in intensive land-use that resulted in the rise in Italy of contractors specializing in the handling and marketing of crops, and notably of the vintage. Columella and others (see below) make the importance of this Carthaginian's influence perfectly clear.

On a big commercial vineyard the crop might be handled in one of three ways: it might be picked and vinified by the owner, a country gentleman or a company of financiers; or by the tenant, who in that case dealt with it exactly as if he were the landlord, but might, if the lease called for it, have to hand over part of the wine to that landlord; finally, it might be, and, if the advice of Columella were taken, probably would be, sold on the vine to a contractor in precisely the same way that the greater part of the Kentish cherry crop is sold on the tree to a contractor. In that case the contractor sent in his own team of slaves to pick and vinify the grapes, and he had to have the new wine off the premises by a date (the kalends of October) fixed by contract and enforced by law. In Cato's time this was unheard of; by Columella's time it was the rule, and we can dismiss entirely all idea of the vintage as a jolly, working-holiday affair; it was strictly business and highly professional, and some contractors worked the vineyards with chained slaves, although as a rule they were off the chain for this purpose. In short, the effects of big capital in the Roman countryside were much the same as they have been in modern times in Britain and the United States. The usual date by which the vintage must be cleared and off the premises was 1st October. But I shall have more to say about vintage dates below; the contract would lay down that if the contractor had not removed the new wine by the specified date, the landlord could confiscate it and sell it himself.

Landlords and tenants who preferred to do their own harvesting and vinification would, in the first century B.C., keep and mature the wine, not selling it until it was in drinkable condition. This entailed the investment of large capital, for example, in vats and amphorae and, by the first century A.D., in wooden barrels.[11] It entailed, moreover, waiting a year or more, perhaps even three years, for any return on a vintage, so that the capital invested in slaves too was relatively slow-yielding. In the first century A.D. and, increasingly, later, with the progress of economic inflation, this sort of integrity in the wine-growing business disappeared: growers wanted their money back quickly; bankers expected a large and quick return on their loans. Very much the same sort of thing is happening today in the Bordeaux country: in the past clarets, for example, were held much longer by the growers than they are today; now, because of the immense cost to the grower of keeping perhaps ten vintages in the cellars at once, they are sold young in bottle. Various rationalizations of this practice are produced by the propagandists of the wine trade, but the cause of the change is at least partly economic. In the Italy of the first century of our era the landlord who made his own vintage sold it within a few weeks, as new wine, to a wine-merchant. The merchant came to the farm accompanied by a wine-taster; or he might have received the taster's report some days before. This would usually be in the first part of September when the vintage had been made in August, as it often was. The price he paid the grower was a matter of striking a bargain, but by the third century prices were controlled as to maxima. The law fixed the conditions of sale, and on their basis the contract between grower and merchant was made. Once again, unless the merchant had removed the new wine to his own cellars by a given date, the landlord or tenant of the vineyard was free to sell the wine himself, and the merchant lost what he had paid.

As we have seen already, until mid-first century B.C. the product of the Italian wine industry was only the *vin ordinaire* of the country, and the great wines were still foreign ones: as well as Chian and Lesbian, the Roman merchants imported for their richer customers Lampsacan, Pergamum and Cyzican from Mysia, Timoleon from Lydia (chiefly for *coupage* purposes, to reinforce Italian wines), Clazomenian and Carian. But in 121 B.C. came the first year of great Italian vintages, the Opimian wines, so called after the consul Opimius, and thus began the golden century of Italian viticulture.

The vineyards which rose to fame and riches in this epoch were quite numerous. The oldest were Sicilian, these exporting Mammertine, Messinan and other wines of quality, such as the Potulan and the Taurominium which, says Pliny, was frequently passed off by wine-merchants as Mammertine, a dearer wine. The Syracusan vineyards produced a fine wine. But Catania was famous only for the quantity of its wine, the vines bearing exceptionally large crops, probably owing to the volcanic ash of Etna in which they grew. Brutium produced much ordinary wine and three named *crus*: Consentia, Tempsa and Rhegian. Later in history this whole province paid its taxes to Rome in kind, that is, in wine. The named and reputable wines of Lucania were Buxentum, Sybaris, Thurium and Lajaria; of Apulia, Tarentine, Babian and Aulonian. Praetutian was the only *grand cru* of the Picenum vine-yards, and Umbria had its wine of Spoleto. According to Martial the Roman vineyards never yielded a tolerable wine, only the miserable *vappa vaticani* of the Vatican hill. But Latium had great growths; Alban, Formican, Gaebian, Praenestan, and several others.

Falernian, Martial's '*immortale Falernum!*', the '*ardens Falernum*' of Horace, was a Campanian product. But it would, I think, be a capital mistake to think of this famous wine as a sort of great claret of the golden age of Bordeaux, or a great Burgundy of the pre-phylloxera vintages. It was, by all accounts, very strong and heady, and it was often and perhaps usually sweetened with honey before drinking. The fact would seem to be that the Roman, or for that matter Greek, notion of a fine wine in no way resembled our own. There were three growths of Falernian: the Gaurian, from the top of the hills from present-day Rocca di Mondragone to Monte Massico; the Faustian, grown on the slopes of those hills, and considered the best; the Falernian proper, from the vineyard at the foot of the hills, the vineyard being on the left of the road to Urbania just past the Ponte de Campania.[12]

All three Falernian vineyards, or at least the Falernian proper, were devastated by Hannibal's soldiers during the Second Punic War, and re-constituted during the peace which followed. The primacy of Falernian lasted three centuries, but under the kind of economic pressure which has already been described, the owners were tempted to increase output at the expense of quality. The story is an old one in viticulture and we are having a new chapter of it in our own time: the name of a wine being firmly estab-lished, and a new class of drinker having risen too fast to learn taste, output is increased to sell to that new class a wine which has the name but no longer the qualities which made that name. Thus Pliny classes Falernian as '*secunda nobilitas*' only, and not much later it was just one of a score of good, reliable wines. Pliny's top-of-the-list was Caecuban and not Falernian. But it should be pointed out, in contradiction of those writers who appear to believe that the practice of increasing output at the expense of quality is foolish as well as wicked, that it is a perfectly logical and financially sound policy: the capitalists behind Falernian made far more money in the late than in the early epoch of the vineyard's career, and the criterion of capitalist-farming is profit and nothing else whatsoever. Large-scale capitalist wine-growing cannot fail to run down quality as soon as it is safe to do so.

The Caecuban which Pliny rated '*prima nobilitas*' was grown in marshy land and the vines were very large, being trained in swags between trees: notwithstanding the poetical encomia, it can only have been coarse and heady stuff; its merit probably lay in its very high alcohol content and not much else. This vineyard was destroyed by the Emperor Nero: he had been told that Dido, fleeing from Tyre, had buried the Tyrian treasure where now the Caecuban wine was grown, and he devised the entirely idiotic plan of connecting the Avernine lake with the sea at Ostia, a perfectly useless canal, as an excuse for digging up the whole area. There was much wailing and gnashing of teeth among the oinophils, and Pliny laments, '*Caecuba non jam gignuntur!*'

There were other famous growths: Pompeii and Cumae had each about a dozen vineyards known for their wines. Tiberius called the wine of Sorrento 'a full-bodied vinegar'; it would, perhaps, have been more to our taste than the Campanian vintages. The most popular wine with all classes was the Setian. Wine from the north was disesteemed: oceans of wine were produced by the marsh vineyards of the Po valley with their fast-growing and short-lived vines, but this wine of Ravenna was 'watery', and Veeian was poor stuff too. There may have been a measure of anti-Etruscan prejudice in such opinions; the older Romans had found nothing to complain of in Veeian. Concerning Sabine wine we have this witticism:

> *Propinas modo conditum Sabinum*
> *Et dicis mihi Cotta: 'vis in auro?'*
> *Quisquam plumbea vina vult in auro?*

Who, indeed, would drink a leaden wine from a golden cup? Tuscan wines in general were despised by the Romans; and those of Cisalpine Gaul were not drinkable at all. But all one can say is that these opinions may have been simply a question of taste and that the Romans clearly liked the southern, syrupy wines, not the thinner ones of the colder north.

By the first century Genoa was producing a very large annual vintage from her slopes, and founded a roaring trade in this wine. It seems, however, never to have been sold into Italy itself, though Pliny gave it a good mark; the customers were Celts—Ligurians mostly—and being half-savages probably did not care what they drank so long as it made them drunk. They were cattlemen who sold hides and meat on the hoof to the Genoese. Pucinum, a wine from Venetia, enjoyed a certain reputation and consequent prosperity, being in demand in Rome because the Empress Livia attributed her longevity to the use of it (she lived into her eighties).

Wine was also being grown by the first century in at least two and probably three Gallic provinces, and in commercial quantities. We come to this in Chapter V, but here it may be said that the vineyards of Massilia, Marseilles, were first planted in 600 B.C. and were far older than the Campanian vineyards. But the Massiliot wine was smoked to preserve it and the Italians considered it vile stuff. 'Cocta fumis', says Martial, 'musta massilitanis', 'Massilot vintage, cooked in smoke', and again, 'Improba Massiliae quidquid fumaria cogunt/Accipit aetatem quisquis ab igne cadus,/A te, Munna, venit', 'It was from you, Munna, that comes what swindling Massilot smoke-holes produce, all those wine jars made to seem old by the flame.' However, the customers for this wine were again Celts and Germans who probably merely wanted to get drunk from time to time. The wine-growers of Narbonne, 'the Province', also had a bad name for faking their wine with herbs, colorants and smoke; Pliny only hopes that the stuff is not actually poisonous. The Allobroges were already growing wine in the valley of the Isère or somewhere in that region, but it does not appear to have been in commerce yet; its descendants are Hermitage and Châteauneuf-du-Pape.

The culmination of this epoch of viticultural expansion was a crisis of over-production and, at last, a fall in prices despite the price-fixing rings operated by the merchants. There is a passage in *The Satyricon* which reveals the fall in prices (see Chapter V). But a bare statistic will do here: in 100 B.C. the price of wheat was to that of wine as 1 is to 2·72; in A.D. 65 it was as 1 is to 0·72; this is a fall in price, *during a period of continuous inflation*, of 350 per cent. In Cato's day it was agreed that though the costs of viticulture were heavier than those of any other kind of farming, the return far more than offset them. These costs rose steadily—for example the price of slaves increased— while the price of wine fell. In mid second century B.C. wine had been so scarce and dear that there were popular riots in protest.[13] About a century later the government was obliged to accept wine-growers' taxes in kind and give wine away with the wheat dole. Although this did not become the general and accepted practice until the reign of Aurelian,[14] Domitian was doing it in the year 90.

In Cato's time few vineyards exceeded fifty jugera, mostly on farms of one hundred to two hundred jugera; by Pliny's day there were vineyard firms like those of Rhemnus Palaemon with six hundred jugera and an annual gross revenue of £10,000 gold, or those of Gellias of Agrigentum with two thousand jugera (one thousand acres), and others of the same kind.

The crisis seems to have ended of its own accord, partly by the vineyard acreage contracting a little, but chiefly by the improvement of viticultural technique which lowered production costs. For this improvement the agro-nomist Columella was largely responsible. But there was another factor, too: the opening up of the French and German markets to Italian wines brought about an up-turn in prices, as demand caught up with and exceeded supply. The evidence for this lies in the growing importance of Lyon during the first century A.D. as an *entrepôt* for the wine-trade. It was, in fact, so impor-tant that many Italian firms of wine-merchants opened offices and ware-houses there, or even moved there completely.

Of the authors on whom we depend for knowledge of the vine in Italy, the one we have now to refer to is by far the most important; only Cato can be compared with him; for Varro, though useful, was really a dilettante, a writer by trade and not an agronomist; Martial, Horace and Virgil, being poets, are more picturesque than reliable; Palladius simply plagiarized Columella; and Pliny was a credulous and uncritical cyclopaedist, invaluable for the sheer quantity of information he published, but industrious rather than intelligent.

L. J. M. Columella was a Spaniard, born in Cadiz in the reign of Augustus and flourishing during that and the succeeding reign. His works on agricul-ture and kindred subjects are in a different class from those of any other Latin writer or from such gentlemanly-amateur productions as those of the Greeks, for example the *Oikonomikos* of Xenophon. His *De re rustica* stands beside such classics of husbandry as Jethro Tull's, Arthur Young's or Jules Guyot's. He would have been at ease with and have talked the same kind of sense as Coke of Holkham or 'Turnip' Townsend. He is not, of course, entirely free from the prejudices of his time: his pest-control recommendations are sometimes as silly as Pliny's or Xenophon's. But the overall impression which he makes on one by his writings is that of a man of science with practical farming experience, a good brain and great integrity. As late as the year 1885, Ottavio Ottavi, a revered authority whose *Viticultora teorica-pratica* is as important as any treatise on the subject ever published, described Columella as 'the inspirer of Italian agriculture', just as Columella himself wrote of Mago the Carthaginian, 'we revere him as the Father of Agriculture'. And that, by the way, is typical of the man: he was scrupulous in referring to his sources and he attributes much of his science to the great Punic agronomist. He was also, besides much else, the first writer, or the first known to us, to publish a good treatise on dendrology, his *De arboribus*.

Columella's work on viticulture was published as part of a general farming manual in about A.D. 65. In introducing it he says that one must first consider whether the planting of a vineyard can still be profitable, and that this preliminary inquiry must, indeed, serve as a basis for his dissertation: 'The more so in that doubt about this is so general, and there are even some who would avoid and are afraid of land planted as vineyard, considering that one should rather wish to have in one's possession meadow, pasture or coppice-wood.' Things had changed indeed since Cato's day.

Both Varro, earlier, and Columella are apt to blame the new unprofitability of viticulture on the loss of the good old virtues; men no longer live on their estates; even less do they work them in person, as their fathers did; and even when they still own and farm land they leave everything to the steward.

This Goldsmithian lament cannot be entirely ignored but does not go to the root of the trouble. In the days these authors are regretting there was an adequate margin to work within; by the year 65, only the most efficient and (to his slaves) ruthless farmer could make wine-growing pay. Columella himself did so, and more; he was no mere armchair farmer.

The figures which follow are Columella's own. But as the labour/land ratio in ancient Italian viticulture was one slave to seven jugera, I have found it convenient to make the unit discussed seven jugera, though of course any

viable vineyard would have been from ten to one hundred times that size.
I remind the reader that a jugera is about half an acre.

|  | Sesterces |
|---|---|
| Cost of 7 jugera of suitable land at 1,000 sesterces per jugera | 7,000 |
| Cost of a skilled slave-vinearoon of suitable age, in good condition | 8,000 |
| Cost of vine plants and their dowry[15] at 2,000 sesterces per jugera | 14,000 |
| Interest at 6 per cent on the above for two unfruitful years | 3,480 |
|  | 32,480 |

That, then, is the capital investment per seven jugera. The price of the land
is about average; the price of the slave is very high indeed, but Columella
justifies this, saying that he has found it pays to buy a skilled man in his
young prime, with a good twenty years of work in him. You can, if you
like, pay as little as two thousand sesterces for an unskilled slave of poor
quality and then try to train him, but it is a false economy.

The key to the following comparison is the interest rate paid by bankers
for money on deposit, or by merchants in safe trades: it is six per cent.

Columella now supposes this vineyard to be as badly managed as it can
be without total failure; and he supposes a price for wine which is the minimum ruling. On these suppositions, the revenue from the investment will be
2,100 sesterces per annum. From a banker you would get 1,920 sesterces
per annum on your money. But this calculation is deliberately based on an
absurd supposition, that of a vintage averaging one culeus of wine per jugera;
in practice, any vineyard yielding less than three culei per jugera should be
grubbed up as a dead loss. So that the smallest gross return per annum would
really be 6,000 sesterces. Now against this we have, however, to set certain
on-costs, while we have also to consider the revenue from ancillary crops:
for example, Columella's vine nursery made 3,000 sesterces per jugera.

But before a proper comparison can be made between the income to be
expected by an investor buying a small estate and planting it to vines, and
that from the same capital simply lent out at interest, the costs of running
the vineyard have to be considered.

## 35

# Italy: Jam vinctae vites

*Early in the first millennium B.C. the civilized Etruscans who settled in what is now Tuscany brought with them viticulture and a wine-and-vine god, Flufluns. Small bronze statuettes show a satyr carrying a wine skin (35) and an Etruscan banqueter reclining with a wine bowl (36).*

36

37

The vine's special importance to the Romans is indicated by examples of its use. A centurion of the northern army carries a vine rod as a sign of his authority (37), for it was regarded as the peculiar privilege of the Roman soldier to be flogged with a rod of vine-wood, rather than with a common stick.

38

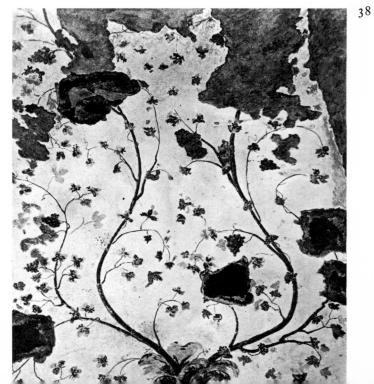

A wall in the catacomb of Domitilla (38) is decorated with the vine, adopted by the early Christians as a symbol of the resurrection.

39

Roman viticulture began as smallholdings, and as modest vineyards on the estates of the well-to-do (39), and grew to be in the main large-scale commercial production based on slave labour. A funerary inscription shows viticultural tools: the bipalium, serpetti and bidens (40).

LEONI INPA
CEQUI VIXI
TAN NISXxx

Ex eodem Cœmeterio.

40

41

42

*Wine was produced in enormous quantities, and was very much a part of Roman everyday life. On the left of the relief (41) servants pour wine from a selection of jars. A slave (42) carries a stoppered amphora and a wine skin.*

43

A 'summer dining-room' (triclinium) at Pompeii, with amphorae (43); in the shop, also at Pompeii, mulled wine was sold (44).

44

45

46

The cult of Bacchus was officially banned in
185 B.C. but Orphic rites were still flourishing in
Pompeii in the first century B.C. A wall-
painting in the Villa of Mysteries shows the
initiation ceremonies (45).

A silver cup from Naples (46) is decorated with
a vine spray. The single handle is an unusual
feature.

The amphora (47) also from Naples, is of blue
and white glass, decorated with amorini frolick-
ing among vines.

47

## 48

The Romans both exported quantities of wine to the Empire and encouraged vineyard planting, until eventually the northern vineyards became rival exporters. Wine vats are being pitched at St Romain-en-Gal, in the Rhône department, one of the most ancient vineyard regions of France (48).

Roman soldiers load wine-barrels on to a Danube boat at a fort in northern Yugoslavia (49). The replacement of amphorae by wooden barrels greatly facilitated the transport of wine.

49

There are two items to be taken into account here, one of which seems impossible to estimate: the depreciation of tools and winery plant; the other cost is a little easier: the maintenance and depreciation of the slaves. To cover the first I propose to offset against it, although no accountant would approve of this rough-and-ready method, the appreciation in the value of the estate due to the planting of the vines; this is a very considerable item: Pliny, for example, records the case of Acilius Sthalenus who sold a running-concern vineyard property for 6,666 sesterces per jugera; a house and out-buildings were probably included, but allowing a very ample 100,000 sesterces for these, the vineyard itself was still worth four-and-a-half times the 1,000 sesterces per jugera for naked land allowed by Columella in his calculation.

If we reckon that a fair period in which to write-off the investment in slaves is twenty years, and take that as the period over which appreciation should be calculated, then the annual rise in value of the property is 175 sesterces per jugera, which no doubt more than covers the depreciation of tools and plant. I shall therefore simply ignore that cost as covered by the rise in property value.

As to the maintenance costs of a slave: first there is depreciation. The slave cost 8,000 sesterces and this must be written-off in his working life, which is twenty years. An 8,000-sesterces slave would not, however, be worthless at the end of twenty years; Columella did not believe in buying very young slaves as they were apt to be troublesome; the skilled slave for which so high a price was paid would probably be about thirty years old, so that he would be only fifty by the time his cost had been completely written-off. If Cato's advice were followed he would then be sold to a slave-dealer who would keep him for a few months, get him into prime condition, and resell him at a profit. We do not know how much he would fetch, however. I shall allow a very low figure, 1,000 sesterces. We have, there-fore, to write-off 350 sesterces a year.

It is not nearly so easy to discover the cost of maintenance, since it so happens that we have no figures for the period in question. The figures we do have are from the reign of Diocletian, and the intervening two centuries had been years of continual inflation. A study of these figures, and of some commodity prices in Pliny's time, makes it fairly clear, however, that if we halve the figures from Diocletian's reign we shall still have a very safe margin, for the inflation was probably a good deal worse than that. From all this we get:

*Annual cost of skilled vineyard slave*

| | Sesterces |
|---|---|
| depreciation | 350 |
| wheat for bread | 200 |
| wine | 80 |
| salt and other food | 120 |
| clothes, including 2 pairs shoes | 40 |
| | 790 |

It is, on the whole, clear that Columella's argument in favour of buying an estate and planting vines rather than simply placing one's money with the bankers was sound; a return on capital, net, of something like fifteen per cent would seem to be about what one might expect. There is, however, one proviso which Columella does not mention; he assumed, as do modern writers who work in the same field, that his own ability and skill could be exactly emulated by the investor, and from personal experience I can say that this is by no means always the case. However, that is an imponderable.

It is interesting to note the great handicap under which the small man must have laboured at this time. Obviously even a vineyard as small as 70 jugera (small, that is, in the first century A.D., it would have been considered large in Cato's day) entailed an investment of 80,000 sesterces in slaves alone. And since, as we have seen, a worker (slave or free, it makes no difference in this context) could subsist on 800 sesterces a year—in fact on 450, if we count only his food and clothing—this is obviously a very large sum. We might get some idea of it this way: 800 sesterces is one hundredth of 80,000. In Britain in 1965 a man's food, clothing and rent or rent equivalent can be reckoned as £300 a year at the least. So that 80,000 sesterces must have been something like the equivalent of £30,000. But if this is anything like right, then commodity prices, on which it is based, are terribly high by our standards, for we find that, using others of Columella's figures, this would make unplanted land cost something like £750 an acre. But however we look at it, 80,000 sesterces for slaves was as far beyond the power of the small farmer as an equivalent sum invested in machinery would today be beyond the power of the fifty-acre freeholder or tenant. But might not the small farmer avoid the buying of slaves by using free labour, the services of day-labourers? He could, but that was also dear. Here again we have figures only from the reign of Diocletian, at which time one had to pay a day-labourer 25 deniers per diem and his meals. This, by the way, shows wages to have been remarkably high, for considering commodity prices from the same reign, far from earning only his subsistence a man working say three hundred days a year could earn an annual income of three times the annual cost of subsistence; probably, however, a man with a family would be living rather poorly even so. At all events, as the period we are considering is about two centuries earlier (say Tiberius or Caligula), we can safely halve the day wage. Our small farmer would have to pay 10 or 12 deniers a day in wages per seven-jugera unit. He might need the men on 100 days a year. As far as I can see his annual wages bill could not possibly be less than 600 sesterces a year per seven-jugera unit, and from this I would guess that whereas the great commercial vineyards were worked solely with slaves, the smaller farmers, if there were any left, employed day labour and owned no slaves, or only one or two very cheap ones.

Vine nurseries, doing a brisk business as the new epoch of vineyard expansion started, were profitable. Columella recommends planting twenty thousand cuttings per jugera; he counted on getting half of these to root. This is very conservative indeed; his methods were identical with our own and my own practical experience shows a better 'take' than that. But sticking to his figures, he counts on ten thousand plants per jugera and he says that an average price was 300 sesterces per thousand. Anyone could expect that; he himself asked and received a higher figure because he had a reputation for being careful to take his cuttings from only the best parent vines, and for making a continuous sound selection for new stock. The work entailed in a vine nursery is much simpler than that in a vineyard, and all the processing of the crop is eliminated, of course, so that 3,000 sesterces gross return per jugera is good business.

We have left taxes out of this discussion because we are trying to compare the return on real estate, planted to vines, with the return on money lent at interest, and everyone had to pay taxes however his income was made. But the taxation of vineyards was a special concern. The vineyard owner had to make a return to the *agrimensora*, a tax office concerned with the agricultural industry only. In this document he had to give:

(i) nature and quality classification of his land

(ii) number of bearing vines planted in it

(iii) income of the past ten years from his vintages or those of his predecessor.

Each district had a tax quota to fill—that is, the government regarded a given district as the taxpayer and how its inhabitants made up the sum required was their own affair. It seems that the amount collected or demanded from each estate or holding was determined by the *decuriones*. It is as if the British government taxed not individuals but municipalities or parishes, and these in their turn decided how much each landowner should pay towards the sum demanded by the fisc. In practice the tax on vineyards was so variable that it must have affected land-values: it might be as low as five per cent and it might be as high as twenty per cent of the revenue, but I do not know whether of the gross or net revenue.[16]

By the end of the first century A.D. the vineyard tax was paid in kind and the wine sold by the State, the proceeds going into the *arca vinaria*. This office employed expert tasters to ensure that the wine offered had not been adulterated or watered down. But the fisc was continually being cheated by wine-growers who used the excuse of bad vintages, inclement seasons and so forth to put off payment until the next season. The arrears owing to the *arca vinaria* were, apparently, always large and became enormous. In the year 400 when the *arca vinaria* was ordered to call in these arrears they were so large that the growers simply had not enough wine in their cellars to meet their obligation, and were obliged to pay in cash instead, at a valuation. The *arca vinaria* used the wine to cover the wine dole[17] and also, it seems, to make gifts of wine to foreign politicians, allies and tributaries, or to threatening barbarians.

The yield of vineyards run on the scientific lines recommended by Columella was much what it would be nowadays. In the modern French vineyards, taking the whole country into account, and good years with bad, the yield is something like thirty hectolitres per hectare. Columella considered forty good and himself usually got sixty per hectare. Italian vineyards generally still yield larger vintages than French ones. Moreover the averages, both for Columella's Italy and for modern France, are the product of figures showing enormous variations in yield from place to place. In both cases, the yield of a vineyard on thin, hillside soil, the vines being pruned for quality wine, may be as low as two hectolitres per hectare; while the yield, again in both cases, from a rich-land vineyard cultivated and pruned for quantity production may be three hundred hectolitres per hectare. The point is, however, that there is no significant difference between the figures then and now; and in both epochs, quantity probably paid better than quality.

The more or less monopolistic organization of the wine-merchants' guilds led to profiteering and price-fixing by the ring, and in 301 Diocletian was driven to fix maximum prices for wine and other commodities by law. He even uttered a Socialist threat: the government would go into vineyard planting and wine-production itself, on a vast scale, if the growers and merchants did not behave themselves more responsibly. The price-fixing gives some idea of the good wines and bad wines available, and incidentally of the disappearance of Greek wines from Italian commerce, and the down-grading of Falernian.

*Maximum prices of wine per sextarius (about 1 litre) in* A.D. *301*

| | |
|---|---|
| Picenum | |
| Tiber | |
| Sabine | |
| Amminaean | |
| Setian | |
| Sorrentan | |
| Falernian | all 30 deniers |
| Ordinary wine, old, first quality | 24 deniers |
| Ordinary wine, old, second quality | 16 |
| Ordinary wine, new | 8 |
| Beer | 4 |

In order that these prices may mean something it should be added that 30 deniers was the price of a pair of chickens or two-and-a-half litres of olive oil, and that good beef cost about 12 deniers a pound. Some points of note: the best vintage wines cost only four times as much as the worst wine on the market; today the factor is at least ten. Taking modern France for purposes of comparison, wine is cheaper today than it was at the beginning of the fourth century. The Romans under Diocletian were paying one-and-a-half times as much for a pound of beef as for a litre of *vin ordinaire*; the factor today is at least two. Falernian is to beef as $2\frac{1}{2}$ to 1; a Château-bottled Bordeaux of a great vintage and at its zenith is to beef as about 7 to 1. But wine had been even dearer before this price-fixing legislation. The reason was the upswing in vineyard planting towards the middle and end of the first century, and the beginnings of viticulture in the provinces which had led to another crisis of over-production. It was represented to the Emperor Domitian's government that the planting of far too many vineyards was leading to a dangerous neglect of bread-grain production—almost certainly a case of successful lobbying by the Campanian and southern Greek-Italian growers and merchants—at all events, in 92 an edict ordered the immediate reduction of vineyard acreage, and prohibited the planting of any more vineyards anywhere in the Empire. As this edict was more important to France than to any other country it will be discussed in the next chapter. Though it was never fully implemented it did force up wine prices; but in 280 Probus repealed it by publishing an edict in the contrary sense. There was at once a tremendous planting of vineyards all over the Empire including Britain, some of it done with military help. It follows that in 301 there cannot possibly have been a wine-shortage to justify high prices. Although the market had expanded enormously oceans of wine were being made in Italy, Greece, France, Dalmatia, on the Danube and in Spain. The only explanation is that the trade was in very few hands and that the merchants, big growers, and perhaps commodity speculators were forcing wine prices to an entirely artificial figure.

The two great associations of merchants which controlled the wine trade of the Empire were the *negotiatores vini supernates*, whose territory was all that served by the Adriatic ports, and the *negotiatores vini internates*, whose territory was the Eastern Mediterranean including Roman Asia. They had their own quarter with warehouses, quays and offices on the Tiber, the *portus vinarius*, and their own market, the *forum vinarius*. They owned ships and lighters specially designed and built for the trade, to carry three thousand amphorae (in this context 'amphorae' is used as a measure of the ship's burden and not literally, since wooden casks became general and displaced earthenware amphorae in the second and third centuries). The load was about 18,000 gallons. The Northern European market was controlled by the *negotiatores vinarii* of Lyon, mostly Italian firms which had opened offices and warehouses in that city as the Gallic and German and British markets became important. These firms were slowly forced out of business in the fourth century as the Burgundy vineyards, placed nearer to the market, began to take business away from them, followed a little later in this by those of the Loire and the Moselle (see Chapter V).

The period of development which we have been considering was marked by the almost complete pauperization of the yeoman-burgess and the disappearance of his small, family vineyard. Even as early as Varro's time, during the last struggles of the Republic, these people were in difficulties. He says of them, '. . . free men who cultivate their own land are for the most part poor men [*pauperculi*] helped by their families.' But at that time they could still subsist, and enjoy their independence if not much else. Within a century they were poor whites; within two they were idle proletarians.[18] Small vineyards had been replaced by two kinds of vineyard estates: the great 'industrial' ones run for capitalists by managers and—in Gaul as well as Italy—the gentleman's property run at a profit, of the type referred to by Ausonius.[19]

The standard of ordinary wine was probably quite high, and the measure bought and sold was fixed and enforced by law. A cask, in contracts of sale of wine, had to be exactly 41 urns; it was called a *dolium*, and was originally of earthenware. The wine offered must be *necque aceat*, *necque muceat*, neither vinegary nor oily. The title of the wine-taster who protected the merchant from the grower at the time of sale was *vini boni arbitoratus*, which suggests that he may have become an impartial public official; the law gave him access to the wine to be sold three days before the sale. The buyer could require the grower to give him a warranty in the form of an oath that the wine was 'conscientiously' made. All this must have ensured a reasonably high standard of quality and have been some protection to the housewife and the toper.

Roman methods of propagating vines were identical with those used in all viticultural countries of modern times until the advent of phylloxera made grafting necessary. Roman vine-dressers did practise grafting, for example they might 'top-graft' a whole vineyard over to a new and better variety, on the old, established rootstocks. Propagation by long cuttings of ripe wood was standard practice. Columella had an amusing multiple-cutting-*cum*-grafting trick for the production of a vine which would bear half a dozen different kinds of grapes. Pliny thought that the stock might be influenced by the scions and vice versa, to change their nature, giving rise to a sort of hybrid; he was right in a way, for the graft-hybrid or chimaera is a well-known though very rare phenomenon.

From Mago's time vineyard planting had been geometrically regular and the question of correct planting distance was much in dispute; it varied from one to four yards. It was Columella's rule to divide the vineyard in half- or even quarter-jugera squares by broad alleys, to give easy access to the vines at pruning and vintage times, and to keep the vineyard well-aired. Every form of training and pruning known to us was in use, and the reasons for each form perfectly well understood. Mago, followed by Columella, had a very sound grasp of the influence of soil and site on the quality of wine. Methods of fast planting of new vineyards—important considering the high cost of skilled slaves and the high wages of free labour—had been developed. Columella himself may have invented the *pastinum* planting tool which he describes: it was an iron bar with a channel cut in the long axis and terminating in two small prongs. The young plant was seized between these at the point of the stem just above the swelling out of the stock; the cane lay in the channel. You thrust the whole thing into the deeply-prepared, soft and friable soil, and then withdrew the *pastinum*, leaving the vine planted. This could obviously be done in two or three seconds by a skilled hand.

What of the vine varieties? There is no point in discussing them all, but a few should be mentioned, and the point made that most of them had Greek equivalents, and many had clearly come to Italy from Greece by way of Magna Graecia. One had come from the Allobroges, a few from Asia; perhaps, ultimately, most came from Asia, for Negrul[20] has shown that there is probably no such thing as a *Vitis vinifera* cultivar of pure Occidental descent.

Pliny's *argitis* has been identified, with some assurance, as our Riesling; his *biturica minor* was probably the Gamay still grown in the Beaujolais, though eliminated elsewhere since the time of Dr Guyot who condemned it, as indeed had the Dukes of Burgundy before his time (see Chapter V). Of one identification I am fairly sure from personal knowledge of the plant: the description of the foliage of the Roman *aminea lanata* makes it our own Pinot Meunier 'Dusty Miller'. The vine is as vigorous and fruitful today— in Kent, Hampshire and Devon as well as elsewhere—as it was two thousand years ago in Italy; it is classed by the French among the *cépages nobles*. Viala and Vermorel[21] identify the Roman *helvenacia minor* as the Pinot Noir of

Burgundy and Champagne. As to table grapes, there was as yet no muscat, but two of the dessert grapes famous on the Roman markets turn up, so I believe, in China some centuries later: the Roman *dactylus* is surely the Mare's Nipple Grape of China; and their *unciaria* that grape as big as a plum which the Chinese had from the Uigurs who probably had it from the Byzantine Greeks (see Chapter VII).

As to cultural practices, it should be emphasized that Columella, following Mago, taught a viticulture as scientific as our own. The ancient Italians had no chemical fertilizers and no chemical pesticides: I make no comment on the fact that their vineyard yields were no smaller, and perhaps larger than ours. But in other respects, they did as we still do. In at least one respect we have only just caught up with them: Xenophon,[22] Mago, Theophrastus, Pliny and Columella all made an important point of the aeration of vine roots. If a tree of any kind be sick, says Pliny, '*afflari radices*'. As late as 1920 a distinguished French authority, while agreeing that the soil should be well cultivated for mechanical reasons, smiled at the notion that plant roots need air. We know now that they do. In manuring vineyards the Romans used everything that English and Scots farmers used in the nineteenth-century era of high farming, excepting Chilean nitrates. The Carthaginian and Roman practice of making much use, in vineyards, of old cow-urine was vindicated when the late nineteenth-century agronomists discovered the importance of potassium for vines. Composts were made of all weeds, straw, oak leaves, road-sweepings, household rubbish and farmyard manure. The Arab agronomist Ibn-al-Awan[23] recommended the use of human urine as a compost-heap activator, but the Romans had known of this valuable property of urine many centuries earlier. Mago insists on the importance of putting back into the vines all that you take out of them, and to this end it was best to use all the wine-press rubbish, the *marc*, as compost material. All the ancient agronomists knew the value of wood-ash (potash). Green manuring was well understood from at least the fifth century B.C.; and from Xenophon to Columella the plants recommended for this are the ones we now know to be the right ones, legumes. Vetches, clovers, lupins and beans were used, and it was understood that they must be ploughed in just before flowering to get the best results.

Pliny says that the reason why the most ancient Roman law-code, the XII Tables, laid it down that only wine of the pruned vine could be used in religious rites was to overcome a conservative (but, I suggest, also religious) objection to cutting vines in any way. Pliny's rule for pruning was '*quidquid materiae adimitur fructuii accedit*', which is a generalization on the right lines. Columella tells his readers to prune for the greatest quantity of fruit consonant with the preservation of the necessary wood for the succeeding crop and with the health and longevity of the plant. Mago introduced and Columella popularized March pruning as a means of holding back the burgeoning of the vine, and so making damage from late spring frosts less likely. Their rule is still in force. Our systems of pruning were all in use then: *in orbem* was the gobelet form; the so-called Guyot system was known, and fan-training common; so were such practices as bending the wood to check sap-flow at a certain point and get growth there; and making incisions above and below buds to discourage or encourage growth and so control the future shape of the plant. Columella favoured the low, shrub-like vines of modern France, but in this particular the Italians resisted his influence and preferred their larger vines with bigger vintages of inferior quality.

The Italian vineyards were afflicted like our own with pests and diseases: the notion that in the good old days 'they didn't have all these troubles' is without foundation. The only chemical pesticide they had, as far as I can discover, was a sulphur and bitumen mixture used by Cato; but bitumen, where obtainable, was widely regarded as a good control of many insect pests. The approach of the ancient Italians and the Greeks to plant sickness and pests differed from our own in that, because they were pantheists, they regarded the plant as very much more alive than we do. We all know that a plant is alive, but the conquest of the Western spirit by the concepts of mechanical technology has led to our treating plants and farm-animals very much more as if they were machines than as if they were people; the ancients, on the contrary, erred in the other direction, and thought of their vines and other trees very much more as if they were a kind of people than as if they were machines. I do not think that it ever occurred to any Greek or Italian of Roman times that man might be a special and separate creation; for them the living universe was a unity; they would instantly have apprehended and endorsed, shall we say, Darwin's theories, instead of having to overthrow the ruling dogma in order to accept them, which was our case; and they would have apprehended, in a way we cannot, the truths of modern physics, for these, too, make the unity of the universe apparent. So that the Roman farmer did not approach a sick or insect-infested vine as a 'thing', a machine which had gone wrong; he approached it as if it were a kind of kinsman, who, like himself, had a soul, an intelligence, smaller than his own but of the same kind exactly. A modern scientist, observing that if you touch a vine tendril with a rod, that tendril presently curls up to lay hold of the rod, invents a whole science and a special and really rather ridiculous jargon to explain what the plant is doing. The ancient Italian or Greek had no such difficulty; it was obvious what the plant was doing; it was doing what he would do in like case.

To my mind this attitude, despite its obvious dangers, was much sounder than our own: the modern phytologist, botanist, zoologist suffers, without realizing it, from the pernicious influence of Old Testament mythology; he still, in other and usually ill-conceived terms, believes in man as a special creation and the animals and plants as things made for his pleasure and use.

As a result of their admirable beliefs the ancients were led into excesses of anthropomorphism in dealing with sick plants, as we are led into excesses of mechanisticism. They did not think it pointless to reproach and exhort an unfruitful vine. (Jesus, when he punished that fig-tree, showed himself a Hellenist, not a Jew.) But the same beliefs led the ancients into some practices which may yet prove to have been well founded: for example, they thought that plants, like people, had friends, favourite associates, and planted certain plants together for this reason; there is some evidence that there may be something in this, albeit of a chemical rather than a spiritual nature. (And do we know for certain that our own affinities are not physically founded?) They believed that disease in men might be caused by the stars; and, therefore, they also attributed some diseases of plants to sidereal causes. But in other ways, their coping with the farmer's usual difficulties was practical and effective within limits.

In ancient as in modern Europe spring frosts often caused serious damage in vineyards. Vines are hardy, but the young clusters of folded leaf containing the flower-bud in embryo are not, and a frost in April or early May can destroy the crop at the burgeoning stage. It is possible that this was a greater danger then than now, for some contemporary descriptions of the climate of France, from which it is argued that vines cannot be grown there, suggest that there was a cold spell of some length in Europe during the first centuries B.C. and A.D. Mago, Columella and Pliny understood exactly the kind of weather which produces such frosts: clear skies and still nights in easterly-wind conditions, with radiation of warmth from the ground surface upwards. They also knew that the lightest of screens, a very thin cloud for example, prevents them. The practice they recommended was to keep masses of straw available round the vineyard and, if frost threatened, set fire to it, thus laying down a screen of smoke between the vines and the sky. There is still no more effective method of preventing or at least minimizing damage, excepting the very expensive one of keeping the vines under artificial rain from sprinklers while the dangerous conditions last. Hail was (and is) another weather hazard, and for this they had no cure; nor have we. Columella advises the planting of very large-leaved vine varieties in regions subject to hailstorms in August and September, which is sound enough.

*Dolor membrorum* was a disease which distorted the nodes and articulations of the vines; it reads very much like the virus disease known as *court-noué*. *Carbunculus* or *rubigo* seems, from the symptoms given, to have been a fungus disease; it was worst in damp vineyards and never seen in high, windy ones. The vines afflicted 'appeared burnt all over'. We may compare this with the 'fireblight' of pears and apples. Billiard suggests that it was the disease we now call anthracnose, but if so it was more virulent then than it is now.[24] The symptoms of *araneum* sound to me like oidium; to the best of my knowledge there is no question, however, that the oidium of the vine, *Uncinula necator*, was introduced from America in about 1845. *Araneum* was perhaps a botrytis fungus. Sometimes vineyards suffered what is described as a 'withering of the grapes before they ripened'.[25] This is so very like the consequences of oidium that some authorities think that this is what it was. But there was a disease of the vine which appeared in Portugal in the seventeenth century, *polvillo*, which is clearly this same one. The Romans treated it by making an incision in the stock of the vine and filling it with a paste of wood-ash and cow-urine (potassium and nitrate fertilizers). If faulty root-action was to blame, this might help. Billiard points out that late in the nineteenth century there was much excitement when a German agronomist succeeded in curing chlorosis of the vine by painting the fresh pruning-cuts, in March, with a solution of sulphate of iron, in short by getting an iron salt directly into the sap-stream, by-passing the roots. But the Romans were using this method— not to cure chlorosis which they seem not to have known, but as a way of force-feeding a sick vine—in the first century A.D. and perhaps much earlier. The recipe appears in the *Geoponica*.[26]

Grey Rot was troublesome in ancient Italian vineyards. This was, and is, *Botrytis cinerea*. The only remedy suggested was to remove the soil about the vine and replace it with gravel and ashes. This is sound enough as far as it goes, for it would improve surface drainage. *Roratio* was 'shanking'; there was, and is, no definite cure. I had a bad go of it in my Devon vineyard in 1964. It is sometimes a result of excessive manuring. The Red Sickness, considered by Pliny of sidereal origin, was obviously a deficiency disease. Columella recommends more manuring, which might help if the manure contained the deficient element. We can do better. Finally, there were various root rots; the ancients destroyed the plant and left the spot unplanted for several years: perfectly sound.

Of large animal pests of the vineyard, those mentioned in the literature are foxes, rabbits, rats, mice and starlings, and of these starlings were the worst; they were, indeed, so troublesome that in an action at law to get one's rent or taxes reduced on a plea of act of God, such as flood or war, a contingency covered in most vineyard leases, a plea of starlings was as good as a plea of flood. I have myself seen a flock of these birds clear a cherry orchard in about fifteen minutes.

Wasps did much damage; they still do. Democritus recommended coating the fruit with olive oil; it might work, but even then it would have been rather costly, especially in labour. There is one completely mysterious pest: Pliny says, '*M. Cicero tradit animalia biuros vocari qui vites in Campania erodunt.*' Nobody knows what kind of beast a *biuros* was; it had never been mentioned before, nor has it since. And Cicero was not a heavy drinker. *Phthiriosis* was an insect pest and when, in 1870, the phylloxera disaster was at its zenith, some French authorities thought that this was it. The consensus of expert opinion now is that *phthiriosis* was *Coccus vitis* (*Dactylopsis vitis*), the cockchafer of the vine; there is an account in Gilbert White's *Selbourne* of a curious appearance of this creature in Surrey in the eighteenth century. *Cantharis* was presumably a coleoptera. *Volucris* was a flea-beetle. *Spondyle* was the larval stage of the common cockchafer. Many kinds of caterpillars ate the vine-leaves and two ate the green fruit. Cato used his sulphur and bitumen specific, burnt as a fumigant, against these and others. Less scientific persons might take ancient advice and have a menstruating woman walk round the vineyard, with feet bare and hair unbraided, whereupon all the caterpillars would fall off. The pest called by Pliny *convolvulus* was probably *Tortrix ambiguella*.

The vintage in Roman-Italian vineyards was made between August and November but where a contractor was employed it must usually have been made in September, for the law called for the new wine to be off the premises by the kalends of October. I find this curious, because the XII Tables laid it down that the vintage was not to be made until the leaves had fallen, which would be November or even December. Of course that law was archaic and was not enforceable, but all the Italian authorities urged growers to leave the vintage as late as possible, and the fact is that with their taste for sweet, heady wines, the ancients persistently overripened their grapes. Obviously a November vintage on the Rhine might be good sense, but in Italy it must often have meant that the grapes were almost raisins. French authorities shake their heads over this 'ignorance' of sound practice but it was nothing of the kind, the ancients simply liked the kind of wine you get from overripe grapes and their favourite vintage today would have been something like Château d'Yquem mixed with treacle. If you leave the grapes so long on the vine in a warm climate, your wine will be very short of acids; it will be insipid to the taste, and it will not keep very well. Falernian was vinted in October which explains its extraordinary keeping qualities; the Falernian served at Trimalchio's table was one hundred years old.

The first process of the vintage is *foulage*; the Romans had no machine to do this and so they still trod the grapes in the ancient manner of Armenia, Mesopotamia and Egypt. Pressing, which comes next, was done with one of three possible kinds of machine: the oldest press was one in which the pressure was obtained by hammering in wooden wedges; after that came a lever-operated machine; but by the first century all the presses in use were on the same principle as our own, based on the screw. Cato describes such a press in detail but it is absolutely impossible to follow his specification. Attempts to do so in practice have failed. But nothing is more difficult than to describe a machine without the help of drawings, and make oneself understood.

To sum up: viticulture began, on smallholding lines, in Sicily, southern Italy, and Tuscany, between the ninth and seventh centuries B.C. The Romans, a people to whom wine was unknown in their primitive phase, had it from the Etruscans of Veii and the Greeks of Magna Graecia. In the first centuries of the city, wine was a subsistence crop with small surpluses for sale, but was more plentiful in the Greek south and the Etruscan north. Viticulture became increasingly important during the Republican epoch and by the first century of our era it had expanded to all the confines of Italy and had crossed the Alps; by the fourth it had expanded to every province of the Empire, despite sporadic attempts to check it.

By the first century B.C. wine had become the daily drink of all Italians, and this may have been so much earlier. Wine was given free or sold below cost price to the urban mob; it helped to ruin the class of yeomen-burgesses; it became a major industry and trade; it contributed largely to the imperial revenue; it was celebrated by all of the few good poets which the Latin language produced, and probably by the bad ones as well. It took the Italian vineyards five hundred years to make men forget that the land of great vintages had formerly been Greece. It was to take the French ones even longer to produce wines with the kind of world-wide fame and special glamour which had distinguished first Chian and Lesbian, then Falernian and Caecuban.

# CHAPTER V

## *The Vine's Great Nation*

IT IS VERY PROBABLE THAT THE FIRST cultivated grape-vines to be established in France were planted by the Phocaean colonists from Greece who founded Marseilles: that is the received opinion, although it is at least possible that Tyrian, Sidonian or Carthaginian plantations, all trace of which has long since vanished, may have antedated these Greek ones. It seems clear from what Thucydides has to say about it that the Carthaginians disputed the Phocaean presence in that part of the Mediterranean. Nevertheless, whatever Carthage may have done to introduce the vine and wine to ancient France, it is quite certain that the first vineyards to have a future were the Phocaean ones. The natives of what is now Provence—Ligurians, Iberians, Celts or whatever they were—began by buying wine from the Massiliotes, but as usual this wine was only for the aristocracy; their poor drank a kind of beer, fermented malt-and-water. But the trade in wine must have been quite brisk all the same, for the geographer Strabo says that the vine flourished all over the hills around Massilia, and that the vines were not trained on poles as in southern Italy, but trailed on the ground.

The relatively swift northern diffusion of viticulture during the centuries immediately following its introduction caused great surprise among observers; and since the culture of the vine north of the Alps had been thought impossible or at least very difficult, it called for an explanation. On this subject Diodorus Siculus[1] says: 'Since the temperateness of the climate of Gaul is destroyed by excessive cold, the land produces neither wine nor oil . . . [But] the Gauls are excessively addicted to the use of wine and fill themselves with the wine which is brought into their country by merchants, drinking it unmixed, and since they partake of this drink without moderation by reason of their craving for it, when they are drunk they fall into a stupor or state of madness. Consequently many of the Italian traders, induced by the love of money which characterizes them, believe that the Gauls' love of wine is their gift from Hermes. For these transport the wine on the navigable rivers by means of boats and through the level plain on wagons, and receive for it an incredible price; for in exchange for a jar of wine they get a slave . . .'[2] An economist, Saserna by name, whose works have not come down to us but who is quoted by Columella, gave it as his opinion that there had been a change in the climate, since many districts which he thought to have been formerly too cold to produce wine had a glut of it at the time when he came to write of them. I shall deal at some length with this opinion, because it has been used time after time, and ever since Saserna first thought of it, to explain the successful northward spread of the vineyards.

During the history of the vine in Europe it is very likely that there have been some changes in climate; rainfall is perhaps lower than it used to be by reason of the destruction of the tree-cover; and there have probably been long periods when summers were warm, alternating with others when they were cool and wet. And this, of course, has had some influence on the extension of viticulture. But it is in the highest degree improbable that there has been a steady warming up of northern Europe to make possible the northward extension of viticulture; or, to put it the other way round, it is highly unlikely that the climate of Champagne or the Rhineland today is like that of Greece and Italy in the last centuries B.C. No; it is the adaptability and genetical flexibility of the grape-vine itself which account for its success beyond its original habitat. The vine, like man, is not so rigorous a specialist as to depend for survival upon an unchanging environment.

What happens, and has been happening now for some thousands of years, is something like this: farmers and gardeners on the periphery of an established viticultural region plant a few vines to provide themselves with wine. Perhaps they are not very successful; in poor summers the grapes fail to ripen; in hot ones, or where the site of the vineyard is particularly favourable, the experimenter gets a vintage. Thus, all along the northern periphery of the region of established and commercially viable viticulture, there is a sort of viticultural marginal zone. Among the vines planted in this zone it will be noticed that some individuals here and there do better than average; this variation is phenotypical, but it can be fixed in a 'strain'. The cultivator chooses an individual vine of superior performance in his climate from which to propagate new stock and he thus establishes, in quite a short time, a clone of plants better suited to the conditions in which he is farming. There is more to it than this, however. As was noted (see Appendix and Notes) by Negrul, there was in France and Italy a native population of *vites*. Very rarely (but it would happen sometimes) there would be cross-breeding between one of these natives and one of the exotic cultivars; that this does happen we know from experience in North America (see Chapter IX) where the first hybrids between native species and *V. vinifera* were the result of chance cross-pollination. It may be that some growers transplanted native vines into the vineyard, mingling them with the exotics. Deliberate, intelligent crossing at that period is highly unlikely, but whatever the scientists may say, it is not out of the question, for peasants have very often made great local advances in technique without their work having any consequences for the world in general. So that there would have appeared from time to time seedling vines better equipped to grow and ripen their fruit in the cooler summers of the north. Finally there would, again rarely but nevertheless often enough, have occurred mutations in the vineyard populations; most of these would have been of no practical value; but now and again a valuable one would happen, and the mutant would be picked out by the cultivator.

What we have here, in short, is evolution immensely speeded up by artificial selection, instead of occurring slowly by natural selection. And this process would be repeated constantly at the periphery of the viticultural area, continuing until the limit, if any (see Prologue), of the vine's variability was reached. We do not know whether there is such a limit; we do know that if there is we have not reached it, for both the Russians and the Germans are having significant successes in the breeding of vines capable of ripening a crop of fair-quality wine-grapes in conditions which would be hopeless for the vines of antiquity, or even for the vines of, say, fifty years ago. It may well be asked, what is the point of doing this? Why not import wine from those parts of the world where it is easy to grow? There are several answers: I suppose that no lover of wine would wish to be without the vintages of Bordeaux, Burgundy or the Rhine, not to mention Champagne; in early Roman republican times these places would have been—indeed were in so many words—considered unsuitable by reason of their relatively cool summers for the planting of vines; as unsuitable as, for instance, Scotland would be considered today. It is a curious fact that the most exquisite, although not the most generous, wines always come from near the periphery of the viticultural region; or else from such an altitude within that region that, climatically, the vineyard in question might be in a much higher latitude. Grapes exposed to too much sun, too high summer temperatures, become excessively sugary and wanting in acidity; the wine made from them will be heavy and heady and coarse. It is the grapes which are sweet enough to yield an adequacy of alcohol, yet acid enough to give the wine character, which yield those wines of real delicacy which the modern palate prefers.

At all events, the vine spread across France much faster than can be accounted for by supposing a change of climate. It was already anciently established in Provincia Narbonensis by early Roman republican times, and by Cicero's day was already so productive there that the provincial government tried to protect the industry by clapping an import tax on Italian wine. This was, of course, disallowed by the Roman government: the export of wine from Italy had become of great economic importance. Cato, in his *De re rustica*, says that the profit per man-hour-acre from vines was at least three times as great as from any other crop; and the result of this was, naturally, over-planting of vineyards, which was in due course to become very serious, a danger to the economy. Italy's need to import bread-grain was owing quite as much to the over-planting of vines as to any other cause. Actual legislation to suppress the competition of French viticulture was not to come until imperial times; but very much earlier one of the conditions for peace which the Romans laid down when negotiating with the transalpine tribes they had defeated was that (in the interests of the Italian export trade) they should not plant vineyards. Cicero[3] comments acidly, 'Fine specimens of justice we are!'

The Celtic or Gallic people who were, both within and without 'The Province', the first wine-growers beyond Italy, were the Allobroges: we shall have more to say about their viticulture, for it had important implications for the future. The centre of their homeland seems to have been the valley of the Isère on the east bank of the Rhône: so that the oldest vineyard in France is perhaps that of Hermitage. Allobrogican influence extended to the east as far as Geneva, and to the west across the river into the land of the Arvernii. Caesar in *De bello gallico* mentions certain Gallic tribes, but much further north and west, whose laws strictly forbade the importing of wine, let alone the growing of it, on the ground that drinking wine softened and corrupted the manhood of the tribe, and so spoilt their military quality. And it is certainly true that the wine-growing Allobroges were no match in war for their formidable Helvetian neighbours, and would have been at the mercy of both those proto-Swiss and of the Arvernii but for Rome's protection. It is curious that the Allobroges should have been so far ahead of the Arvernii in the civilized arts of wine-growing; for the Arvernii were famous among the Gallic tribes for their wealth and for the opulence of the court of their kings, and one would have expected so rich a people to grow their own wine. They may, however, have been prevented from doing so by one of these treaties which Cicero mentioned with such scorn for Roman justice; whereas the Allobroges, if as is possible they had their vine, their *allobrogica*, from Massilia much earlier, could hardly be deprived of it so late in the day, even by the Romans.[4]

Caesar's conquest of Gaul hastened the northward march of the vines. Within an astonishingly short time French wines of certain regions were to be making a great name for themselves. The wines of the Rhône valley about Vienne and the wines of the Garonne/Gironde were the first to do so.

It should be made clear at this point that the factors which made certain regions of France viticulturally successful, and so enriched their inhabitants, were not only matters of soil and climate. A tremendous amount of nonsense has been talked about this; there are many parts of France where the vine would have grown as well, and the wine been as good as in the regions now long celebrated for their wines. It is not even—in fact not at all—true to say that by some extraordinary feat of prescience the peoples of the Gironde estuary, or the Burgundian hills, or the Rhine valley, knew that their soil and their climate would yield the finest wines in the world. The quality of the wines from Bordeaux, Burgundy and the other great wine centres is a product of time and skill, of fitting the vines and the techniques of growing them to soil and climate. What, then, was the reason why the particular regions in question were chosen, rather than others? The answer is simply, transport. To have a chance of commercial success, viticulture had to be established preferably on a navigable waterway, or at least on one of the great main roads, the military roads on which the great lumbering carts which carried the wine out could travel with some degree of ease and safety (*plates 52, 53*). Of course, it was not enough to have this advantage; there had also to be suitable vineyard sites, viticultural knowledge, supplied by some experienced and enterprising foreigner from the South who would have played an important part. But, as we shall see, this matter of transport of the vintage was of such importance that it was, for example, to give the Moselle valley a tremendous start, in point of time, over that of the Rhine.

The fact that the earliest French vineyards of commercial importance were established on the sea, on the Gironde estuary and on the Rhône enabled the planter or his merchant to ship out his product so easily that French wines could and soon did compete, even in Rome, with the home product. But much more important, these vineyards were nearer by hundreds of miles to the newly-developing markets in the North on which Italian viticulture, notably that of Campania, had come to depend for its profit, the home market being grossly over-supplied. Thus it was that, '*Quand, sur les maîtresses voies par ou s'acheminaient leurs vins, les trafiquants Italiens dont parle Diodorus Siculus trouvèrent installés les vignerons de Vienne et ceux de Bordeaux, ils comprirent que désormais pour eux l'ère des brillantes affaires était close.*'[5]

As a consequence of the success of wine-growing in France there was a serious fall in the price of wines throughout the Empire in the second half of the first century. Trimalchio, the newly-rich tycoon of Nero's day, boasting of the indifference with which, so rich was he, he had endured the loss of five shiploads of wine in the past, ends his boast with: '. . . *tunc erat contra aurum*', meaning that wine in those days was worth its weight in gold. The implication is that it was cheaper now; and in fact it was much cheaper. It had been falling in price throughout the lifetime of Trimalchio's creator Petronius.

In the century which followed Diodorus Siculus's account of the Italian export trade in wine, the direction of that trade was reversed. Not only was wine entering Italy from France and being relished by good judges, for after all the Italians had such vintages as Falernian and Caecuban to compare it with (Falernian remained the standard of quality long after it had vanished, I think; for it is used as such not only by Ausonius, but even by Gregory of Tours); wine was also coming into Italy from Spain (see Chapter VI), and from the eastern Mediterranean. Both Martial and Plutarch bear witness to this reversal in the direction of the wine trade; and Columella[6] says that the wine one drank in Rome, '*vindemeas condimas ex insulis cycladibus ac regionibus baeticus gallisque*'—'comes to us from the Cyclades islands, from Baetica and from Gaul'. This does not mean, of course, that Italian viticulture was given up: the reverse is true; to meet the foreign competition the Italian industry was forced to extend its plantations, that is, to increase annual output, in order to maintain profits at their old level though selling at a lower price. Either the consequence of this development really was very serious for Italian agriculture and the economy in general, or—which may rather have been the case—the wealthy and powerful Italian wine-growers' lobby contrived to persuade the government of the Emperor Domitian that it was so. There is, however, another explanation of the restrictive legislation which Domitian was to introduce, as will appear.

Suetonius says (in *Dom.* vii) that Domitian was convinced that the superfluity of wine and shortage of wheat were the effect of excessive pre-occupation with viticulture and a consequent abandonment of arable farming. (See Chapter IV touching the real economic causes of this legislation.) It was not merely a case of abandonment, however: good wheat-land produces poor, coarse wine, but plenty of it, and vineyards both in Italy and France were being extended into soils far too good for vines; they were not only flooding the markets with wine, but lowering the standards of quality, much as Algerian wine has done in our own time. The Emperor therefore issued a decree which prohibited any new planting of vines in Italy, and ordered the grubbing up of half the vineyards in all the provinces of the Empire.

It is quite certain that this law was never strictly enforced as to the grubbing of vineyards. The aim and the consequences of this law have been absurdly exaggerated and misunderstood by many French writers. In Chaptal's nineteenth-century *Traité théorique et practique sur la culture de la vigne* there is a bitter lament over the 'total destruction' of French viticulture in A.D. 92 as a result of Domitian's law; it is accompanied by the shocking statement that '*nos pères, par cet édit désastreux, se virent condamnés a ne se désalterer qu'avec de la bière, de l'hydromel, ou quelques tristes infusions de plantes acerbes . . .*' But no such condemnation to the quenching of their thirst with beer, mead or the wretched infusions of acrid herbs was ever inflicted upon the fathers of M. Chaptal and his fellows. During the nearly two hundred years that this law of Domitian remained on the statute book, not only did the great vineyards of the Gironde and the Rhône continue to flourish, not only did Provence still supply the demand for rough wine for the people, but the beginnings of the great Burgundian vineyard were made in the region of present-day Nuits and Beaune. By the golden age of the Antonine emperors, Lyon had become a great centre of the wine trade (it was to be ruined by Burgundy), so much so, indeed, that as we have seen, Italian export merchants, overwhelmed by this competition, moved their businesses to Lyon. By the sixties of the first century the wines of Vienne were as famous as are those of Bordeaux today; our authority is Pliny the elder; and there is not a trace of evidence that the Rhône industry ceased to flourish after the decree.

On the other hand, Suetonius was certainly exaggerating or over-simplifying when he said that the Emperor altogether gave up the idea of trying to enforce his wine law (*nec exsequi rem perseveravit*). The decree called for the destruction of *half* the provincial vineyards; it would have been quite easy and very sensible to carry out the statutory grubbing of vines where they really did not matter very much to the government or to the locals, while leaving alone the established commercial vineyards in the great and prosperous centres. Even had the good sense of the imperial bureaucracy not made sure of this result, their notorious corruptibility would have done so; the French growers and merchants could well afford to pay substantial bribes to the enforcement officers and magistrates.[7]

But that there was some enforcement of the law, and that it certainly restricted, and seriously, new planting at least in Gaul is clear from the following facts: the Emperor Probus had a very short reign, from A.D. 276 to 282. In that short reign he inflicted a total defeat on an important section of the barbarian forces which were closing in on the Empire. This achievement was of such importance that one would suppose nothing else he did worth mentioning. Yet his edict repealing that of Domitian and giving full liberty to the Gauls to plant the vine where and when they liked is mentioned by every biographer and in every account of that Emperor. This certainly would not have been so had the edict not been a striking one with important consequences; it follows that viticulture had indeed been under some kind of governmental restriction in France, from which it was freed in A.D. 280 after nearly two centuries.

Roger Dion[8] goes too far, I believe, when he says that the aim of Domitian's edict was to maintain the quality of Gallic wine, though no doubt it had that result. It can be compared in its results if not on its intention with a whole series of such laws and edicts issued by French governments during the next eighteen hundred years, which continue to be promulgated even now, and which were at least in part designed to improve the quality of French wines, or rather to prevent that quality falling by preventing the planting of vines in rich, arable soils. Before taking up the tale of the diffusion of viticulture throughout France, perhaps we may take a look at these laws, in one or two examples which can fairly be compared with Domitian's.

Towards the end of the reign of Louis XIV an author named Delamare wrote a book of great value to social historians entitled *Traité de la police.*[9] In it, among much else doubtless of more importance, he made a comparison between the edict of Domitian and later laws and decrees of the same tendency. It is apparent from his collation that at all events from the fourteenth century onwards, decrees similar to Domitian's, and justified by the same argument which Dion if not Suetonius attributes to that emperor, were not uncommon, and were published not only by kings of France but by dukes of Burgundy. In 1622, for example, at the instance of the Burgundian States General, there was a royal proclamation prohibiting the planting of any more vines in Burgundy and ordering that all vines planted within the past twelve years be grubbed up; the reason given was that the extension of the vineyards into arable land was a cause of famine; a reason not given was that established wine-growers were anxious to restrict competition. In 1682 Colbert was writing: 'His Majesty considers that one of the disorders of his realm is the too great multiplication of vineyards on land which is not proper to the vine.' The same sort of thing is repeated at surprisingly frequent intervals: in 1724 the Crown's intendant at Bordeaux advised the central government in Paris: 'It is considered that vineyards should be grubbed up on all land suitable for growing corn, flax, hay . . . leaving only those vineyards on lands which are only suitable for the production of good wine.' And later the Napoleonic government was repeatedly being called upon to forbid the planting of vines on arable land in Champagne, Alsace and in the Rhineland generally.

A remarkably wise and prudent improver of wine by legislation was Philip the Good, that duke of Burgundy who was allied to Henry V and his successor the regent Duke of Bedford, and whose vassal John of Luxemburg sold Joan of Arc to Bedford for ten thousand gold crowns. As ruler of Burgundy, Franche-Comté, and most of the Low Countries, Philip was a much more important monarch than the king of France. His family had a lot to do with wine legislation: his grandfather, Philip the Bold, had issued an interesting edict in 1395 against that variety of the wine-vine which was to receive its *coup de grâce* at the hands of the great Dr Jules Guyot five centuries later, the Gamay. This vine produces a great deal of poorish wine in many kinds of soil; but, as an instance of the fact that good vintages depend very much upon finding the right vine for each soil, the Gamay yields good Beaujolais. Philip the Bold in his edict stigmatizes it as the '*très mauvais et très desloyaux plant nommé gamay*'. His grandson, in this as in most business, was much more cautious: called upon to order the grubbing up of all vine-yards whatsoever in the rich plain lands of Burgundy, so confining the vines to the *côtes*—this was in 1441—he would not go so far as that. He ordered only that no more vineyards be planted in such soils; for as a ruler who knew his people, he knew that once a vineyard is established the owner will find fifty unanswerable reasons for leaving it there. The Duke's example was followed by French governments during the next four centuries. Had it not been followed, half France might now be covered with vines.

This will serve, then, to establish that the diffusion of the vine throughout France was not left to accomplish itself without interference. From the earliest times efforts were made by governments to control it; and on the whole such legislation was wise and good. Nevertheless, Probus, who emancipated the vine again two centuries after Domitian had tried to restrain it, is also deserving of praise. It is very well, in a great Empire with free trade between its parts and with open, easy communications over a whole continent, to concentrate each crop where it will do best, and to rely thereafter on trade to distribute the products. But in the Europe which emerged from the chaos of the Empire's collapse, and which we have had to endure ever since, a Europe of mutually hostile small powers usually at war with each other and often at war each within its own frontiers, no man could count upon import-export trade as a means of supplying the necessities of life. It was therefore as well that Probus enabled the vine to resume its march to the north, for a time was coming when a community which grew no wine too often went without.

The northerly limit of viticulture in France at the end of the first century was a line drawn from Bordeaux to Geneva, the easterly wine country being the territory of the Allobroges.[10] This people, as has been said, are of the very greatest importance in viticultural history: it is at least very probable that their vine, the *allobrogica* mentioned by Pliny the elder, was the prototype or parent of those new, hardy and forward plants which made possible the planting of vineyards further to the north. The first of the important northerly developments was in Burgundy. For reasons it would be tedious to discuss here it is probable, in my opinion, that there had been at least a beginning of viticulture in that country before the edict of Probus in A.D. 280. But it is also certain that the real importance of the Burgundy vineyards did not begin until that edict had been promulgated.

Very strong evidence for this is provided by the third-century prosperity of the wine-export trade in Lyon. The wine merchants of Lyon would not, of course, be selling the bulk of their wine back into the viticultural South, though some French wine went to Italy, any more than the coal merchants, say of Berwickshire, sold coal to Newcastle: it follows that they were buying in the South and selling in the North, and that their trade would hardly have been the tremendously profitable one it was, if between them and their markets (and therefore, nearer to those markets) lay a great wine-growing and wine-exporting country.

On the other hand it is certain that by A.D. 312 the wines of Nuits and Beaune had made a name for themselves. In 1952 a notable Latinist and historian, M. E. Galletier, published a collection of Latin panegyrics among which is one in the form of a diatribe combined with a speech of thanks addressed by the people of Autun to the Emperor Constantine. It specifically mentions the *pagus arebrignus*, which is now the Nuits-Beaune *côtes* and surrounding country, as having been *for some time* noted for its wines: 'This famous canton, distinguished for the culture of the vine.' The rhetor of Autun, speaking for his fellow-citizens, says that the said famous canton is, however, far from deserving the envy with which it is regarded; he goes on to describe its unhappy situation, dominated as it is by rocks and forests swarming with savage beasts, while below it, the plain of the Saône, which was formerly indeed rich agricultural country by reason of the drainage works, has fallen back into the condition of a pestilential swamp because of the neglect of the drainage canals owing to the 'devastations'. As for the vines, the admired and envied vines, they are, the rhetor assures the Emperor, so *exhausted by age* that they hardly respond at all to the vine-dresser's care (my italics). 'Their roots, whose age we no longer know, have in the interlacings of their thousand ramifications, formed a mass which prevents digging the furrows to the required depth, so that for want of sufficient cover the *provins* are exposed to the rains which drown them and the rays of the sun which burn them . . .'[11]

And so on: the rhetor even complains of the appalling and dangerous conditions of the great main road through the region—one of the *viae militares*—which prevent them from getting their vintage away to market even when they have one: 'We have indeed more trouble in exporting a small part of our harvests than have other cities in distributing the greater part of theirs.'[12]

A *provin*, referred to by the rhetor, is what English gardeners call a 'layer'; and the practice of *provignage* was an important part of viticulture until modern times, although now no longer in use for reasons which appear in the Epilogue. A new and properly ripened shoot of the old vine is bent over in a hoop and its severed tip is thrust into the soil and secured there, where it roots. In due course the old root of its parent plant dies; but this renewal of the plant by *provignage* makes each plant virtually eternal (but see Epilogue).

How much of the Autunois complaint was the truth—or shall we say, how much was justified? Not very much. No doubt the roads were in a shocking state and no doubt the plains had gone back to marsh; but the part about the vines is nonsense. The fact is that the purpose of the address to the Emperor was not merely to give thanks for help received but to ask for much more help in restoring the Burgundian economy, either by subsidies or by remission of taxes. It was true that the province had been devastated by war, by barbarian invasion. But as to that business about the age of the vines and the interlacing of the roots: first, the latter is not good evidence that the vines were of great age, the condition could have been produced in less than half a century especially on a thin soil; second, it is not a hindrance to good cropping. All the cultivators needed to do was to go on sticking in new *provins*: in due course the old, dead roots would have rotted and the new, live ones would have been feeding on their decay. This system was still in use in Burgundy only a little more than a long lifetime ago, and the foregoing was the verdict on the rhetor's complaint delivered by experienced growers who had practised it themselves in vineyards of enormous age. What the rhetor's complaints do prove, if anything, is that the people of Nuits and Beaune had *not* been vine-dressers for more than a lifetime, for the terms of the complaint clearly indicate a want of long experience. If the people of Autun had called in an expert from further south he would have told them that the condition of their vineyard was perfectly normal and nothing to worry about, and that in so far as the vineyards were perhaps a little too crowded with plants, that was their own fault and the remedy was obviously to dig some up. It is quite clear, not perhaps to an historian but certainly to a vine-grower, that the people of Autun were novices at the trade.

On the other hand I cannot believe that the Nuits and Beaune vineyards can have got into that state between A.D. 280 and 312, that is, in thirty-two years; nor that thirty-two years would have sufficed to make a great name for their wines. A man's lifetime is the least one can reasonably allow for these things to have happened. I therefore believe that the great vineyards of Burgundy were begun not later than A.D. 250. But at that time the edict of Domitian was still in force; and we have argued that in all probability the vineyards spared by it when it was promulgated in A.D. 92 were only such as were of some commercial importance. It is hardly possible that the Burgundian vineyards were of great commercial importance until after A.D. 300, when the wine-trade of Lyon began to decline for the same reason that that of Italy had formerly become less profitable—a powerful competitor established between the trade centre and the principal markets. In all probability, then, the business was established in a small way as an extension of the Allobrigican wine-producing industry from some time in the first century, and it did not become a serious menace to the more southerly producing regions until after 300 when Probus's edict had freed the growers from government control and the Burgundian vineyard could expand.

The citizens of Autun got their remission of taxes. We have seen that one of their complaints was the state of the main road. But the very fact of having to use road-transport at all in sending their wine to market is put forward in the address to Constantine as a serious handicap. Other, happier cities had a river which served the purpose; these were on rivers whose current set towards the markets and not, as in the case of Autun and the Saône, away from them.

This is a case in point to support our argument above, that viticulture tended always to develop where there was a river to carry the wine away to market. For as a rule, by no other means could the vintages reach the markets at a competitive price.

It is likely, but I cannot prove it, that the establishment of viticulture on the Loire, or in the valley of that lovely river, was as much influenced by the transport which the river offered as by other considerations of site, of soil and climate. I take it next in order to Burgundy for the following reason: that although we have no direct evidence for the date at which viticulture became of commercial importance on the Loire, we do know that by the second half of the fourth century vineyards were many and productive and their wines in good repute, not only as far north as Paris but also along the course of the Moselle (see below). Now it is in the highest degree improbable that the much more southerly Loire vineyards, with the great convenience of a navigable river for the carriage of the vintages, should not have antedated those of Paris and the Moselle.

I have explained the method by which viticulture was extended northward—the selection and propagation of suitably adapted individual vines among established populations of vines. It was this, combined with the selection of good seedlings produced by chance inbreeding in effectively isolated vine communities and occasional and chance outbreeding with the wild vine, which gave rise in the course of some thousands of years to the enormous number of varieties of this single species, and to the startling diversity among them. But the point I wish to make here is that as a rule the new vines which were obtained, and which in their forwardness and hardiness offered the opportunity for northward extension of vine-growing, were only marginally superior in tolerance of cooler conditions and could not exempt the cultivator from attention to every climatic, and therefore geographical and topographical consideration. Generally, all that the latest new vine would enable the cultivator to do would be to move a little further into the region of cooler summers. From time to time, of course, there might be a mutant or hybrid so strikingly superior in this respect that a big jump forward could be taken by the industry. This must have been very rare, however. But there is one other factor not yet discussed: it might from time to time strike an observant traveller that the local (or as the scientists say, micro-) climate of his home parish, although that parish was much further north, was very like the climate of the viticultural region in which he happened to find himself. He might then take home with him a bundle of vine-cuttings; and from such a small beginning, a new vineyard might be established far to the north of the main territory of the cultivated vines (see, for instance, page 161 below, Gironde vines planted on the Loire). For all these reasons I think that the Loire vineyards were well established early in the fourth century, and perhaps late in the third.

'True, it is not until the Merovingian epoch that the vine, and wine trade, are first mentioned in the Loire valley. But it certainly then displays features which had already been fixed for several centuries . . .'[13] Chroniclers of the early Middle Ages, far from confining their observations to politics and war, often had a good deal to say of interest about the weather and the crops. And for good reason: even today these are by far the two most important matters to the vast majority of the human race. Gregory of Tours was no exception: and being 'of Tours' he is a most useful authority for the viticulture of the Loire. In his *History of the Franks* he makes several references to the damage done to the grapes by bad weather, and in these cases he refers to this damage as to a serious public disaster. He would not have done so unless not merely the daily wine, but the livelihood of the people was in question. This of itself argues some degree of antiquity for the viticulture of the region. But the truth is that no facts anterior to the reign of Chilperic II are available for this region, and I shall therefore say no more about it.

The antiquity of the Moselle vineyards is established by the accident of a poet's interest in the beauty of that river and its countryside. Ausonius was a Gallo-Roman of, he says, Viviscan stock, and was born in Bordeaux, the capital of the Bituriges-Vivisci, in the first quarter of the fourth century. His *Mosella* is a pleasant descriptive and encomiastic poem in 483 lines. The most agreeable passages in this work are, to my mind, his descriptive list of the fish of the Moselle. But what concerns us here is that by noticing the vineyards beside the river he establishes for us a fact we might otherwise not have known: the presence of viticulture on the Moselle in the fourth century; and by noticing the river traffic he also gives us the clue to the manner in which the vintages were sent to market. '*In speciem quin me patriae cultumque intentis Burdigalae blando pepulerunt omnia visu, culmina villarum pendentibus edita ripis et virides Baccho colles et amvena fluenta subter labentis tacito rumore Mosellae.*'[14] Or, in the English of Hugh G. Evelyn White: 'Nay more, the whole gracious prospect made me behold a picture of my native land, the smiling and well-tended country of Bordeaux—the roofs of country houses, perched high upon the overhanging river-banks, the hillsides green with vines, and the pleasant stream of Moselle gliding below with subdued murmuring.' And the poet hails the Moselle as: 'river whose hills are overgrown with Bacchus' fragrant vines'. And again, of the utmost importance to the wine-traffic and by favourable comparison with the too turbulent Rhine: 'Thou, with calm waters onward gliding, feelest not any murmurs of the wind nor check from hidden rocks; nor by foaming shallows art thou forced to hurry on in swirling rapids, no eyots hast thou jutting in mid-stream to thwart thy course . . .' As to that traffic of barges or lighters whereby the wine was conveyed to the cities: 'For thee, two modes of voyaging are appointed: this, when boats move down my stream with current favouring and their oars thrash the churned waters at full speed; that, when along the banks, with tow-rope never slackening, the boatmen strain on their shoulders hawsers bound to the masts . . .'

Having told over and described all the fishes of the Moselle: '*Iam liquidas spectasse vias et lubrica pisces agmina multiplicesque satis numerasse catervas*', Ausonius proceeds: 'Let show of vines lead on another pageant, and let Bacchus' gifts attract our wandering gaze where lofty ridge far-stretching above scarped slopes, and spur, and sunny hillside with salient and reëntrant rise in a natural theatre overgrown with vines . . .'

This passage is followed by a series of comparisons between the viticultural landscape of Moselle and the most famous wine-countries of the Empire. He mentions, too, the people of this smiling countryside—they were, by the way, Belgae of the same people as had conquered and settled south-east England about four or five centuries earlier—'The people, happy in their toil and the restless husbandmen are busy, now on the hilltop, now on the slope, exchanging shouts in boisterous rivalry. Here the wayfarer tramping along the low-lying bank, and there the bargeman floating by, troll their rude jests at the loitering vine-dressers; and all the hills and shivering woods, and channelled river, ring with their cries.'

There is a pleasant passage in which Ausonius describes the verdant hills and the details of vines, their tendrils, leaves and clusters of fruit, mirrored upside-down in the waters of the river (a passage imitated by Alexander Pope in his description of the Loddon, as Ausonius' translator points out). From the description of the country houses, each in its fine grounds, each having its bath-house with smoking chimney and *tepidarium*, *caldarium* and *frigidarium*, it is clear that this was a rich and highly-civilized countryside.

# France: the Vine's Great Nation

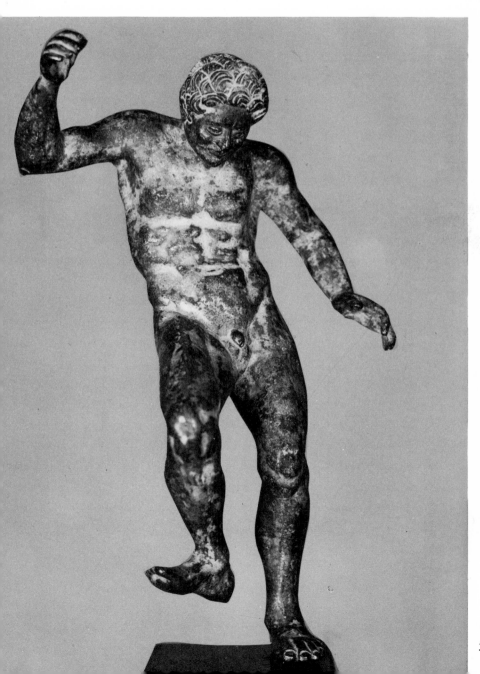

Gallo-Roman bronze
wine-treader.

51 *A wine-shop in Dijon, already a great vineyard centre in Roman times. The merchant pours wine through a funnel in the counter.*

52

*Viticultural regions such as those of the Rhône and Moselle which could use river transport (52) had a great commercial advantage over those which were obliged to use carts (53), especially when the decline of the Roman imperial economy led to the neglect of the roads.*

53

Within image: ISTI PORTANT:ARMAS:ADNAVES:ETHIC TRAHVNT:CARRVM CVMVINO:ETARMIS: + HIC:WILLELM:

54

55

In 1066 William's army, setting out to conquer England, carried a provision of wine as well as weapons (54). From the Bayeux tapestry.

Eating grapes (55), and the grape harvest, the Labour of the Month of October (56), both from the romanesque church at Vézelay in Burgundy. The date of the vintage would be fixed locally according to the variety of grapes grown and the weather. Right, picking and treading grapes in September (57), a wall-painting from the church at Pritz, in western France.

56

57

58

A fourteenth-century wine press from Burgundy (58) has a capstan-operated wheel and screw. Screw presses had been in use since at least the third century B.C.

The King had his vine trellises on the Ile de la Cité, Paris, in the sixteenth century (59). Vine planting about Paris dates from the fourth century A.D.

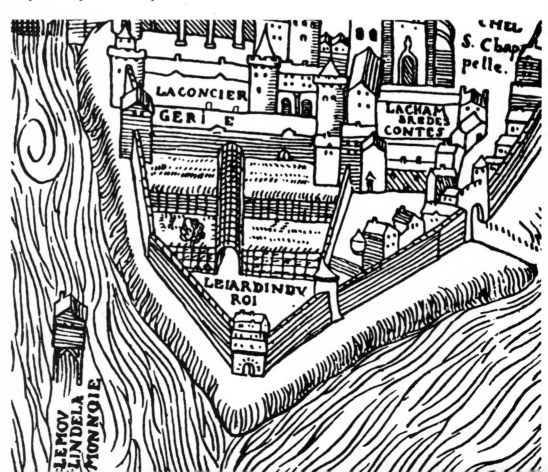

59

60 *In a romantic spirit of fete champêtre, lords and ladies help with the vintage in the Loire Valley. From a tapestry woven in the late fifteenth century.*

61 *Clos Vougeot, one of the vineyard-surrounded châteaux of Burgundy.*

And the riches, the polish, were undoubtedly founded on the profits of wine-growing.

Not much needs to be said about the region of Paris. Its vineyards were established early in the fourth century, but at no time were its vintages of any commercial importance. Grapes are still grown in the same parishes where masonry has not ousted them; but these are table grapes, usually of the famous variety *Chasselas doré de Fontainebleau*, miscalled in English gardens Royal Muscadine. (It is not a *muscadine*, but of pure *vinifera* stock.) This ancient and admirable variety is now being displaced at long last by some of the new hybrid table grapes, but it is still of some economic importance.

For the antiquity of vine-growing about Paris we have imperial authority: the Emperor Julian, called by Christians 'the Apostate', was perhaps the first of an interminable line of distinguished men of parts who have conceived a passion for the town of Paris. He could find no fault with a place which was, in his day, a small town, nor with anything belonging to it. And he spoke highly of the Paris vintages. By upbringing he was no doubt a competent judge of wine; to what extent his prejudices in favour of Paris influenced his judgment, we cannot know. But there is no technical reason why the wines of Paris should not, in fact, have been as good as those of, say, the Rhine, especially in a period of warm summers.

When a period of very hard winters, cold springs, and cool, wet summers set in, then the story was different, and it becomes clear that growing grapes for wine was as 'marginal' in the region of Paris as in southern England, and in the north-western peninsulas of France (see below). For example, the first half of the fifteenth century was one of the periods of great cold in northern Europe, and in the *Journal d'un bourgeois de Paris sous Charles VI et Charles VII*, which covers the period 1405 to 1450, we find that good vintages from the vineyards round Paris were rare, and that in very many of these forty-five years there was no vintage at all, the burgeoning of the vines being destroyed by sharp frosts in May; or the grapes failing to ripen in summers of continuous rains and low temperatures; or the ripe grapes being destroyed by wet weather in August and September.

There seems also to have been rather frequent trouble with caterpillars (probably of a moth of the genus *Tortrix*), and with *hannetons*, that is, cockchafers.

I should perhaps say at this point that pests and diseases of the vines seem to have had very little influence in checking the diffusion of the plant in the Old World. In the past, cultivators took damage to crops by insects and diseases so much for granted as an unavoidable affliction that they rarely said much about it. Chroniclers note that in the year in question the grapes or the vines were ruined by such and such a pest. The experimenter planting vines to the north of the principal vineyard regions probably had less trouble of this kind, at least to begin with: pests and diseases of plants build up to epidemic—and occasionally pandemic—proportions where monoculture on a vast scale provides the parasite creature with unnaturally favourable conditions for increase. But new plantations in a region where the pests and diseases were not yet present would not have much trouble from them until the eggs and spores on the original cuttings had had time to give rise to a population of the pest species and the disease species, the pathogen or its vector. So that the long-established vineyard would be far more likely to discourage attacks from parasitic organisms than the new vineyard, which might moreover be in a climate less favourable to the pests and diseases in question. It may be, indeed, that really serious, and at that time uncontrollable, infestations of vineyards by pests and diseases promoted the extension of viticulture by forcing the grower to try a new situation, to move, in short, out of the recognized viticultural region.

For Paris, then, we can conclude that the vine had reached that city by A.D. 350 and did not thereafter retreat from it even following the supposed climatic change after 1350.

One would have expected the Rhine valley to have its vineyards no later than the Moselle valley; but what is now the important section of Rhine vineyard in France, that in French Alsace, was not as a matter of fact planted until some centuries later. The reason for this was that whereas the Moselle gave the vine-growers a means of exporting their wines, the Rhine in Alsace was not navigable, although the navigability of the Doubs made possible the carriage of goods by river as far as the Alsatian border. 'The difficulties', says Roger Dion, 'opposed by the Alsatian reaches of the Rhine to river traffic, and the convenience of such traffic on the Moselle, meant that the route by the latter river from Chalon-sur-Saône to Coblentz, even taking account of the overland stage as far as Toul, was shorter and easier than the route by way of the Doubs and the Belfort gap, used by the moderns.'

The Belfort gap referred to is the Rhône–Rhine canal. Until the Germans dredged and embanked it after 1870, the Rhine through Alsace was broad, manifold, shallow and very swift, the fall of land along its course from Basle to Strasbourg being 0·86 metre per kilometre. These reaches were so subject to flooding that the great towns of the region did not develop on the Rhine but on other and calmer rivers. It was not until the seventh or eighth century that the very skilful Frisian river-sailors with their flat-bottomed craft opened a traffic between the mouth of the Rhine and Strasbourg, in the search for markets for their country's cloth manufacturers. Then, and not until then, was it possible for the eastern slopes of the Rhine to be exploited by the planting of vineyards whose vintages could be carried out to a rich market by the Frisians returning home. But by the time that this trade had been established, the Corporation of *nautae mosallica*—the Moselle Lighter-men's guild as we may call it—had been carrying Moselle wines to market for at least three centuries.

But in tracing the speed and direction of the vine's diffusion from an ancient centre of origin, this belatedness of the Alsace vineyards is not really relevant; for although the vines were not established in Alsace until later, they were established beyond it on the Rhine in Gallo-Roman times, and perhaps as early as in the Moselle valley. There were Roman settlements at what are now Germersheim, Speyer, Altrip, Worms and elsewhere; and there, where the river was steadier and deeper, archaeology has unearthed pieces of carbonized vine wood, dating from the fourth century or there-abouts, and the character of this wood relates the ancient vine from which it came to the modern Riesling. But that belongs rather to the tale of the vine in Germany than in France.

It may safely be assumed that while the great vineyards, important not only commercially but for the steadily improving quality of their wine, were being established between the first and eighth centuries, so that the vine had its colonies at the furthest extremes of France as we now know that country, the vine was also spreading across the country to fill up the spaces between the great viticultural regions. Away from the principal commercial vine-yards it remained thin on the ground, collected into small vineyards in odd corners cultivated by peasants for their own provision of wine, and rarely for sale. And this applies likewise to the extreme north-west provinces of France: Brittany and Normandy had their subsistence viticulture but it is most unlikely that they ever had commercial vineyards with a market beyond the nearest town.

In both the Atlantic seaboard duchies the cider apple was of importance, certainly as early as the sixth century and perhaps earlier. Cider competed with the local wine, was in due course preferred to it, and may have been superior to it. Of Norman viticulture I can find nothing of interest or importance: it was probably of monastic origin and it can be compared for character with the viticulture of medieval England (see Chapter VI). No Norman wine of merit ever seems to have been developed.

The establishment of vineyards in Brittany was late and unimportant. Too much has been made by some writers of the fact that the Emperor Probus, according to what we are told by his biographer Vopsicus, specifically called upon the 'Bretons' to plant vines and thereby to enrich themselves. But the people Vopsicus refers to are quite clearly the *Britons*. Brittany was not so called, of course, until after the invasion and colonization of Armorica, its ancient name, by Britons who were apparently running away from the Saxons and other invading Germans. There is an odd kind of evidence for the persuasion that Brittany had no vines until the seventh century at the earliest: Gregory of Tours says that almost every year during the reigns of kings Chilperic II, Gontran, and Childebert II, the Bretons raided the vineyards about the town for the purpose of carrying off part of the wine-grapes, which they then vinted at home. On one occasion, he records, the raiders, under a chieftain named Waroch, were able to hold the vineyards long enough to gather the grapes, press and carry off the fermenting must, and complete the process at home in Brittany. Clearly, there would have been little point in such raids if the Bretons had had their own vineyards. In A.D. 610 when Columba, subsequently canonized, embarked at Nantes on his way to evangelize the Irish, he was able to provision his ship with a wine purchased locally; but Columba's provision of wine could have been and probably was imported from the Loire valley.

Roger Dion has cleared up another source of great confusion touching the matter of viticulture in Brittany. One of the principal vines of the Loire valley vineyards was then and is often still called the *breton*. This *breton* vine is one of the *plants nobles* and no experienced vinearoon would for a moment entertain the notion that a plant of such quality could ever have been selected or bred in Brittany. We have it on the authority of Rabelais, moreover, that *breton* wine was not, in fact, Breton: '*Ce bon vin breton*', he says, '*poinct ne croist en Bretagne, mais en ce bon pays de Verron . . .*'[15]

Then how came the vine and the wine to be called *breton*? Dion points out that it was the practice, before mechanical transport made the movement of goods quick, easy and general, to name a commodity by the place whence it was most readily bought. (A good English example is that of Stilton cheese, named for the place where it was bought, not the place where it was made.) The vines which the planters of the Loire valley were using to furnish their vineyards reached them from Bordeaux by sea: the port they came to was Nantes in Brittany; they called the vines Breton. What were they, in fact? The *breton* vine is a strain of the famous *cabernet* of the Gironde *graves*; but to the planters of Chinon and Saumur, it was still the *breton*.

Nevertheless, by Rabelais' time Brittany had long had her own vineyards and the Bretons drank wines of their own growths. A distinction is made in the nomenclature: *vin de Breton* was wine of the Cabernet Breton d'Anjou which got its name, no doubt, in the fashion described by Dion. *Vins bretons* were the wines of such *cépages* as Gamay and Folle Blanche planted in the Nantaise. It is possible to get some idea of the age of these vineyards; there is a record of a very considerable planting made near Ronceray at the orders of Geoffroy Martel, Count of Anjou, in 1055; trading concessions granted by one Count of Anjou in 1135, renewed by another in 1253 and by Charles V in 1366, indicate that some Breton wine was actually exported inland. The English bought wine in Nantes early in the fifteenth century and it may well have been the local product. And finally Richelieu, at the instance of an abbot of Fontevrault, caused considerable vineyards to be planted in Brittany.

The youngest vineyard of France is almost certainly that of Champagne. But like Alsace, Champagne has no significance for the diffusion of the vine: for it was a backwater, filled up long after the mainstream of viticulture had flowed further north.

It can be said with some certainty, then, that having set out upon its great career in France in about 600 B.C. when the Phocaeans were founding Marseilles, the vine had colonized the whole of suitable parts of the country by A.D. 600. Despite Saserna's opinion, twelve centuries seems a long time to take in covering a relatively small region; but as we have noted, the north-ward movement of the vines was restricted by laws. Even had this not been the case, there was another obstacle to its progress. The selection and propagation of vines suitable for planting in country where the summers are relatively cool takes time; so does the raising of more or less barbarous populations to that point of civil settlement at which plantation farming of any kind becomes possible. It may fairly be said of France that both men and vines had to adapt themselves very considerably before they could form a profitable partnership.

It will perhaps be interesting to glance at the manner in which the people in this partnership changed the ancient techniques of cultivation and wine-making to suit the conditions in which they worked; and how, at the same time, the vine itself changed its nature to fit itself for the climate of northern Europe.

The process of *provignage* has been briefly described: it consists in hooping over a young but lignified shoot on an old vine and burying its severed end in the soil, where it puts out roots. There is no limit to this process (in the absence, however, of phylloxera; it becomes impossible in the presence of that aphis; see Epilogue), and an entire vineyard could be and probably often was planted by *provignage* from a single mother-vine. The technique is a northern one in practice, although Columella knew it. The vine as it was known in nature and in the earliest vineyards is not a scandent shrub, but rather a scandent tree, a large woody plant needing the support of a tree or large pole, bearing a large number of big bunches of big berries. What a vine of a variety which, as commonly met with, is no larger than, say, a stool of blackberry, can do in favourable conditions can be seen, for example, at Hampton Court near London (*plate 75*) where a single specimen bears three thousand bunches of large grapes annually. The fact that this vine is under glass has nothing to do with its size, excepting that it happens to be in England where the climate is not favourable: the microclimate of the greenhouse simply reproduces the ordinary climate of, say, Morocco or Baja California, where, in the nineteenth century, there were single vine-plants two hundred years old covering as much as an acre each. If you take cuttings of one of these vines and plant them out of doors in cool conditions, the plant grows much more slowly and bears fewer grapes.

Those individual vines, mutants or extreme variants from the type which were selected to give rise to clones more suitable for northern plantations, were, without reference to their pruning, smaller, slower-growing, and bore fewer and smaller bunches and smaller berries than the southern vines from which they derived. Moreover, the sugar content of their grapes, even when these were fully ripe, was lower. But this was the circumstance which gave the wines of the North their character and their delicacy. The ultra-sweet grapes of the South yield a wine very high in alcohol, for alcohol is made of sugar and nothing else. These wines were, therefore, heavy; and, being short of acids, they were also of little character and no delicacy. In England we think of wine as a product of the burning southern sun; but the best wines are the product of more temperate climates, and too much sun is as bad for wine as too little of it.

Since the individual vine yielded less wine in the North, especially when pruned to enhance the quality of the fruit, the technique of *provignage* was adopted in the first place to increase the crop-per-acre by increasing the number of plants per acre. But it was found to have two other advantages; a multiple-rooted vine has more rigidity than a plant on a single root, and therefore requires less support from stakes; and in crowded vineyards the damage done to the burgeoning vines in May by a late frost, a very frequent occurrence throughout northern and central France, and even in the South, is reduced.

The northern migration of the vine, then, turned it from a large, sprawling or clambering plant into a relatively bushy and quite small one, bearing a rather different kind of fruit: the change was progressive, beginning in Italy, going further in France, and culminating in Germany. And other, subtler changes occurred. In 1949 I found, growing on a house in Kent, a vine morphologically indistinguishable from *Pinot Meunier*. I took cuttings of it: they have given rise to a clone of this variety which, grown side by side with *Pinot Meunier* plants imported from France, ripens its fruit two weeks earlier. How does this kind of change come about? By selection; a grower finds one vine of a plantation earlier than the rest, he propagates it as more suitable for his cold climate; it becomes established. It is, moreover, probable that the very hard pruning to which vines of the North are subjected every year was also something new. Some pruning there must always have been; but whereas in the South, and on vines of the ancient form, this would have been quite light, a matter of shortening back the seasonal growth, in the northern vineyards, beginning in Italy under Columella's influence, pruning came to consist in removing all but a very few new shoots; in a single season of growth a vine may produce several hundred 'eyes' or buds each capable of yielding at least one and often more bunches of grapes in a year's time. In the northern vineyards it became the practice to reduce these to perhaps a dozen. By so doing the vine was persuaded to mature a small crop perfectly; had the large crop which was normal in the South been allowed to develop, it would never have matured in the cool summers of the North.

The process of change in the vine itself may very likely have started in the land of the Allobroges, and with the *allobrogica* vine mentioned by the elder Pliny as the prototype. The people who cultivated this vine in the first century of our era were not, it is true, much concerned to extend their vineyards towards the north; but they were concerned to expand into and to grow good wine in mountain country, and they were therefore on the watch for variant or mutant vines which gave better results in conditions of high altitude. Little of their country was below 1,000 feet above sea level, and much of it was over 4,000 feet. Climatically, high altitude equals high latitude. In short the vines of the higher Allobrogican vineyards were good material for planting further north but at a lower altitude.

All that has hitherto been said here touching the vine's relations with climate, refers to summer climate. Something had better be said about the vine in winter, for there is a widely held but mistaken belief that *Vitis vinifera* is not a hardy species, and that the relative difficulty of growing it in the North due to its inability to stand the cold of the northern winter. There is no substance whatever in this belief. No doubt there is some variation in the degree of hardiness from variety to variety; but broadly speaking, the dormant plant in winter can stand without any damage whatever something like 20, and probably more like 30, degrees of frost Centigrade. (That is to say, about 50 degrees of frost Fahrenheit.) About one winter in a hundred will kill *some* vines in northern French vineyards; the much milder winters of England do not, of course, damage the plant in any way. It should be made clear that this applies to all varieties—there are several thousand— of the species. Vines of varieties which are completely unable to mature and ripen their grapes in the northern summer are nevertheless perfectly winter hardy.

The North produced no significant changes in the making of wine until the machine age arrived. The wine-press used in France is of very great antiquity of design. It was noted in Chapter II that the Egyptians did not press grapes; they wrung the juice out of them. But we have already noted that the press was used in ancient Greece, and of course in Italy. It was complained of the early wines of France, notably of Burgundy, that they were pitched (compare the resinated wines of Greece today). This pitching of the vessels in which wine was stored and carried was a preservative measure. But far from being a new and barbarous French practice, it is of enormous antiquity; vessels treated with pitch on the inside, doubtless for the storing of wine, have been dug up by archaeologists on the most ancient sites of civilization. Sir Mortimer Wheeler has even found one in the Indus valley.

The principal change introduced into the handling of wine by the 'new', that is, northern wine-growers, was in the use of wooden vessels. The wines of the most ancient Near East, of Egypt, of ancient Greece and of ancient Italy, were stored and carried in earthenware amphorae or, locally, in sewn-up skins, that is, in leather vessels. Amphorae and skins were the only wine vessels in use in Europe until the second century of our era. But archaeology finds no wine vessels of this kind, and no shards of such vessels on any northern vineyard site. Moreover, such material begins to be scarce on more southerly sites at levels equivalent to the third century. This circumstance gave rise to a singular series of mistakes in one chapter of viticultural history. X. M. Thevenet, a distinguished student of the antiquities of Burgundian wine-growing, dated the importance of the Burgundian vineyards from the end of the first century A.D. by the following argument: he found many shards of wine-amphorae at levels corresponding to dates before about A.D. 100; he then found a quite sudden disappearance of such shards. The presence of shards, and their nature, had enabled him to say that for the epochs in question wine had been imported into Burgundy from such and such centres of the wine trade, chiefly from Italy. The absence of shards meant, then, that such imports had ceased. Why? Clearly, he reasoned, because Burgundy was growing its own wine and had no need to import any. Therefore Burgundian vineyards on an important scale must have been in production by about A.D. 100. But this argument ignores the possibility (it is, however, more than that, in fact an established certainty) that earthenware was giving way, and soon gave way entirely, to wood in the making of wine vessels. Probably the country exporting wine to Burgundy at the end of the first century was Allobrogica; or it could have been Bordeaux. It was in these regions of the wine-trade that the wooden cask was pioneered in Europe.

Pliny the Elder says that the practice of storing and moving wine in wooden casks was of Allobrogican origin. There is no truth in this; it was quite widespread long before Pliny was writing about it. Strabo says that huge wooden casks, as big as houses, were used to store wine in Cisalpine Gaul; and that the Illyrians brought their wine from Aquileia to various markets in wooden casks. In a Note in his *Wanderings of Plants and Animals*, Victor Hehn has a philological argument which throws a good deal of light on this subject. The Provençal word *tona*, French *tonne*, English *tun* must, he says, be derived from one of the Alpine languages, Ligurian or Rhaetian. It has passed into all the Celtic and Teutonic languages, but is wanting in Italian, which is significant. He also gives the derivation of our words cooper, cooperage (and, I suggest, perhaps copper). The original word is Greek *Kugīh*, from which comes *cupa* which became good Latin: 'When Maximin, in the year 238, was about to besiege Aquileia, but could not get his army over a tearing, rain-swollen river, he was assisted by the extensive wine-trade of the place, for he found a quantity of large empty wine-barrels of which he built a bridge' (Herodian 8.4.9). The word *cupa* was in use for these. 'Julius Capitolinus, reporting the same event, calls these enormous casks *cupae* (Maximin 22. "*Ponte itaque cupis facto . . .*" etc.).'[16]

Hehn says further that the Massiliotes must have had such barrels very much earlier, for when Caesar besieged their town they rolled them, filled with burning pitch, down from the walls upon the enemy positions. This, in fact, appears in Caesar's own account of the war, and again the word used is *cupa*. The tradesmen who made and sold the casks were called *cuparii*. (They also made sacks, for they were likewise *saccarii*: evidently there was an industry supplying the carrying trade with packs, then as now.) Our English word 'cup' is a later derivative from the same root. None of these authorities, however, refers to what must be the earliest reference to wine-casks made of wood, which the reader will have noted in Chapter II. That Pliny should have overlooked Herodotus' account of the Armenian-Babylonian wine-trade in palm-wood barrels is curious.

While we are on this subject, we may as well dispose also of the words 'bottle' and 'cork'. Bottle comes originally, but through either French (*botte*, *bouteille*) or German (*Butte*), from a Greek word *Bovtis*. But this seems to have conveyed a much larger and probably wooden vessel: in fact, again, some sort of barrel or cask, since the same original, developing along a different line, has given us in Irish *bothy*, and similar words meaning hut or house in Old Prussian and other tongues. The bottle as we now know it, made of glass, did not come into use until the fifteenth or at earliest the fourteenth century. And glass bottles (although the Phoenicians made some very beautiful ones) for general, cheap use were of North European not Mediterranean origin (see Beckmann, *Beiträge*). But it is possible that the North Europeans had bottles from an Arabian, ultimately Phoenician source, from the Tartars by way of Hungary. In this connection the reader is referred to Chapter VIII (page 239) where he will find an account of wine in glass bottles at the tented court of Ogdai Khan.

For closures the ancient vintners used various materials, usually wax: obviously you could not close a wide-mouthed amphora with a cork, and in any case nobody had thought of it. The *cupae* were bunged with wood. The Italians, and perhaps the Greeks as well, both sealed wine-jars with wax and floated olive oil on top of the wine to keep it from contact with the air; and this is still a useful practice, especially if you buy your wine in the wood, do not want to bother to bottle it but wish to draw it from the wood as you use it. For by this means the air-tight seal sinks with the wine as the level falls. The cork oak, *Quercus suber*, is a Spanish and west North African plant. Cork as a closure for wine-vessels came into use in late Roman republican times and Pliny describes its use for bungs, *cadorum opturamensis*.[17] Corks as we know them (the word is from *cortex* through the Spanish *corcha*) came into general use with glass bottles in the fifteenth century.

The archaeological evidence is determined by the fact that the wood and the iron of casks quite soon decay and leave no trace; whereas the shard of earthenware, unless pulverized, is eternal. There is no reason to doubt Pliny's attribution of the practice of using wooden casks to the Allobroges, provided it is not suggested that these people had just invented the cask or cooperage; both are older. The reason for not using casks in the South had been that they are very difficult to keep in good condition when empty, in the hot and dry climate, and that they are relatively difficult to clean. The cheap palm-wood casks of Babylon were perhaps broken up after a single use. But given summer conditions in which preventing the wood from drying out is not very difficult—in such mountain country as Dauphiné for example—wooden vessels have great advantages, the greatest being that they do not break if you drop them. This, and advancing techniques for summer storing, and possibly also cheapness, led to the extension of the Allobrogican method all over the viticultural world, although it was many centuries before the amphora quite vanished from Greek and south Italian usage.

The adoption of wood—usually oak or Spanish chestnut—had its effect on wine. I think it probable that it was responsible for the disappearance of the pitching technique. The wood itself plays an important part in the maturing of wine; for one thing, it is porous to air which is filtered through the wood, and this has an influence on wine's oxygenation. (I am very doubtful about the porosity of earthenware vessels referred to by H. Warner Allen in his admirable history of wine.) Wine aged in wood is not the same as wine aged in earthenware. In the ageing of brandy—which did not become a problem until the Arabs had perfected distillation—and of fortified wines, wood plays an even more important part, so that where today it is convenient to make use of vessels lined with glass or even plastics, oak shavings are often added to the wine or spirit.

In short, the fine French vintages of our own time, derived from small, relatively acid grapes and relatively low in alcohol (about twelve per cent as against about sixteen per cent), and matured in the wood, can bear little resemblance to the great vintages of antiquity, whether Egyptian or south European, derived from large, ultra-sweet grapes of low acidity (consequently difficult to keep, and therefore to mature), matured, in so far as they were matured at all, in glazed earthenware or even in leather, and preserved with pitch and spices. And the changes which made this great difference between the wines of antiquity and those of our time were for the most part accomplished in France and in Northern Italy (as they now are) between 600 B.C. and A.D. 600.

# CHAPTER VI

## *The European Periphery*

THE CENTRAL AND MOST SOPHISTICATED TERRITORY of the wine-vine seems always to correspond to the central and most sophisticated territory of Western civilization at any given time. While Greek thought and Greek art dominated the Mediterranean world, say from 500 to 150 B.C., then the heart land of wine was also Hellas, and the great vintages were Greek. When leadership passed to Rome, Italian wines, as we have seen, ousted the Greek ones, both in general commerce and in special excellence. In the seventeenth century, when France emerged as the leader of European culture, French viticulture began to be something more than a mere branch of agriculture in that country, and by the nineteenth, had become what Italian and Greek viticulture had formerly been. It may even be possible, if a little far-fetched, to discover an association between the great age of German scholarship and music, and the great age of the Rhine wines of Germany. And the reason is self-evident: a preoccupation with the highest excellence in a community is general, not particular, and an epoch which, in some particular place, produces the greatest master-works of art and thought, will also produce the finest wines where the vine can be cultivated at all.

Although I do not want to push this argument to the point of absurdity, perhaps it is not too fanciful to see the wines of Spain as very representative of Spain's peculiar role, and that of Portugal, in European culture. The Iberian countries have never taken a central position even at the time of Spain's political and military domination of Europe; both Spain and Portugal have contributed great works to the body of European art, yet the growing point of European culture has never been located in either country. The Italians, the French, the English and the Germans have at times led the way for the rest; Spaniards and Portuguese have, as it were, run a parallel course, sometimes stretching a little ahead, sometimes lagging, never followed excepting in the matter of navigation and geographical discovery—and even there, although this is too often forgotten, it was the Genoese who led. Spain and Portugal have each produced one great wine, in variety; in both cases a special kind of wine, not in the main line of viticultural and oinological development.

In the period between 800 and 600 B.C. when the Phoenicians and the Greeks were sailing the Mediterranean, trading with the savages of its remoter countries and founding, first trading factories and later colonies in the west, it seems the Iberian peninsula was rather sparsely inhabited by Bronze Age people of Iberian (whatever that may mean), Celt-Iberian and Celtic stock. Presumably this people was less rather than more advanced in the arts of civilization than, for example, the Iron Age shepherds who were 'founding' Rome at this time; especially as in Spain there were no Etruscans to show the way in city-building and the arts generally. *Vitis vinifera* is, or was, native to Spain as to France and Italy; but there is no reason to suppose the primitive Spaniards capable of domesticating it, or even of noticing it, although where the plant was abundant some tribes may have gathered the wild grapes: and may even, perhaps, have discovered or been taught how to make wine with them. There is no evidence that they did so.

It is very likely that their mentors in planting the vine were Phoenicians, though they may have been Greeks. It seems likely that the Phoenicians of Tyre and Sidon and Byblos traded with Spain even before the new Phoenicians of Carthage were doing so. But Gades (Cadiz) and New Carthage (Cartagena) were Carthaginian, not Tyrian or Sidonian settlements. There were other settlements, including some, no doubt, on the Atlantic coast as far north as the present Portuguese frontier; but whether these were plantations or merely factories is not possible to say. On the whole, whereas the Carthaginians concentrated on trade, and might perhaps have preferred to continue selling wine to the savages rather than show them how to grow it, the Greeks made real settlements, plantations in our eighteenth-century sense, and to that extent are the more likely to have been the teachers of viticulture to the Spaniards. There were very early Greek colonies at Maenace on the south coast and at Hemeroscopium on the east coast of Spain. No doubt these colonies were of the same character as others elsewhere on the Mediterranean coast—that of the Phocaeans at Marseilles, for example—and in that case they would have included vineyards. But just how much the primitive Spaniards learnt from these colonies is an open question: one receives the

impression that even at that time the Iberian pepeols were resistant to foreign
influence.

One gathers little about these people from the classical authors. Diodorus
Siculus,[1] writing in the first century B.C.—towards the end of the century,
however—says that the Spanish Ligurians drank nothing but water, and he
describes them as in a very primitive phase of agriculture, still semi-nomadic
in that they shifted their ground from time to time as they exhausted the soil
of a particular site. Yet he describes these same primitives as trading in their
ships as far as, for example, Sardinia; and from other sources it seems that
Ligurians may have traded right up the Atlantic coast of Europe to Brittany,
and that they acted as middle-men between the Cornish tin-miners and the
Carthaginian merchants. Perhaps some of the first wine to be drunk in Britain
was Spanish-grown. After all, at about the same time Caesar encountered
in the Veneti of Brittany a people who were certainly backward in agriculture
but whose sailing vessels were in advance of anything the Romans had.

On the whole we can take it that the first vineyards were planted in
Spain before 500 B.C.; and that while the vine thus early obtained a small
foothold in Spain, its advance was very slow. We cannot now trace it. At
the time of the earliest real documents in the case, viticulture in Spain is
already an advanced and more or less sophisticated art. It is true that Punic
civilization seized upon the whole of south Spain in the third/second centuries B.C. But was the Spanish empire of the Barcas really much more than
a lightly-connected sprinkling of strongly-held military posts? The native
Spaniards might serve in Hannibal's armies for pay; it does not appear that
they were in any real sense Punicized. And I think it more likely that it was
later, under the Roman rule, that the taming of the Spaniards went a stage
further, and that viticulture, with the other arts, began to make progress.

We can guess that the Spanish provinces in which the vine made its
earliest real progress were those in which it had firmly established itself in
historical times. These were Tarragona, Andalusia, and the Balearic Islands.
If forced to give an opinion, I should say that the viticulture of the mainland
was of Greek origin but was really developed under Roman influence; and
that the origin of Balearic viticulture was Punic; for those islands had been
for a very long time of the first importance to the Carthaginians, not only
for the Carthaginian merchant and armed navies, but because they drew from
them their best missile-soldiers: the slingers of the Balearics were famous,

and their sling was of their own invention. They played an important part
in scores of battles against the Romans, but like all the armies of Carthage,
they were mercenary troops, and in the end turned on their paymasters.

The two most famous vineyard regions of Iberia, Jérez and Oporto, have
no ancient history; they were not of classical, but of medieval establishment.[2]
By the first century A.D. Tarragona had become an exporter of wine in some
quantity, but only a single vineyard of distinction is mentioned by Pliny:
that of Laurona, whose wine is said by him to be of high quality. The
Balearic wines, on the other hand, are all said to have been wines of distinction, well able to compete in the market with the best Italian growths.
The two southern provinces of Turdetania and Betica (Andalusia) were
viticultural[3]—the town of Julia Traducta minted a coin on which grapes were
depicted—but nothing is known of the quality of their wines or the extent
of the vineyards.

Catalonia, the north-east, may well have had its vineyards as early as the
southern provinces, for the Massiliotes expanded their territory along the
coast and round the corner into that province, forming settlements some
way inland as well. And wherever these Greeks went, the vine went too.
But there is no mention of Catalan wine in any early authority. The fact is
that for the period in which we are interested there are no documents.

For Portugal the case is the same. We have nothing but this: 'In the
Hellenistic and Roman republican age the famous wine of Lusitania—perhaps from the region of Oporto—was astonishingly cheap, since ten gallons
were sold for the equivalent of ninepence.'[4] No source is given for this
statement; Billiard would hardly have missed this remarkable fact, if it were
one. The Lusitanians of the first century B.C. were warlike savages, remote
from any centre of civilization or trade, not plantation crop farmers.
H. Warner Allen, the admirable historian of port and sherry as of so many
other great wines, has this to say: 'It seems highly unlikely that even as late
as the Empire any wine worth exporting was made in Lusitania, as Dr
Seltman suggests, and it was certainly not famous and not from the Douro
region.'[5] My own guess is that no wine of any kind whatsoever was made in
Portugal until the fourth century A.D. at the very earliest. It must be remembered that not even Bordeaux was making wine before the first century,
since the Gauls were barely civilized enough to practise viticulture. Perhaps
the Lusitanians traded some of their mead to the Spanish Ligurian seamen.

62 *The vine obtained a foothold in Spain in Roman times and perhaps even earlier. The conquering Visigoths used the vine to decorate a capital in a church at Zamora in eastern Spain.*

# The European Periphery

63

*An eleventh-century Spanish illustration of the final harvest, from the Book of Revelations, shows men gathering 'the clusters of the vine of the earth' and letting them fall into the wine-press of the wrath of God (63).*

*A large wine-jar from the Moorish period has an incised vine pattern (64). Similar jars are seen in Persian miniatures (see plate VII).*

64

65

Northern European viticulture depended on navigable rivers as trade routes, and the Moselle valley was producing wine in Roman times, as described by Ausonius. A funeral monument (65) is shaped like a Moselle boat laden with wine-casks.

Capitulū. xx. De appa-
ratu vindemie.

Capitulū. xxvij. Quali-
ter vinū mittendū sit in dolijs.

Capitulum. xxix. De co-
gnitione si mustū vel vinum babeat aquam.
et qualiter separabit ab ea.

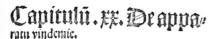

66  Fifteenth-century German woodcuts show coopering, cleaning the barrels, and wine tasting.

67

68

The vine was grown in England in late Roman Imperial times, but wine was certainly imported much earlier. The Roman amphora (67), about four feet tall, and the silver wine-cup (68) come from the burials of Belgic chieftains of the fourth century B.C. Wooden casks started to replace amphorae in the first century A.D. The six-foot Roman barrels of silver fir (69) were found in use as well linings near Silchester, in Berkshire.

69

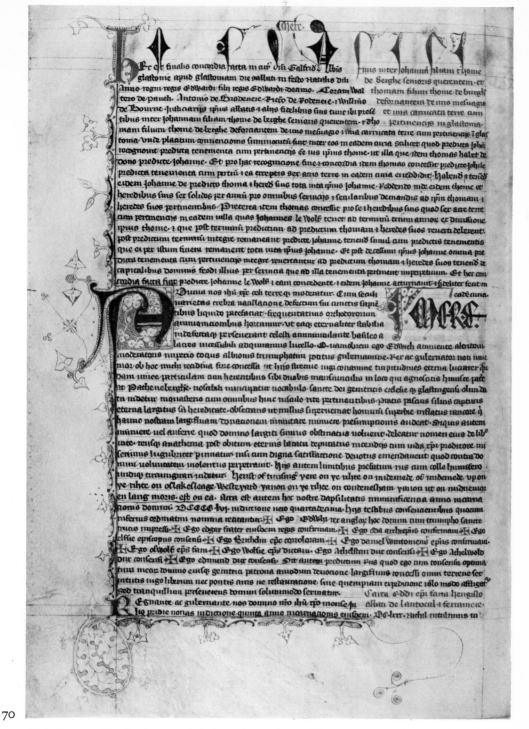

*Viticulture in England expanded from the early Middle Ages onwards. The fourteenth-century document (70) records the grant of a vineyard in Somerset, made by King Edwy to the monks of Glastonbury Abbey in 955.*

71 *Vintaging, from a misericord in Gloucester Cathedral. Gloucestershire was described in 1125 as a county 'more thickly planted with vineyards than any other in England'.*

72 *Detail of the wine ornamentation on a fireplace in the Abbot's Parlour at Muchelney Abbey, Somerset.*

73 *An angel gathers the mystical vintage, from an early fourteenth-century Apocalypse MS. The vine is trained in an arbour, as it doubtless was in the monastery's vineyard. English viticulture was at its zenith in the fourteenth century.*

*Pargework on a sixteenth-century cottage at East Dereham in Norfolk (74) imitates a trained vine. Below, the Great Vine at Hampton Court (75), two centuries old.*

Much later, in the late seventeenth and eighteenth centuries—ignoring the great development at Oporto, a case of a great wine being brought into existence by a political treaty, the Methuen Treaty—the vine played a curious and rather terrible part in the economic history of Portugal. There was a kind of explosive expansion of vineyards throughout Portugal. Vines were planted by the million, and everywhere, in the richest alluvial plains as well as in poor mountain soils. This expansion was not the product of prosperity, but of the most miserable poverty, of an economic distress—by-product of very depressed agricultural prices—so severe that the wretched peasants turned to the vine as the only plant which would yield them a cash-crop.

But in this attempt to save their families from starvation they defeated their own ends, for soon there was such a glut of wine in the country that it, too, could not be sold.[6] There were whole provinces in which by about 1750 viticulture had simply ousted agriculture entirely. This extraordinary state of affairs was remedied, as usual, not by giving the farmers a fair price for their work, but by a government order which must have condemned many to death by starvation. The Marquis of Pombal, at the time virtually dictator of Portugal, simply ordered the vines to be uprooted and wheat to be grown instead; and, moreover, this is one exceptional case in which a ukase against the vine was carried out to the very letter. The order was confined to certain provinces, chiefly the Tagus valley, and did not affect the Douro vineyards as far as I can discover.

It is even more difficult to deal with the introduction of the vine to eastern Europe, and for the good reason that it is very improbable that viticulture was ever 'introduced' to countries so near to the most ancient of the European vineyard lands; the vine made its way in the Balkans by a kind of social osmosis; but in the Germanies the case is different, as we shall see. Dealing first with the Balkans: it is true that respectable authorities give the credit for the first planting of vineyards in Pannonia and Moesia, covered by modern Yugoslavia, Hungary and Bulgaria, to the Emperor Probus. And it seems to be a fact that in about A.D. 281, after the general promulgation of his edict which emancipated the vine from the chains with which the Emperor Domitian had tried, with only very partial success, to load it, that simple soldier set his idle army to clearing land and preparing fields in the Balkans for the planting of vines by means of which, the Emperor believed, the people could enrich themselves.[7] But while this may well have been so in the more northerly and westerly parts of the territory in question, it seems rather unlikely that the countries which marched with Macedonia and Thrace, both very ancient lands of the vine,[8] should have waited until the third century A.D. to plant vineyards.

On the other hand, the advancement of settlement and manners among the peoples in question was slow, and it is at least possible that they were in no condition to receive the vine and the arts of growing it and using its grapes until the time of Probus.

There is a curious story which may belong here geographically, although it is difficult to place and may really belong in Asia. The Getae (who seem to have been the ancestors of those Turkish Uighur peoples, Avars and Magyars, who ultimately settled in Hungary) were notorious in antiquity with the Thracians, Dacians and Scyths for drunkenness. This is said to have been so prevalent among the Getae, either on imported wine or on some native brew of beer or mead, that no political or military organization of the people was possible.

Not long before the time of Strabo[9] one of their shamans or witch-doctors effected a reform. The man's name was, in Latin, Decaeneus, no doubt a civilized version of some less euphonious barbarism; according to Dio Chrysostomus[10] he arose during the dictatorship of Sulla, and travelled in Egypt where he learned the art of prophecy, giving him a hold over his fellow-countrymen upon his return home. What follows implies that the Getae were practising viticulture and had long done so at this time, for the story says that, acting on the orders of this witch-doctor, the Getae rooted up all their vines and abjured wine as the cause of their ruin. The shaman had the backing of the Getic king Boerebista, who was thus able to turn his people into soldiers and to found an empire. Hehn[11] remarks that this makes Decaeneus a forerunner of Mahomet; and it is true that both men turned peaceful, laughter-and-party-loving sensualists into fanatical soldiers who were a misery to their neighbours and to themselves until they began to relax again and pay proper respect to the vine.

Most of the peoples of eastern Europe north of Macedonia were, in fact, wild and barbarous into the third century, although nearer home civilization was taken to them much earlier. The Romans were taking steps to bring order into Dalmatia as early as 135 B.C. and vineyards were planted there before the birth of Christ. Twenty years later Roman armies were on the Danube, and unless their influence was less than was usually the case, it does not seem likely that the natives were still without their vineyards four centuries later. We can, however, take it that serious viticulture did not begin in those lands which are now Hungary, Rumania and Bulgaria until the fourth century of our own epoch at the earliest.

Hungarian historians say that when their ancestors, who came from the region of the Don, occupied the land which is now Hungary—and which had been devastated and depopulated by Charlemagne in his successful effort to drive out or destroy the Avars who had dominated the region for three centuries—they found the vineyards which had been planted by the Romans still bordering the rivers. There would be no point in making this claim if there were no grounds for it; no doubt it is true. The Uighurs, the most brilliant of all the Turkish peoples, were among the few central Asiatics who practised viticulture; they even had a hand in trying to introduce it to China (see Chapter VIII). The Avars were of that stock and may well have maintained the old vineyards, or made sure that some more anciently native and now subject people did so.

It is true that the new ninth-century incomers, the Magyars, were like all the Asiatic horse-nomads unsympathetic to and even contemptuous of the notion of turning farmer. But quite soon after they overran Hungary they were at war with the Germans. The Emperor Otto the Great defeated them but the Magyars had taken prisoners from his armies; not later than 920 there were German colonies in Hungary, originally formed by such prisoners of war. These colonists taught their barbarous masters the arts of agriculture. To them fell the task of renewing the old Roman vineyards. German influence was paramount in civilizing the Magyars for some centuries. But it is to Italian influence, rather, that we owe the one really great viticultural achievement of ancient Pannonia and Moesia: Tokay.

It was the Grand Duke or King Stephen of the great Arpad dynasty who by his example—he was subsequently canonized, of course—led the Magyars into the Roman, rather than the Greek, camp of the Christian Church. By so doing he put an end to Magyar paganism, against which German missionaries had made little headway, and initiated an epoch of Italian influence which soon obliterated the older German one. The country was

Christianized, latinized; and Italian advisers, merchants and colonists migrated to Hungary in considerable numbers. It was under this influence that ancient vineyards on the River Theiss, about one hundred and forty miles east-north-east of Budapest, were renewed, the best *cépages* propagated, and expansion started until the vineyards extended over an area as large as an English county. The best wines came, as usual, from mountain sites—in the Hegyalja range—but the central town of this viticultural province is Tokaj.

What is extraordinary is that the Italian promoters of this enterprise, in an age when great vintages were unknown—were phenomena, almost legendary, of the remote past—should have set themselves to the creation of a great, and not merely a good, wine. It is, of course, possible that while the fine Tokay which is dry and bears the German name of *Ausbruch* goes back to the very early epoch of these vineyards, the imperial Tokay *Essence* is a later, no longer Italian but properly Hungarian wine; but the fact is that the making of it entails a practice followed in two viticultural countries only; in the making of this sweet wine the grapes, allowed to overripen in the old Roman style, were not pressed; only that juice was used which ran from the grapes under the pressure of their own weight.

Other parts of ancient Moesia and Pannonia came under other influences: in the ninth century the country which is now Bulgaria, and that which was formerly Serbia, were emerging into nationhood as Turkish states, effectively autonomous but in principle provinces of the Eastern Roman Empire. So that even if nothing had remained of the older Roman civilization, they were Byzantinized; and by the time of the short and glorious career of the Bulgarian Empire and during the reign of the Emperor Simeon, viticulture was not only ancient but renewed and prosperous in a domain which, in any case, included such very old wine-lands as Macedonia and the Epirus. In Rumania, likewise, it is impossible to find any break in the viticultural traditions and practices from ancient to later Roman times; and it is certain that at no time between the third and twentieth centuries has that country been without vineyards.

The exact date of the introduction of viticulture into England is not known; it is probable that Roman and Romano-British villas had the first vines in the country, more by way of an ornamental re-creation of the Mediterranean atmosphere than for the grapes which they yielded. But it was noted in

Chapter V that the exhortation of the Emperor Probus to provincials, to plant the vine and grow rich, was addressed to the Britons among others; this was in A.D. 280. Tacitus had earlier declared[12] that the vine could not be grown in Britain because the climate, though free of extreme cold, was 'objectionable', damp and misty; but, as we have seen, precisely the same thing was said of Gaul some centuries earlier, and the fact is that Italians were unable to believe that their plant could possibly thrive in a climate which depressed them. That the vine was in fact introduced in Roman times is very probable; for the Venerable Bede, in his opening remarks, says that: 'Britain excels for grain and trees and is well adapted for feeding cattle and beasts of burden. It also produces vines in some places, and has plenty of land- and water-fowls of several sorts . . .'[13]

Now it is on the whole unlikely that the Saxons had themselves introduced the vine; they probably came from a part of Europe which knew not vineyards. The conclusion must be that they found it growing here when they arrived. Nevertheless, it was certainly not growing in such abundance and under such care that the Britons, and after them the English, could find themselves in wine from their own vineyards. For both the Frisians—those great merchants of the so-called Dark Ages, the skilled boatmen who, by managing to navigate the Rhine, made the development of the Rhenish vineyards worthwhile by giving the planters an outlet for their wine in the north-west—and the Anglo-Saxons themselves, also a mercantile people, were importing wine into England as early as the seventh century.[14] Here is a Saxon merchant of about the seventh century speaking: ' "I go on board my ship with my freight and row over the regions of the sea, and sell my goods and buy precious things which are not produced in this land, and I bring it hither with great danger over the sea and sometimes I suffer shipwreck with the loss of all my goods, barely escaping with my life." And what he brings are "purple and silk, precious gems and gold, rare garments and spices, wine and oil, ivory and brass, copper and tin, sulphur and glass and such-like things . . ."'[15]

Wilson[16] says that from the seventh century onwards we have evidence of pottery imported from the Continent, and he associates it with the German (Frisian) wine-trade. He claims that the great relief-band amphorae, some of them three or four feet in height, can have been used for no other purpose than transporting wine. I am not happy about this statement. By the date in question it seems to me very doubtful indeed that amphorae were still in use for transporting wine: the use of wooden casks had started to displace that of amphorae in the first century, and it is particularly the case that the wine of the north European vineyards was transported in wood and that no amphorae were used; for example, the few images we have of the Moselle wine-trade show clearly that the *nautae mosallica* used barrels, and it is as certain as anything can be that the Rhine vineyard-owners would have followed suit, being relative novices and having to learn the trade from those of the Moselle. Moreover, even supposing that the wine was brought from Italy, which it may have been since the Anglo-Saxon merchants had trade treaties with the Lombard kings, it would by that time have been in wood, not in earthenware.[17] Perhaps the great amphorae were used for the transport of oil, rather than wine; archaeologists would find few vestiges of casks because wood and iron are so perishable.

The fact that wine was imported does not mean that none was being grown. It has always been the case in those countries where the native wine is small that the rich have preferred to buy foreign wines as a luxury; thus the Italians before 150 B.C. bought much Greek wine, in a country with a large domestic production. It seems most probable that at some time between that remote age the first century B.C., when Belgic chieftains in Britain were buried with whole amphorae of Italian imported wine to save them from thirst in the Celtic heaven (*plate 67*); and the fourth century A.D., the first vineyards were planted in Britain; and that probably this happened early in the fourth century rather than in the third.

There is, however, another possibility to be considered. We have noted that the vine early became necessary to Mediterranean man in his religious rites; and well into modern times a primary reason for the swift urgency with which vineyards were planted in lands newly colonized by Europeans was the need for the provision of Mass-wine.[18] Missionaries of Christianity, setting out to evangelize the heathen, had, of course, to take a provision of wine with them, like Columba setting out from Brittany for Ireland with a cargo of Loire wine. When St Augustine landed in England in A.D. 596 he was landing in a country which, as regards its British inhabitants, was Christian; but his object was to evangelize the English who were heathen, as well as to persuade the British of the superior excellence of the Roman rite. The British Christians may have imported Mass-wine; but they may also have grown it, for trade was unreliable at that date, bedevilled by piracy and war. Augustine probably brought his own wine for the Mass; he may also have encouraged the planting of vines when he saw that they would grow and bear in England, and I think it likely he did so. It is at least probable, then, that the expansion of viticulture in England, reaching a zenith in the fourteenth century as we shall see, was coincident with the rise and spread of religious establishments here, as it was to be twelve centuries later in, for example, California.

By the ninth century vineyards had become sufficiently commonplace in Wessex for them to make an appearance in the law-code of Alfred the Great: '. . . *si quis damnum intulerit alterius vineae vel agro, vel alicui ejus terrae, compenset sicut illud aestimet . . .*'[19] We have a record of the grant of a vineyard at Pathensburgh in Somerset made by King Edwy, Alfred's great-grandson, to the monks of Glastonbury Abbey, in 955 (*plate 70*).

From the ninth to the twelfth century the vineyards expanded, rather slowly and sparsely in so marginal a vine-land as England, as far northward as Norfolk in the east. By the time William the Conqueror's great land-survey was being made and collated as Domesday Book, there were thirty-eight vineyards in the territory surveyed, a territory which was much smaller than the whole of Britain. Contrary to a received opinion the vineyards were not all monastic property; nor were they all so small as to be insignificant, for in considering their size one has to remember that the population of Britain at the time was probably less than three million people. At Bittesham in Berkshire, Henry de Ferrieres had a vineyard of twelve arpends, about ten acres.[20] Other considerable vineyards were at Wilcote, Wiltshire; Holborn, London; Westminster, Middlesex—this one is noted as newly planted in 1084; Cheneton, Middlesex; Ware, Hertfordshire; Hantum, Worcestershire. There was a large vineyard at Wdelsford in Essex belonging to a man called Sweyn, presumably a Dane of the old Danelaw. Ralph Baignard had eighteen arpends of vineyard in the same county, and he was engaged in expanding his business, since there is a note to the effect that of these, seven arpends were not yet bearing fruit, which means that they had been planted within the past three years.

The slow but steady expansion of the viticulture established by the Saxons, to whom, in southern Wessex, October had even become known as *Wyn moneth* because it was the month of the vintage, continued. In about

1125 William of Malmesbury was writing of Gloucestershire: 'This county is more thickly planted with vineyards than any other in England, more plentiful in crops and more pleasant in flavour. For the wines do not offend the mouth with sharpness since they do not yield to the French in sweetness.'[21]

Elsewhere this author again refers to vineyards; in a passage about Thornly he says: '*Nulla ibi vel exigua terrae portio vacat, hic in Pomiferas arbores terra se subjugit; hic praetexta ager vineis quae vel begulos palos in celsum surgunt.*'[22]

The neighbouring county of Worcestershire was also rich in vineyards. The light clay and sand over the Lower Liass of the Vale of Evesham is good vineyard soil. Both Worcester and Pershore Priories had their vineyards and there were others at Droitwich and Grimley. The Pershore vineyard, having passed into lay hands at the Dissolution, was still being cultivated in 1544. Other old vineyards planted by the monks but passing into lay hands were maintained, although many seem to have been given up about 1350. The wines grown by Sir Henry Lyttleton at Upper Arley were famous, competing with French imports. Further east, Kent was viticultural, and here again the Canterbury Cathedral Chapter gave up growing wine in the fourteenth century and their vineyard became pasture let to a grazier. Although there is some evidence for vineyards as far north as Edinburgh, the most northerly to achieve reputation was that of Ely; apparently the Normans referred to this island as *l'Isle des Vignes*.[23]

Viticulture received considerable attention from English horticultural writers, beginning in the sixteenth century with Barnabe Googe.[24] His work includes a curious little mistake of the kind which can give rise to a whole fabric of nonsense about 'the good old days'. The book is in dialogues; one of the speakers, Marius, says: 'As touching the easiness of husbandrie and the greatness of the gaine, the old writers have ever preferred the vineyard afore the corne feelde: for as Columella reporteth Siserna writeth, that the labour of one man is sufficient for eight acres of vines, or at least seven . . .' To this his interlocutor, Thrasybulus, grumbles: 'Marry, sir,

*V A lord and lady watch vintagers at work in the Loire valley in the late fifteenth century. The press is unusual in that it has no superstructure. Tapestry woven in the Loire valley.*

at this day one man thinks three acres too much for him.' In fact, of course (see Chapter IV), Columella allows one slave per seven *jugera*, that is, about three-and-a-half acres.

Although it is clear from all this, and much more which it would be tedious to particularize, that the vine had secured a footing well north of the 50th parallel of latitude by the seventh century at latest, and was firmly established in England for about a thousand years, it is a fact that viticulture in Britain, in Germany excepting on the Rhine, and in Flanders, is marginal and precarious. This is so for climatic/economic reasons, as will appear. The climate does not preclude viticulture; it simply makes it relatively unprofitable, and consequently the extent of vineyards north of latitude 50 degrees North at any time is a function of agricultural prices in general. In Britain, as distinct from Germany (again other than the Rhineland), there has been one other influence at work: English culture in general owes more to the South than to the North, the English upper class and English artists and writers have looked south, to the Mediterranean; there has very often been a special feeling for the vine, an enthusiasm found not only in such gentlemen-vinearoons as Hamilton of Painswick who grew his own sparkling white wines in the eighteenth century, but in such professional gardeners as John Rose, head man to Charles II, whose *English Vineyard Vindicated*[25] is still a sound little treatise on the subject.

The vine was first planted in what is now Germany, on the Rhine, in the fourth century. Archaeology has revealed a number of Rhineland vineyards on the German side of the river which can be attributed to *c.* 350, albeit rather roughly and speculatively. The settlements, later towns, were of course Romano-German, and may even have been Gallo-Roman and not German at all. We have already seen that viticulture on the turbulent and shallow Rhine was very restricted and centuries behind that of the Moselle, but that when the Frisians overcame the difficulty of navigating the river, probably in the seventh century, they offered the Rhinelanders a German,

*VI In Europe as in the Middle East, vineyards were often let out to tenants in exchange for part of the crop. The Parable of the Vineyard, here illustrated in a tenth-century German MS., tells of tenants who refused to pay rent and instead killed the landowner's servants.*

Flemish and English market and stimulated the planting of the Rhineland vineyards.

The general history of the vine in Germany is very much like that of the vine in England—with the important exception of the Rhineland vineyards. Dealing first with the exceptional case, the persistence of the Rhenish viticulture has been due to two factors: first, once the Frisians had opened a market in Rhine wines, that market remained faithful to its special source of supply; the conservatism of the market gave a special and artificial advantage to the Rhineland growers, sufficient to offset the disadvantages of cultivating the vine in relatively unfavourable conditions. Second, the loving care and Teutonic thoroughness with which the Rhineland vinearoons turned their disadvantages into advantages, by developing the special properties of wines grown in cold climates, created for Rhine wines so high a reputation that it was possible to sell them at prices which were apparently uncompetitive, but made the Rhineland vineyards economically viable. Had the growers at that latitude been forced to compete in terms of price, the industry must have been unprofitable.

It should be made quite clear that while the sites chosen for the Rhineland vineyards are, as it were, microclimatically the best that the region can offer the vine, the whole region offers no special advantage to viticulture. The grapes very often fail to ripen properly and the practice of 'chaptalization'—sweetening the must with cane-sugar—is legal and very usual. And if a comparison be made, for example, between the weather over a period of ten years in the Rhineland vineyards, and the weather for the same period in south Sussex, the Isle of Wight, parts of the coast of Devonshire, Cornwall and Pembrokeshire, the advantage, from the vine's point of view, will be found a shade on the British side, and the soils of the British places are in no way inferior for wine-growing.[26] This means that had the vineyards of certain parts of England been favoured by a special market and had the English vinearoons worked with as much love and conscience as the Germans, there might very well, today, have been wines of Sussex and the south-west generally as famous and profitable as the Rhine wines. But did not the English have, in their own country, such a special and favourable market? Oddly enough, no; during the period of the Franco-British Plantagenet empire wines entered England from Bordeaux, a city longer faithful to the idea of the dual monarchy than any other in France, at a price which made English wine-growing unprofitable. English growers had no reason, therefore, to persist in their efforts, and although enthusiasts continued to cultivate vineyards here and there until the nineteenth century, so that we find, for example, Pepys referring to the soundness of wines grown in Walthamstow, Hamilton passing off his sparkling whites as champagne, and the Marquis of Bute still with his twenty acres of vineyard in Glamorganshire, at Castle Coch, well into our own century, the infant English industry was overlaid at birth by its immensely vigorous Gallic mother.

But if we except the special case of the Rhineland, the experience of wine-growers in Germany was so like that of wine-growers in Britain that, having given a few arguments to support this case, I shall not go into it in detail. In Germany beyond the Rhineland the dominating influence on vineyard acreage at any time from the ninth to the fifteenth century was that of agricultural prices in general, and the influence of climate was only very secondary. Indeed, the influence of prices of staple crops on vineyard acreage was often very marked even in France, although viticulture was, of course, more resistant there than elsewhere, just as wine prices, as if still responding to Cato's rules, were more stable than those of almost any other crop. After the great fall in cereal prices between 1350 and 1450, for example, which caused a general depression of long duration in agriculture, rents of farmland in general fell much more steeply than vineyard rents. An example taken from the viticulturally marginal region of Meudon shows:

| Period | Rent of arable land in denarii | Rent of vineyard in denarii |
|---|---|---|
| 1360–1400 | 84 per acre | 76 per acre |
| 1483–1515 | 36 per acre | 48 per acre[27] |

The unprofitability of grain-growing when prices fell so steeply, then, almost automatically led to the planting of vineyards in Germany in places which, with bread-grains paying, would have been regarded as unprofitable for the vine. The estate farms of Stolberg-Wernigerod in the Harz mountains provide an example of a movement which was certainly fairly general during the late fourteenth century.[28] There, not only did hops replace grain crops but: 'The same cause led to an expansion of wine-growing in the late Middle Ages. In Germany vineyards were planted in the north and east, in parts where they had hitherto been unknown. On the above-mentioned estates in the Harz there was extensive wine-growing but it was discontinued in the sixteenth century, an economic consequence of rising cereal prices.'[29]

From this and much more evidence of the same kind it is clear that without any reference to climate, commercial viticulture ebbed and flowed in the Marks of Brandenburg, in Austria (where, however, it persists, again owing to a special cause), in parts peripheral to the Rhineland vineyards, in the Swabian Alps, in Saxony and elsewhere.[30] And this ebb and flow was clearly influenced by the prices of cereals. There was, of course, another factor: wine was not the only plantation or industrial crop that could be used to replace corn when corn prices were too low; it has already been noted that hops were planted in the Harz. Elsewhere in Germany such crops as woad, madder, meat and dairy produce were grown, and from this we can make two guesses: first, that wine must have paid fairly well or it would not have been preferred to these others; and second, that the local climate did have some influence on the German farmers' choice of crop.

It is frequently written that the retreat of the vineyards in Germany as in England in the late Middle Ages, or at the end of the epoch so called, can be attributed, as in England, Belgium and parts of France including Flanders and Normandy, to a climatic change for the worse; I have mentioned this theory elsewhere and there can be little doubt that there was such a change; but all it can have done was to make the crop, and therefore the value of viticulture as an economic safeguard, less reliable. It did not make it impossible, and the price relation remained the more important influence. For example, there is no doubt whatsoever that the period 1150 to 1300 was one of increased vineyard planting in England, Germany, Flanders, notably Brabant and Luxembourg (from which country, indeed, the vineyards have never retreated). Now during this period there were, at least in England— and doubtless, therefore, in Germany where extremes of weather are much greater, but the weather is generally of the same kind at any given time— fourteen severe winters; ten winters of heavy snowfall; sixteen serious floods; forty-nine years of very heavy rainfall; twenty-four years with periods of drought; and only seven hot summers. The one hundred and fifty years before this period saw only very slow viticultural growth in England and probably also in Spain and Portugal, and was not a period of viticultural growth in Germany, in which country all provinces with the usual exception of the Rhine had yet to receive their first vineyards; yet it was a period of much more equable, more viticulturally suitable weather, suffering fewer extremes. And during the period 1300–1450, one of sharp decline in English viticulture and stagnation in Germany, there were also fewer extremes of weather: only thirty-one wet years, only twelve periods of drought, and although fourteen winters were severe there was heavy snowfall in only six of them.[31] This should, in short, have been an epoch of expanding viticulture in Germany if climate were the dominant influence, whereas the reverse is true.

Thus rising cereal prices in the sixteenth century drove back the outposts of the vine in Germany and confined that always ambitious plant to the Rhineland; the influence of bread over wine was indeed so strong once again that it even triumphed in some French provinces; in Maine, vineyards had replaced wheatfields in the fourteenth century; in the sixteenth the corn came back and the vineyards disappeared, probably for ever.[32] Nor was this a purely medieval phenomenon: Slicher van Bath[33] points out that in *southern* France between 1676 and 1734 in the region of Sete and Montpellier, where viticulture was ancient and stable, vineyard acreage increased by twenty per cent at the expense of cericulture as a simple reflection of the wine/bread price ratio, when the cereal prices fell once again.

It should be noted that the effect of high cereal prices in depressing viticulture in the peripheral zone, and particularly in Germany, was cumulative. Until very modern times bread, all over Europe, was of such importance in the poor man's diet that prior to about 1830 it represented well over half, often three-quarters, of his provision of calories. Any rise in the price of bread must instantly produce a reduction in the demand for every other kind of food and drink excepting water. Wine was the first commodity to suffer and fall in price; the vineyards shrank; and only two kinds of vineyards can (or, in the past, could) withstand this shock; those where for climatic reasons the vintage was abundant for a small expenditure of labour, and where the population was one to which life was almost unthinkable without wine; and the vineyards which, producing fine wines regardless of cost, were catering for a class too rich to be affected by a rise in bread prices.

In our own time there is a new factor favouring the vineyards, and accounting for the immense expansion of viticulture outside Europe; this is the steadily rising standard of living of the great masses of people, who, in the times we have been considering, could expect to do little more than maintain themselves and their families just above the level of actual want. But at the same time the equally tremendous advancement of international trade and in means of transport have given an advantage of a new kind to those countries, such as south Australia, South Africa and Chile, where the climate favours viticulture in the best and easiest conditions. It is unlikely that Germany will ever again be a viticultural country beyond the Rhineland. In England there are, at the time of writing, two small vineyards producing wine for sale (Hambledon and Beaulieu); and some others are projected, notably in South Wales. But these are and will be the product of that special feeling for the vine by which some Englishmen express their 'Mediterraneanism', and only by selling their wine at a price which has nothing to do with ordinary economic laws can they be made financially viable. Finally, the brilliant viticultural agronomists of the Soviet Union are making possible by a programme of breeding and selection the northward extension of Soviet viticulture far beyond the limits of those very ancient wine lands which fall within the Soviet boundaries. But this, again, is a reflection of national pride, of a policy of very restricted trade, and of the mania for technological ingenuity. Economically the Soviet Union would do better to provide her people with wine by importing from France, Italy, South America and Australia, to supplement the output of the Crimea and other viticultural provinces.

Apart, then, from these two very special cases, it seems likely that the present limits of viticulture in Europe, in the periphery of the European viticultural region, are the extreme ones; and that the vineyards will make little, if any, progress in future beyond the territory they have already conquered. The much more ambitious advances of six hundred years ago were made possible by conditions which are most unlikely to occur again, and although the annual consumption of wine will continue to rise as a function of the rising standard of living, it may be severely checked and forced to decline again, and perhaps eventually to diminish to nothing, as rising world population makes ever-increasing demand on land for food-growing. Meanwhile, we will examine the progress of *Vitis vinifera* far beyond its ancient Eurasian habitat.

# CHAPTER VII

# *The Abode of Islam*

IT IS A SINGULAR CIRCUMSTANCE IN THE HISTORY of viticulture that the vine was to meet with and be checked by its sternest enemy in the lands of its most ancient prosperity. So well established in our minds is the notion of the antipathy between Islam and wine that we now never associate Syria and Arabia and Iran, for example, with vineyards and vintages; whereas, as we have seen, until the eighth century, or at all events the seventh, almost every country of the eventual Dar-al-Islam was vine country, and even the Yemen exported wine to India. It ought really to surprise us more that this is no longer the case than that it was ever the case: for not only is Iran, in its broadest meaning, the homeland of the vine, but the countries in question mostly belonged, and still do belong, to that complex of cultures, of which the notion 'wine' is an attribute, which we think of as 'Mediterranean'. In many versions of the Dionysus myth Nysa, birthplace of the god, is placed in Arabia. Nobody today would think of Jordan or Anatolia as wine countries. Yet in both the culture of the vine and the cult of wine were important there for thousands of years; and Anatolia is one of the places where the wild *V. vinifera* is still to be found. The communities of men who were to become Moslems made to the Mediterranean culture in general contributions entirely characteristic of Western civilization—among others the alphabet, algebra, trigonometry and chemistry; and these were swiftly assimilated into the body of Europeanism in a way that, for example, nothing Chinese or Aztec could have been.

Thus far more tragic in its consequences than the great schism in Western Christian civilization called the Reformation, was the seventh-century one which split a culture common to the successor states of the Roman Empire, first into two Christianities, and then into Christianity and Islam.

Mahomet's strictures on wine, which will be examined in their place, were something very different from the Chinese and Japanese and Indian indifference to the wine-vine examined in Chapter VIII. A deliberate act of self-denial was called for, and was not by any means always forthcoming; in Persia, for example, the very existence of the ban on wine gave rise to a special romantic attitude to it, and to a poetry of wine. And there is something more: Mahomet's distrust of wine was in a very ancient Semitic tradition; it manifested itself, as we have seen, in Babylon, and among the Israelites. Finally, how pleasant it is that they were probably Moorish scientists who perfected the ancient technique of distillation, and who thus found out how to extract from wine the spirit which was exactly what Mahomet had against it; and that this spirit, *al kohl*, alcohol, should bear an Arabic name.

It was the opinion of Diodorus Siculus that Osiris, with whom he doubtless confused Dionysus, for to the Hellenes the two became one and the same in course of time, discovered the grape-vine and how to use it; and that he did so at Nysa. But this Nysa was not in Syria or Anatolia; it was in 'Arabia'. This is at least a recognition of the fact that Europe had vine and wine from the East.

This historian says: 'Mention is also made of Nysa by the poet in his Hymns', that is, the Homeric Hymns, 'to the effect that it was in the vicinity of Egypt, when he says,

> There is a certain Nysa mountain-high.
> With forests thick in Phoenice afar,
> Close to Aegyptus' stream . . .

And the discovery of the vine was made by him', that is by Osiris, 'near Nysa, and that having further devised the proper treatment of its fruit, he was the first to drink wine and taught mankind at large the culture of the vine and use of wine . . .'[1]

Later, and this I quote as evidence from popular beliefs for the claim, made in an earlier chapter, that wine was an earlier invention than beer: 'And if any country did not admit of the growing of the vine Osiris introduced the drink prepared from barley which is little inferior to wine in aroma and in strength.'[2] This barley beverage is obviously the Egyptian beer which Diodorus elsewhere calls *zythos*.

As for the location of Nysa, that singularly wandering place, the 'far Phoenice' of the Homeric Hymn may perhaps refer rather to the country of the Nabataeans than to the geographical Phoenicia. Petra (see below) was their capital city, and it was quite well known for its vineyards in later times. At all events it is clear that some Arabian lands were very much a part of the most ancient vine country.

It is not possible to arrive at even an approximate date for the introduction of the cultivated vine into Arabia: there are no documents, or if there are any they have not yet come to light. But a date can probably be arrived at if archaeologists are able to establish, in due course, a date for the earliest settled, farming communities either in the Yemen or in Dhofar, now a dependency of Oman. The epoch of that settlement will almost certainly have been the first epoch of the vine in Arabia. In only a few parts of that country can it ever have been possible to cultivate the vine at all. The extent of mere desert, the terrible heat, the want of rain and even of water in much of the land, all make for the confinement of viticulture to a few favoured regions. Still, the very places, the fertile valleys of the Yemen and Dhofar whence came frankincense, where perhaps the first Arabian farmers settled and grew prosperous, provided good vineyard territory in their hillsides, although the climate must always have made this culture difficult, or at least made its product something very different from what we understand by the word 'wine'.

The little we know of the viticulture which Mahomet was to check in Arabia all belongs to historical times. It is probably needless to point out that the only evidence we need that Arabia had her vineyards and vintages is that Mahomet ever found it necessary to lay down the law against wine. Of course, the Arabians might have been importing from Syria; in fact they were. But there is evidence for Arabian vineyards five hundred years before Mahomet's time.

About the year 80, say half a century before the Emperor Claudius added Britain to the Roman Empire, a master merchant seaman of Alexandria, the greatest commercial city in the Western world, wrote a small handbook about the seaborne trade of his time which seems to have been intended as a guide book for fellow-sailors. We do not know his name, but his book is known as *The Periplus of the Erythraean Sea*,[3] and its language is, of course, Greek. Among much else this book gives a few details of trade with Arabian ports. At the time, trading with the East in general, notably with India, had been made easier by the observations of a navigator named

Hippalus, who published about mid-century the fact of the existence of the monsoon, long known to Arab seamen. By taking advantage of this absolutely regular wind, merchant seamen could shorten the voyage between Alexandria and the nearest Indian ports to only two months; and the author of the *Periplus* would probably take about three weeks between Alexandria and Aden.

The *Periplus* advises merchant seamen to load only a little wine for Arabian ports, as the country has plenty. This does not, of itself, prove anything; Arabia could and did import wine from sources nearer than Egypt and the captain might therefore have been referring to the competition of these imports. But he also says that the great port of South Arabia, Muza, '. . . imports both grain and wine, but not much because the country produces a fair amount of wheat and a larger amount of wine.'

As to the kind of competition in wine, and also as to the charter cargoes which might be picked up in Arabian ports (for that, I think, is the point of some of the observations in the *Periplus*), the captain says that on the one hand Arabia is importing wine from Italy, Laodicea and other parts of Arabia (by which he may have meant Syria); and on the other she is exporting her own wines to Barygaza in India.

The *Periplus* makes one very interesting point touching the import of wines into the Mapharitic states of Arabia, where it is obvious that wine could not be grown, for the people were nomadic savages—or at least, the author calls them savages—and in any case the climate was unsuitable: 'There is imported into these markets . . . at some places . . . a little wine . . . not for trade but to serve for getting the goodwill of the savages.'

We have here, then, a repetition of the ancient trading device of the Tyrians and Sidonians and Cretans in Thrace; of the Carthaginians in Spain and North Africa; and of the Europeans, or rather Americans, in their dealings with the North American Indians, excepting that the latter used spirits instead of wine.

But the Muza of the *Periplus*, which is our Mocha, was a very different matter, and so too were other Arabian or near-Arabian ports. The export of Arabian wines from Arabian vineyards to Barygaza, the modern Broach on the Gulf of Cambay, may have been a fact. But the out-port for this trade seems to have been Oraea, and as far as I can make out this was on the modern Shatt-al-Amara. The author also mentions dates and rice as exports to be shipped at the same place, and in that case the trade is not relevant to our subject, for the wine was almost certainly date-wine, which had great commercial importance, both then and earlier. This may explain why Arab importers, according to the *Periplus*, gave preference to wine from the Italian and Laodicean vineyards over that of Arabia, a point of great importance to Greek shipping firms in the first century, for they were nearer to the sources of supply than their Arab and Indian rivals.

It should be made clear that the reading public to whom the *Periplus* must have been addressed, the commercial community of Alexandria, was at this time an interloper in the wine-trade with the East, or for that matter in all trade with the East. The discovery of the monsoon and how to use it in trade across the Indian Ocean by that Hippalus already mentioned, a sort of Vasco da Gama of antiquity, is placed by Schaff, the admirable American editor of the *Periplus*, at about A.D. 45. But it seems certain that both Dravidian and Arabian merchant seamen had been using it for many centuries, and had managed to keep this very valuable trade secret to themselves, thereby excluding the Greeks from the immensely profitable Oriental trade with the Roman Empire.

A paper in the *Journal* of the Royal Asiatic Society for 1898 places the start of this Red Sea–Indian Ocean trade at the beginning of the seventh century B.C.; and it is entirely possible, in fact it is probable, that Arabian and Syrian vineyards were exporting wine to India eight hundred years before the *Periplus* was published. Certainly the vineyards of Laodicea (see below) were very ancient.

At all events, Hippalus enabled his countrymen to get a share in the trade in Arabian-grown wine for India. And the author of the *Periplus* had been himself as far as the Arab-dominated states of what is now Tanzania, if not to the delta of the Ganges, with such cargoes.

There are a few place-names in Arabia which connect the communities in question with viticulture. The Bata' people of the Wadi Dahr are said to have cultivated a vine peculiar to themselves, and this may well be so, for it is in isolation from other vineyards that vines, inbred, can realize in their seedlings genetical permutations which may bring out valuable characters; and oasis-culture might provide the perfect conditions for such breeding which would, however, have been fortuitous at that time. According to Pliny the Elder, Petra, the 'rose-red city half as old as time', had its vineyards.

In fact it must have had them long before his time. It is clear that the Nabataeans, whose capital was Petra, were in many ways as civilized a people as
the Jews of the Maccabean monarchy. Despite their Bedouin manners, the
people of Petra may have had viticulture for nearly as long as the Jews or the
Greeks. Other vine places are Sam'a, G'enwan and 'Oman. The two last-
named were celebrated for the great size of their grapes, so famous in fact
that news of them reached China, and annalists reported them as being 'as
large as hens' eggs', perhaps an exaggeration. Both Pliny and Theophrastus
in his *History of Plants* refer to a remarkable wine which comes from the
'Island of Tylos in the Arabian Gulf'.[4]

The grapes of Arabia were of the large, very sweet, pulpy kind which are
delicious when eaten fresh and which make the best raisins. Muscat grapes,
of which there are scores of varieties now, were of Arabian origin. But such
grapes make a heavy, very strong, rather syrupy wine. In fact one Arabic
word for wine, used at least by the North African and Spanish Moors later,
is *xarop*, and presumably this is the origin of our word 'syrup'. It seems to me,
however, uncertain whether European authors are correct in taking this
word to mean wine. For a product of the Arabian vineyards of equal importance with wine was the boiled-down must of the grape, reduced to a
third, even a fifth of its original bulk, to produce a thick but still liquid
grape-sugar. I have a little more to say about that below; such syrups were,
of course, free of alcohol.

Although the vines of the Yemen produced some white and some amber
wines, Arabian wine was typically a deep red. The best wines were properly
aged, although whether in wood or earthenware does not appear. A reference to the muscat flavour—we have it now not only in grapes, but in the
best 'aromatic' apples, pears and melons—which is equivalent to the scent
called musk (though the nominal equivalence is coincidental), seems to
appear in the following verse from an Arabic poem to be found in a collection and translation made by Sir Charles Lyall, *The Dīwāns of 'Abad ibn
el-Abras*:

And oft-times the wine in fragrance like broken pieces of musk;
Long time has it spent in the wine-jar, year after year passing by;
Have I quaffed in the morning before the dawn shone forth to our mirth,
In the tent of a man rich in bounty, pouring it freely to all.[5]

The verse reveals that at least some Arabian wine was aged in amphorae. There was not a great deal of Arabic wine-poetry until the Persian (see below); but a contemporary of the Prophet (whose strictures on wine were not pronounced at the beginning of his career), the poet al-A'sha of Bakr, celebrates in verse the pleasures of the vintage at a place called 'Anâfit. This must, I think, be the same as the 'Anâfit in the Yemen that the great Arabian geographer Idrisi (who was born at Ceuta in 1061 but who studied and taught at Cordova) described as surrounded by vineyards in his time, more than three centuries later. Being in Arabia proper, these vineyards would by then have been producing raisins and grape-sugar syrups rather than wine, for though the Koranic prohibition (but, as will appear, it was not quite that) was only honoured in the breach in such lands as Persia, in the Prophet's homeland it was usually respected.

Arabia, then, was one of the ancient vine lands. And Syria, to become another country of the Dar-al-Islam, was, as we have seen, one of the most ancient of all. The geographer Strabo (XII. II. 9) says of Laodicea on the Syrian coast sixty miles south of Antioch that it '. . . abounds with wine, most of it exported to Alexandria. The whole mountain overhanging the city is planted nearly to the summit with vines.' And for evidence of earlier date we may refer to Ezekiel xxvii, 18, touching the vineyards of Damascus. This is also true of Iran, of Anatolia, of Palestine, and of Egypt. But what of the North and North-West African countries, now Tunis, Algeria, Morocco and Mauritania?

Near-Eastern Mediterranean civilization was carried to North Africa, in just-prehistoric times, by the people whom the Greeks called Phoenicians and who called themselves Sidonians; their great centres were Tyre and Sidon. They were Semites with a language closely akin to Hebrew; it seems they invented alphabetic writing, the most important single invention in the history of the human race; they probably invented glass. One of their cities was the Byblos of Chapter II, that is, one of the three most ancient centres of commercial viticulture. They were a people who never seem to have had much land, only cities with a little land round them; this very fact may possibly account for their forwardness in viticulture; it would pay them far better to plant their few acres with vines and sell the wine in exchange for grain and other necessities, than to grow their own grain. As everybody knows, these Phoenicians were the greatest traders and seamen of Mediterranean antiquity. And one of the principal Phoenician exports was, during many centuries, wine.

Men of Tyre, and perhaps of the other Phoenician cities, early founded, not exactly colonies, but trading stations (factories) on the coast of North Africa, on the south coast of Spain, in Sicily and on other Mediterranean islands. There is some conflict of opinion as to when these foundations occurred. The classical Greek authorities believed that the Phoenician settlements were much earlier than the middle of the eighth century B.C. From these literary sources we would infer that the imperial city of Tyre, whose king, Hiram, was one of Solomon's allies, had founded Gades (Cadiz) and Lixus in Morocco as early as 1200 B.C.; and that other settlements belong to about 1000 B.C. But it seems that no object found by archaeologists on North African sites of ancient Punic settlement can be dated earlier than, or even as early as, the eighth century B.C.

The earliest settlements did not include any kind of planting, any real colonization; they were established as havens for ships from the home cities, at which masters could water, leave and draw trade-goods. They were, in short, factories. The method of trade was peculiar: the so-called 'dumb-trade'. The people of North and North-West Africa, and the Celt-Iberians of Spain, were barbarians; the former lived a nomadic life and were what the ancients called Nubians and, further west, Berbers; the Spaniards may have been more settled, for at an extremely early date, as we have noted, they were trading in ships as far north as Brittany. With the savages of North-West Africa and of the West African coast, the Phoenician method was to place trade-goods on a beach and withdraw. The savages then came down and placed an amount of gold beside the goods. The Phoenicians then landed again and, if satisfied, took the gold and departed; if not, they withdrew again and gave the savages a chance to add to the gold offered. This method was successfully worked for centuries and it had the great merit of avoiding the brawls and consequent ill-will which were apt to break out where personal contact was established. I suppose the 'dumb-trade' may have been even older than Phoenician merchant adventuring, it was very much in the character of the great merchant oligarchies of Tyre, Sidon and Byblos, and it is at least possible that it was first used by them in those contacts with Thrace which led to the introduction of viticulture, wine and

Dionysus to the Hellenes. It is also possible that such trading-posts as were first established in the western Mediterranean region would have left very little for archaeologists to dig up later; and that the objects which have been found and which have caused scholars to revise the dating of Phoenician settlements, belong to a later, more truly colonial epoch.

There can, I think, be no doubt at all that the Phoenicians took the vine to western North Africa. Some viticulture may well have spread along the African coast from the Nile delta very early indeed; and the Greeks were quite early colonists in Cyrenaica; but not as early as the Phoenicians further west. The steps in the introduction of the vine would have been much as they were in Thrace: first wine is sold; then the natives, having become very fond of it and perhaps addicted to it, want more than they can buy; as soon as they begin to settle and farm—that is, as civilization spreads to them—they plant the vine. More often, a trading-post develops into a small, true colony, with plantation. The vine is one of the very first plants to be established, because wine is not only easily made with very little gear, but is an immensely profitable object of trade. From the colonial vineyard the plants make their way in due course into the still-independent native country.

By far the greatest of all the Phoenician colonies, in North Africa or anywhere else, was Carthage, which was founded about 800 B.C. and was destroyed after seven centuries by Rome. The Carthaginians first rented the land they settled, but later conquered a very considerable territory which they farmed. Vineyards were an important part of their plantings; the wine in which they traded with the natives of both the African and European shores of the Western Mediterranean no longer had to be fetched from Byblos, or Tyre, or Egypt. It was home-grown, and with it as a part of their cargo they traded further than men had ever done before in the Western world. Hanno, a member of that class of rich merchant-oligarchs who were to become land-owning gentlemen, the class from which the Shofetes or Sufets who governed Carthage with a Senate were drawn, took a fleet of armed trading ships and transports carrying colonists to plant, right down to within five degrees of the equator. However, the southernmost vineyards planted under Punic influence were those of Lixus.

The pattern of viticulture in the Carthaginian and other Punic colonies, which became independent of Tyre and Sidon even before the imperial epoch of Carthaginian history, reminds me of the pattern of cotton and tobacco production in the southern United States late in the eighteenth and early in the nineteenth centuries. There is some evidence that the ruling class of Carthaginian merchants, like the great merchants of nineteenth-century England, having enriched themselves by trade, tended to buy estates in the country and drop their connection with trade to become 'improving' land-owning gentry. But what makes them more like the gentry of the United States is that their farms, including their great vineyards, were worked by a teeming people of chattel-slaves. In at least one sense, however, this slave-economy was more liberal than that of the United States: the slaves were of all colours.

This social movement of the great Carthaginian oligarchs is curiously reminiscent, slavery notwithstanding, of that which took English gentlemen like 'Turnip' Townsend and Coke of Holkham from the city into the country, to experiment with farming and teach all Europe to farm better, in the eighteenth century. I have no real doubt that it resulted, in ancient Carthage as in modern England, in great advances; in the Carthaginian case, viticulture was a beneficiary. It seems clear enough from the later comments of Columella[6] (see below and Chapter IV), who knew what he was talking about, that Carthaginian viticulture and agriculture became the most advanced in the Mediterranean basin. Contemporary Greek comment on the beauty and high-farming of the Carthaginian gentlemen's estates (which were, however, quite small, like those of England) is full of wondering admiration.

Mago, the agronomist referred to in Chapter IV as having by the influence of his treatise helped to transform Italian viticulture, was probably a landed-gentleman of this kind, perhaps a member of the great Magonid family which seems to have dominated Punic political and naval life until the rise of the Barca family. The book was translated from Punic into Latin by D. Silanus, for distribution among landowners, and also into Greek.

*VII Despite Koranic prohibition, sophisticated Persians did drink wine. In the early sixteenth century the great painter Sultan Muhammad used a verse of Hafiz as the occasion to caricature a contemporary drinking-party, with the angels themselves decorously taking part. The verse illustrated, from the 'Diwan', is: 'The Angel of Mercy took the cup of delight, and dashed the dregs like rosewater on the faces of Hur and Pari.'*

*Vitis Labrusca.*

But although the influence of North African plantation-industry, in viti-culture chiefly, was financially good, it was socially vicious. The Roman economy, like that of all ancient civilizations excepting those native to the Americas, was based on chattel-slavery; but in the early centuries of the Republic, the centuries of the subsistence-farming burgesses, there was at least a measure of humanity in the relations between master and slave, who daily worked side by side at the same tasks. But the much more efficient Cartha-ginian system of exploiting viticulture as an industry was pure capitalism at its atrocious worst. Mommsen, in his history of the Roman Republic, pointed out (in 1859, eleven years after the publication of the Communist Manifesto) that such a system is cruel and ruthless. He had before his eyes the hideous spectacle of the first great capitalist industrialism in England, before the trade unions had asserted the workers' humanity. Copied in Italy, the social consequences of Punic viticulture were, as we have seen, appalling. As a consequence of 'rationalization' of the wine-producing industry under Carthaginian influence, viticulture made much greater pro-gress in Italy; and the lot of countless thousands of wretched slaves became far worse. The story has been told in Chapter IV.

The Carthaginians were themselves heavy drinkers of wine, and since their wines, like North African wines today, were heavy and heady, as their taste became more refined they took to drinking wine imported from Italy and Greece as well as their own. It is a pity that the city was destroyed about four centuries too soon for the Punic epicures ever to have tasted the vintages of France. It would appear that drunkenness became a social problem; for, like Mahomet, and like the United States Congress thirteen centuries later, the Carthaginian government tried a measure of prohibition, very much in the Semitic tradition of temperance already discussed. Wine was forbidden to four classes of the community: slaves, soldiers, magistrates and Senators. I have no doubt that this law was unenforceable and that it was later abro-gated by tacit agreement.

It is safe to conclude that viticulture had been firmly established in Tunis, in Algeria and in Morocco—not, of course, all over those countries, but in

*VIII* Vitis labrusca. *One of the first American vites to be introduced to Europe, bring-ing with it phylloxera, oidium and mildew (see Epilogue). It is a parent of many American cultivars, including 'Concord'. Engraving by Nicolas Jacquin, 1797.*

many vineyards throughout the whole region—not later than the sixth
century B.C., and as to some part of it, earlier. The destruction of Carthage
by Rome and the turning of North Africa into a Roman, instead of a Punic
(and in places Greek) colony, or rather province, in no way interfered with
the vineyards, or not, at all events, until the first century A.D. when the
spread of the vine may have been checked and perhaps some vineyards
destroyed for economic reasons (see Chapters III and V). But when the
Punic, Numidian and Berber lands became part of the Dar-al-Islam, viticulture was severely restricted and in places totally ceased; and it was left to the
French to restore it when they followed Tyre, Rome and Islam into North
Africa as an imperial power.

The only other country of the Dar-al-Islam with which we need concern
ourselves in this chapter is Iran.

Persia, like Syria and Arabia, presents us with another case of a land into
which viticulture was introduced so early that dating is impossible. Persia
is virtually part of the original homeland of the vine, so closely allied in the
past with the country in which the cultivation of the vine, or at least the
making of wine, was first developed, that it can hardly be separated from it;
in the same way it is cheek by jowl with Anatolia, land of origin of so much
wine mythology. In short, its earliest history is certainly to be placed in that
group of countries which we can perhaps call Iranica.

Throughout historical times these countries have been famous for their
vines and wines; they contributed largely to the immense wealth which
enabled men like Cambyses, Cyrus, Darius the Great, Alexander and his
Seleucid successors and the Parthians, to build great empires in Iranica.
From some of the lands which belonged to the Iranian culture-complex we
have accounts of vines flourishing in a way which is peculiar to those few
regions where they can give of their tremendous best—ancient Morocco
and modern California are others. Of Khorasan, of ancient Aria, and of
Bactria, Strabo recounts not only that the vines were of colossal girth and
fabulous fruitfulness, but that the wine which these giants yielded was of
such substance and quality that it would keep and improve in unpitched
vessels for three generations, which is to say seventy-five years.[7] There is
nothing impossible about this, but Chinese accounts of the wines of Parthia,
Sogdiana and Bactria, from the end of the second century B.C. until the

seventh A.D., seem to average out at about thirty years for the age of many such. The Book of Esther provides a fairly early reference to the product of the Persian vineyards, if that work should, as some scholars maintain, be assigned to the fifth and not the second century B.C.: 'And they gave them to drink in vessels of gold, the vessels being diverse one from another, and royal wine in abundance, according to the state of the king.'

Herodotus, and he is followed by Athenaeus, says that the couch-throne of Darius the Persian was overshadowed by a grape-vine wrought of gold, and that this had been given to him by Pythius the Lydian: 'Now there lived in this city [Celaenae] a certain Pythius, the son of Atys, a Lydian. This man entertained Xerxes and his whole army in a most magnificent fashion, offering at the same time to give him a sum of money for the war. [Xerxes was on his way to conquer Greece.] Xerxes, upon the mention of money, turned to the Persians who stood by and asked them, "Who is this Pythius and what wealth has he that he should venture on such an offer as this?" And they answered him, "This is the man, O King, who gave thy father Darius the golden plane-tree and likewise the golden vine; and he is still the richest man we know in the world, excepting thee."'[8] The vine in question was not only made of solid gold, the bunches of grapes which it bore were wrought of precious stones. But Pythius could evidently afford it; he told the king that he had two thousand talents of silver and four million wanting seven thousand of daric staters.

Xenophon, who had much to do with the Persians and who in the *Anabasis* and *The Education of Cyrus* wrote about their manners, says that at the court of Cyrus the cup-bearer was an officer of the first rank. He tells how Cyrus, when he had tasted a wine of exceptional excellence, would drink only half the flagon, sending the rest to a friend, with a note saying: 'For some time Cyrus has not found a pleasanter wine than this; and he therefore sends some to you, begging you to drink it today with those whom you love best.'

Such a flagon would have been a *congius*, a measure equal to six pints: and of these, according to an inscription at Persepolis, fifty of sweet wine and five thousand of ordinary wine were delivered daily to the Royal House-hold of the Persian Empire. Production of wine in Persia must have been large. But if this seems a lot for one household to consume in a day, a matter of four thousand gallons, doubtless there the word 'household' implied the military establishment, including the 'Immortals', the Life Guards of the

Persian Emperors. But evidently the domestic wines were not those most esteemed by the gentry in Persia; that, at least, is what Athenaeus says, and he adds that their favourite was the Chalybonian wine grown near Damascus.

If we are to believe Herodotus (and in this story he is confirmed by Strabo), the Persians put their vineyards to a use which must be unique, using their wine rather as some Amerindian peoples use mescalin (*peyotl*), deliberately to release the inhibited subconscious judgment. We have been taught by Rabbinical moralists that strong wine is a mocker; and on the whole, despite the antithetical Latin opinion that there is truth in wine, we believe them and are a little uneasy about getting drunk. But the Persians: 'It is also their general practice to deliberate on affairs of weight when they are drunk; and on the morrow when they are sober, the decision which they came to the night before is put before them by the master of the house in which it was made; and if it is then approved of, they act on it; if not, they set it aside.'

I know of no other people who have made this deliberate use of the judgment of their drunkenness, checking the truths of their intoxication by the judgment of their sobriety: it is as if they had realized both the use and the danger of that release so beautifully and atrociously displayed in the *Bacchae* of Euripides. But the Persians' drinking was in any case excessive, and Xenophon says that they were often carried out from their banquets because they were no longer able to stand, a state of affairs which had been commonplace in Egypt some thousands of years before, and was to be so in England a couple of thousand years later. And in Persia as elsewhere, and albeit the Persians were 'Aryan of Aryan descent', it gave rise to a temperance movement and to harsh punishments for public drunkenness.[9]

The Persian vineyards were in no way like those to which we are accustomed. The vines were allowed to grow as large as they would, although some pruning was certainly done, possibly in the nature of modern 'spur' pruning. The plants were not bushes, but scandent trees, propped as necessary or trained over timber- or fruit-trees (*plate 84*), and along ropes connecting these in long swags. It seems likely, too, that the old Egyptian system of training on pergolas, often ornamental ones of fine mason's work, was in use. Irrigation was general and necessary.

When the strictures on wine uttered by Mahomet, first at Medina and later at Mecca, became part of the Moslem canon, they did not extend to the vine itself. It is true that many vineyards, in Persia as elsewhere, were grubbed up; and this was probably socially desirable, for as we have shown elsewhere the vine always tends to encroach on corn land and thus to cause serious food shortages. But many vineyards in all the eventually Moslem countries were retained, for fresh grapes were valued, raisins were an important article of commerce, and the grape-sugar syrups described below were of economic importance. For these reasons the Moslem attitude to wine had an interesting effect upon the vine, that flexible plant, itself. Attention being given to the kind of grapes which had long been recognized as better for dessert than for wine, improved varieties were selected and propagated. We have already noted that the very many Arabian varieties of the grape which have the muscat flavour were probably produced in the eighth and ninth centuries within the Dar-al-Islam; and a great boost was given to the propagation of seedless mutants. A case in point is the Kishmish (*cišmis*) grape still grown in Anatolia by the Turks for the production of seedless raisins and introduced into California in the nineteenth century of our era. This vine is of astonishing antiquity; for it was known to the Chinese, and introduced into China by way of Turkestan in the seventh century.[10] It was therefore older than the wine-ban, but became more important economically after that ban.

Although there is a clear distinction between wine-grapes, table-grapes and grapes for drying, a distinction made fairly early in the history of viti-culture, it is of course the case that you can make wine with any grapes. Consequently, those people within the Dar-al-Islam who wanted wine despite their Prophet and their Koran, had the means to make it. Even the continued existence of vineyards in the peasant communities of Arabia might not lead to the breaking of the law, for simple people are cowed by religious sanctions. But the sophisticated man of the great and ancient city in the heart of the west Asiatic wine country was a very different kind of human being. Among such urban types, and excepting during short periods of fanatical faith, there is little power in religion to impose self-denial of a usually harmless pleasure. In Moslem Persia the vines continued to yield wine.

Thanks to Edward FitzGerald, we are familiar with the quatrains of Omar Khayyam, and no quoting of his work is necessary to establish that he regarded wine, at least in his poetic moments, as man's best and perhaps only consolation for his condition. If his feelings were those of his class, it is obvious that the latter would be very unwilling to treat their great and ancient vineyards as a mere source of raisins. Yet no doubt in other respects this Persian mathematician in the service of the Seljuk Malik Shah was a respectable Moslem; but perhaps, as a distinguished scientist, an intellectual, his religious observances were a matter of good manners and social expediency rather than of faith. Moreover, his Seljuk masters were very fond of wine, and belonged to one of the peoples which, long before Mahomet's time, had introduced the cultivation of the vine into the heart of Asia.

The Persian city which had, in its long day, the reputation of producing the best wine in the country, Shiraz, also gave birth to the greatest of Persian lyric poets, Hafiz or, to give him his real name, Mahomet Shams-ed-Din. He was born early in the fourteenth century and died in 1389, and the point of bringing him in here is that a very large number of the short odes written by this 'son' and namesake of the Prophet, this lapsed Moslem puritan (he had been a monk of a dervish Order but had come to his senses when confronted with ascetic practices), celebrate wine, drinking and bibulous conviviality (*plate VII*). His work proves, if proof were needed, that the Persian vineyards and wineries continued in being; but also, and this is true, too, of Omar Khayyam's poetry, that the act of breaking a religious law every time you drained a cup of wine introduced into wine-drinking an element of glamour, of romanticism, which is only to be found in countries where a feeling of guilt accompanies wine-drinking. An entertaining circumstance touching the wine-poetry of Hafiz is that there exist works of criticism by Moslem writers quite as absurd as those which contrive to see in the Beloved of Solomon's ravishing if rather too opulent erotic poem, the Song of Songs, none other than Holy Church. These commentators of Hafiz interpret the poet's vinous sensualities as mystical statements to be understood only according to certain rules of Sufi theology.

Every country which eventually formed a part of the Dar-al-Islam was vine country, so that Mahomet's rule against wine dealt a serious blow against viticulture and, after Domitian's edict examined in an earlier chapter and before the rise of the North American aphis, *Phylloxera vastatrix*, was the sharpest check the vine had received since some thousands of years B.C. It is therefore worth while to examine its nature.

The Koranic strictures on wine are not prohibitions in so many words. They are two in number, and both very short. Before we come to them—

what gave rise to them? Since they were put into the Koran they are not simply laws of social hygiene promulgated by a secular government; they are part of the Prophet's revelation, and are law with religious sanction. But this statement needs qualifying; the fact is that among the Moslems, as among the Jews much earlier, it is not possible to separate secular and religious law; there is only one law, and it has religious sanction; it is not the government which forbids you to do this or that and enjoins you to do the other; it is God. It is, therefore, not necessary to suppose that Mahomet had any personal and peculiar objection to wine. There is apparently reason to believe that his strictures on wine were first promulgated as a measure of military discipline. It is very likely that his simple Bedouin soldiers, raised under very harsh conditions, might when they overwhelmed the cities of the sown, and entered upon lands flowing with wine, have got dangerously out of hand. On the whole, then, we can take it that these anti-wine pronouncements were practical measures, not mystical ones. There may, however, be more to it than that. If Mahomet shared the Rabbinical hostility to wine, he will have been all the readier to help his generals to keep the troops in order by pronouncing against it. But what was the basis of this hostility? It was, surely, the close connection between wine, wine-drinking, wine-mythology, and the worship of deities detestable to the stern and sad monotheism of the Semite. The Rabbinate had always had the greatest difficulty in keeping the Jews from whoring after strange gods; they were apt to start worshipping any deity but Jehovah, even when that entailed such revolting practices as sacrificing their own children to Bel-Marduk of the Phoenicians. Dionysus was a dangerous enemy. The Christians were cleverer than the Moslems; for whereas the latter tried to prohibit wine and stop the drunkenness which was also a Dionysian rite, the former took over, and civilized, in the Eucharist, part of the wine-ritual and made it their own. (Orphism had made a similar use of the Dionysian cult in the sixth century B.C.) So successfully did they do so that one finds in the attitude to wine of certain rather self-conscious Roman Catholics a touch, more than a touch, of the reverent awe or the religious gladness proper enough if the object of your religious thought and feeling is the Vine made flesh and spirit. This Vine-worship sits rather awkwardly, indeed, on some English Catholics; there is more than a little of the ridiculous in, for example, some of Chesterton's work, or in Ernest Dowson flinging roses riotously with the throng.

Whatever their origin, here are the Moslem rules in form: in the Chapter of the Cow, in the Koran, it is written: 'They will ask thee concerning wine and lots. Answer, in them there is great sin and some things of use unto men; but their sinfulness is greater than their use.' Wine-drinking and gambling, coupled, are here frowned upon. But they can hardly be said to be forbidden. One can always repent of a sin. Also, this passage reads as if some edict or sermon had already been published against drinking and gaming, and was fairly generally known. Next, in the Chapter of the Table, also in the Koran, it is written: 'O true believers, surely wine, and lots, and images and divining arrows, are an abomination of the work of Satan; therefore avoid them, that ye may prosper. Satan seeketh to sow dissension among you by means of wine and lots, and to divert you from remembering God, and from prayer; will ye not, therefore, abstain from them?'

And that is all: we have the usual and already at that time very ancient Jewish Rabbinical hostility to soothsaying and image-worship; and the condemnation of drinking and gaming, once again coupled together. The impartial reader will, I think, conclude that both these passages rather deprecate social drinking and gaming than prohibit a moderate and proper use of wine.

It is, however, a common experience that the followers of a Prophet are often more royalist than the king: hence total prohibition among the fanatical.

But not all Mahomet's followers were so very bigoted; how could men of breeding and education, and of an ancient tradition of literacy and art, entirely surrender their judgment to an illiterate member of the lower classes, albeit possessed by the divine spirit? Hence Persian bibulous poetry and the salvation of the vineyards. It may be amusing to glance at the Koranic passages by which the more liberal Moslems justified their continued use of wine. In the Chapter of the Bee grapes are listed among God's gifts to man, but this is not much to the point, since you can use them otherwise than in the wine-press; but later in the same chapter comes: 'God sendeth down water from heaven and causeth the earth to revive after it hath been dead. Verily, herein is a sign of resurrection unto people who hearken . . . And of the fruit of the palm-tree and of grapes ye obtain an inebriating liquor, and also good nourishment. Verily, here is a sign unto people who understand.'

76 A delegation of Syrian traders, one in the bottom row carrying a large amphora, from a Theban tomb-painting. In the ancient world Syria was famous for its wine, and this fame endured, despite Moslem domination, into the Middle Ages.

# The Abode of Islam

77  *A stylized vine-leaf appears among the decoration at Leptis Magna in Roman North Africa.*

*The small terracotta statuette (78) shows that the Romans in Syria used camels to transport amphorae of wine.*

78

On a votive stele from the region of Carthage
in Tunisia the dedicant holds pomegranates and
a large bunch of grapes; second century A.D. The
vine was brought to Carthage by the Phoenicians, and after 800 B.C. Carthaginian viticulture became the most advanced in the entire
Mediterranean basin. The greatest viticultural
authority of antiquity was a Carthaginian,
Mago, whose textbook was translated into Latin
and Greek after the destruction of Carthage by
the Romans.

79

The floor mosaic at Sabratha in Libya shows birds eating the grapes of a great vine (80). Below (81) the Triumph of Bacchus, a mosaic from Thysdrus, now El Djem, in Tunisia.

82 *Carved on a cliff at Ivriz, in modern Turkey, an eighth-century Hittite vegetation god, to whom a king pays tribute, holds corn in his left hand and a grape-laden vine in his right.*

83

*The Persians have gone down in history as great drinkers of splendid wines. But when the strictures on drinking uttered by Mahomet became part of the Moslem canon, many Persian vineyards were grubbed up and—officially at least—the remaining vines were grown for table-grapes and raisins. Some Persians fled from the Arab conquest to Mazanderan, where they paid tribute to the Khalifs for one hundred years to preserve their own faith and customs. The seventh-century silver dish from Mazanderan (83) shows a banqueter drinking under a vine, with a wine skin at the lower left. The mid-sixteenth-century garden scene (84) in Islamic Persia shows a vine trained on a living tree.*

85

*Despite Koranic prohibition sophisticated urban Persians continued to drink wine. A page sits dreaming with wine cup and bottle, in a sixteenth-century painting from the city of Qazwin.*

This passage was, and perhaps still is, used by wine-loving Moslems as a text. There is more: George Sales, translator and redactor of a good English edition of the Koran, describes in his long Preliminary Discourse the really rather repulsively gross paradise offered to true believers, in which the feasting, in its lush abundance, is rather like that of the plutocratic English Edwardians. As a part of the post-mortem and eternal *dolce vita*, the blessed, '. . . will also be supplied with [as] many sorts of liquors in vessels of gold; and to complete the entertainment there will be no want of wine which though forbidden in this life will yet be freely allowed to be drunk in the next, and without danger since the wine of paradise will not inebriate . . .'

I was once, in a health-food shop, offered deodorized garlic . . .

The final result of these rather mild strictures on social drinking was to check the advance of the vine and even force it to retreat. Vineyards in the Dar-al-Islam were saved by the wine-loving inhabitants of sophisticated cities; by the trade in raisins; by the market for fresh fruit; and by the need for grape-sugar syrups. These were obtained by boiling down the must instead of fermenting it. These thick, dark *defrutum* syrups, called *arrope* in Jerez where they are still in use to make *vino de color*, are of impressive antiquity, perhaps nearly as old as wine: they were made and sold in Tyre and Sidon and Byblos; and it has already been suggested that the arrangements for heating the must apparent in some Egyptian inscriptions may have been used in the making of *defrutum*. In numerous early works, especially in Chinese, we come across 'wines' having the consistency of honey. These would have been a mixture of *defrutum* and wine—in fact the *vino de color* referred to above, or some similar oinological curiosity.

Finally, Islam, despite the Prophet, had a good deal to do with the introduction of spirits—brandy. But as it is often written that the Arabs, or the Moors, invented the technique of distillation of spirits from wine, which gave a new stimulus to viticulture by finding a new use for even more grapes, it will be worth a page to point out that they did not. The principle of distillation, for example of sea-water, was understood in the fourth century B.C., and perhaps earlier. It was first put to some kind of practical use by the experimental alchemists of Alexandria in the second and third centuries A.D. It appears that the principle and some kind of basic apparatus were carried abroad, but chiefly to the East, by Nestorian Christian alchemists. Among the people who learned alchemy from these missionaries were the Arabs. I have found a small amount of evidence that the Chinese, who either invented distilling for themselves or had it from the Nestorians, may even have been distilling the spirit out of wine earlier than we were (see Chapter VIII). It is not claimed that the alchemists of the Eastern Roman Empire were the first to distil wine into brandy; only that they had stills in their laboratories. But would it not be rather odd if they had never had the curiosity to see what happened if you put wine into the still? Perhaps not, for they were not scientific chemists, and they were probably putting the cart before the horse, trying to do in practice what, on irrational grounds, they had decided you could do in theory, rather than seek the truth by experiment. If the Chinese were, in fact, distilling wine before the thirteenth century, they could have had the technique of distillation not directly from the Nestorians, but indirectly through the Turkish peoples who were settled and growing the vine in Iran.

What the advanced school of alchemists among the Spanish Moors did do was to carry the technique further, to improve the apparatus, and to make use of it to extract the spirit from wine—that spirit which the Chinese (see Chapter VIII), when they 'distilled' it by freezing instead of by boiling, thought would fly to a man's armpits and then kill him. The first, or perhaps, rather, the most eminent, of the Christian pupils of the Moorish schools was a Spaniard, Arnaldo de Villanova, who died in 1311. But at about the same time there seems to have been a number of people who were distilling spirits from wine, the 'recipe' was being published, and there was a separate introduction of the art from, probably, Byzantium into Italy. The reason we use the Arabic words 'alcohol' and 'alembic' is that when Europeans became civilized enough to take up alchemy—another Arabic word of course—they received it at the hands of Arab masters: so that Paracelsus, for example, had from Moorish books what their authors had had from Alexandrian ones; and he introduced these words for phenomena which had no names in the European languages.

During the relatively brief period in the thirteenth century and into the fourteenth when the coincident impact of Asiatic paganism and Latin Christianity in arms—the conquests of Jenghiz Khan and the first Crusades —recaptured parts of the Dar-al-Islam in the Levant for Dionysus, viticulture enjoyed a great restoration. But perhaps in some of these countries it had never been very much affected by the Koranic pronouncements. Thus

Syria was as famous for wine in the thirteenth century A.D. as in the thirteenth century B.C.; its best medieval vintages came from Neffin or Aneffin in the county of Tripoli. What is more remarkable, Tyrian wine, by far the most ancient in commerce, was still in good repute. It is curious that England had something to do with the last flicker of viticultural prosperity in the vineyards of Tyre. For until about the mid-fourteenth century Venetian shipping-houses were buying wine in Tyre for sale in the English market.[11] So that, as late as 1400 at least, Syrian Arabs, as well as Christians, might still be drinking their glass of wine and perhaps citing the Koran in justification.

Not all Moslems were as lucky. The gentry of Egypt had been drinking wine for at least four thousand years and probably longer when Mahomet saw fit to declare war on Dionysus. They were obliged to see their ancient vineyards destroyed by the same barbarians as burnt the library of Alexandria. By the late Middle Ages they were having recourse to bootlegging. There were two islands which, being still Christian, were still oinophil, and were conveniently close as sources of wine: Cyprus and Crete. Now Cyprus, at this time, had a tremendous reputation for wine: Heyd[12] and Schulz[13] give ample authority for saying that in the thirteenth and fourteenth centuries Cyprian wine was regarded as unquestionably the best in the world. For some reason, however, the Egyptian bootleg cargoes were not run in from Cyprus but from Crete. The bootleggers were almost certainly Genoese, for the Genoese shipping-houses had, at this time, something like a monopoly of the Cretan trade: and such part of their purchases from the Cretan wine-growers as were not quietly landed somewhere in the Nile delta without troubling the officers of the customs department, were carried to London and Southampton,[14] from which ports they were distributed to the English wine-shops as Malvoisie, or Malmsey.

One way and another, it does not look as if any man in the abode of Islam who really wanted his bottle of wine had to do without. Nevertheless it remains true that Mahomet did triumph over Dionysus: the very heartlands of the god were robbed of their wine-bearing vines and his most ancient worshippers have long ceased to be people of the vine.

# CHAPTER VIII

## *The Far East: Dionysus Rejected*

THE VINE-GROWING AND WINE-MAKING COUNTRIES of the Mediterranean and
their neighbours are linked to the East by that group of countries which has
sometimes been united into a single empire, which includes the ancient
native land of the vine and wine at its central, southern limit, and which is
best called Iran, although here the name designates rather a culture than a
geographical and political entity. The word is used to include, for example,
Sogdiana (Turkestan), Bactria (Afghanistan), parts of ancient Armenia,
Azerbaijan, all the lands of the south-western Asian plains and mountains.
All this country was, as we have seen, vine and wine land, even after it has
been conquered by the Moslems, or at least by Islam. Much of it is now
within the U.S.S.R.

We have already glanced at the fate of the vineyards in those Iranian
territories which became part of the Dar-al-Islam, that 'nation' which cannot be defined by geographical reference. Those parts to which Islam did
not penetrate, or from which it was driven by Tartar and Mongol hordes
subsequently Christianized by the rise of Russia, kept their vineyards if they
had them, or acquired them as they became civilized. Viticulture is therefore
of enormous antiquity in parts of the principal vineyard country of the Soviet
Union: in Soviet Armenia, for example, on the shores of the Black Sea
generally, and in the Crimea. The Appendix deals briefly with the investiga-
tions made by Negrul among the ancient vine populations of those lands.
But in other parts of south Russia the vine came later; and it seems to have
been introduced by Greek colonists and settlers of both the ancient Hellenic
world and of Byzantium.

The peoples of the vast central steppe, whether shepherds or horsemen,
did not practise viticulture, since only settled, farming communities can do
so and these Tartars, Mongols, Turks and Huns were all nomads. When
these people first came into contact with wine their reaction to it was often

hostile or at least suspicious. And well it might be, for civilized peoples have repeatedly made use of the power in wine to lower the resistance of barbarians to conquest or pacification. (Compare Chapter IV, the weakening of Gallic resistance to Rome by wine; and the attempts of some Belgic tribes to prevent the drinking of wine among their men.) Herodotus has an entertaining story of the way in which wine might be used as a weapon against barbarous nomads, and the way in which this was resented. When Cyrus the Persian was operating against the Massagetae, that is, the Huns, he set a trap for one-third of their army commanded by Spargapises, the son of the Hunnish Queen Tomyris, by leaving his camp unguarded and set with a banquet, including wine. The Massagetae took the bait: 'When they had eaten and drunk their fill and were now sunk in sleep, the Persians under Cyrus arrived, slaughtered a great multitude, and made even a larger number prisoners. Among the last was Spargapises himself.'

The infuriated Queen Tomyris sent an envoy to the Persian who delivered the following *note verbale*: 'Thou bloodthirsty Cyrus, pride not thyself on this poor success: it was the grape-juice—which when you drink it makes you so mad, and as you swallow it brings up to your lips such bold and wicked words—it was this poison wherewith thou didst ensnare my child . . .'

However, when any of these nomad peoples settled and took up farming as a way of life, they planted the vine, and in some cases became great viticulturists, as witness those Turks who introduced wine to China (see below); and, of course, the Magyars.

The present south Russian vinelands were formerly the home of the Scythians, nomad horsemen with a taste and talent for art which has attracted much attention and admiration from archaeologists. By the fifth century B.C. some of them, the poorer communities apparently, had settled down to farming. They grew wheat but not, as far as one can discover, the grapevine. It is true (see below) that the Chinese report a Scythian people as wine-growers, but that was a thousand years later, by which time viticulture had long since been introduced, probably repeatedly, by Greek settlers. Even when the Scythians at their zenith took to building cities, they do not seem to have planted vineyards, although one cannot be certain of this. Their city of Neapolis in the Crimea was flourishing from about 300 B.C. until the early years of the Christian era; amphorae dug up by archaeologists on its site reveal that wine was imported from Rhodes, Cos, Cnidus and Sinope. It is not very likely that the Neapolitans of the Crimea would have been importing so much wine had they been also growing it at home. But as a matter of fact it is by no means impossible, for the later history of the Crimea reveals something of the kind.

It is possible that the cultivated vine had been introduced to the Crimea at a time so remote that we have no knowledge of it yet; but it is unlikely. What is certain is that the Greeks of the sixth century B.C. had much business with the Crimea, and with the Scythians. Greek goldsmiths and other crafts-men settled in Scythia and made their living by producing those articles of gold for which the Scythian nobility had such taste, and there were Greek trading and artisan colonies on the Black Sea—Ponticapaeum, for example— as early as the seventh century or the sixth at latest; since the Greeks never failed to plant the vine wherever they went, it is safe to assume that they started viticulture in the Crimea and elsewhere on the Black Sea before the fifth century B.C.[1]

Was this culture continuous thereafter? That is to say, are the Crimean vineyards about twenty-five centuries old or were they lost, to be replanted perhaps more than once later in history? On the whole it seems likely that these vineyards, their plants renewed from time to time, of course, have endured. I cannot find any evidence that there was until very recently any considerable seaborne trade in wine coming from the Crimea. But this is not of any real significance, for the natural markets for Crimean wine lay inland, especially as the power and wealth of Russia, growing out of the Grand Duchy of Moscow, increased. For the same reason, the fact that, for example, in the thirteenth century the Genoese were taking wine *to* the Crimea, never bringing it away from that country, is not evidence that the old Greek viticulture had been lost. If the Genoese took wine to Caffa in the Crimea, rather than some other commodity, it must have been because there was a brisk demand for it. But this wine may not have been for local consumption: it may well have been exported overland into Russia. For the fact is that in the fourteenth century the Genoese became masters of part of the Crimea, and they then found that viticulture was flourishing in parts of their territory and that the terms used in connection with it were Greek: for example, the special vineyard tax was the *ambelopatico*.[2] One cannot abso-lutely assert that this Crimean viticulture was continuous with that started by Greek settlers in the Crimea and elsewhere on the Black Sea in the seventh or sixth century B.C. There may have been Byzantine settlements. But on the whole we may take it that the Crimea had been vineland for two thousand years when the Genoese got control of it.

But the Crimea and neighbouring countries were and are the eastern limits of serious viticulture.

Beyond, Mongolia and Manchuria, China, Indo-China, Northern India, and finally Japan, all have one or several species of *Vitis*. Asia as a whole seems to have about a dozen *Vites* (see Appendix). The one most familiar to British, American and West European gardeners is *Vitis coignetiae*, which is grown for its value as an ornament, and which sometimes bears large crops of small black grapes looking very like those of a wild *vinifera*, but the taste is insipid and the grapes are rather sour. If there has ever been a systematic attempt to cross-breed any of these vines with *V. vinifera*, it has had no economic consequences. There is one exception to this: the Russians have been making some use of *V. amurensis* to produce a hybrid of extra hardiness for their northern vineyards.

It is very difficult to tell from the Chinese and Japanese literature whether the use made of the fruit, leaves and parasitic grubs of *VV. coignetiae, thunbergii* (*plate 89*) and *flexuosa* (and perhaps others) led to the vine's domestication and cultivation, or whether it was a matter of gathering the wild harvest as we gather blackberries, and as the seventeenth-century colonists of North America gathered the grapes of *V. rotundifolia* and *V. labrusca*. But as far as I can discover, no Asiatic vine has ever been taken into cultivation seriously and on a commercial scale. Moreover, as will appear, there is evidence that until the introduction of *V. vinifera* drew their attention to the genus, the Chinese hardly knew of the existence of their native vines. And this can surely only be because the peoples in question, the far Asiatics, saw no merit in the vine; the Hindus, the Chinese and the Japanese were all in advance of Europe in their horticulture, and just as closely in touch with the lands of primal viticulture.

They were, in short, better placed than Europeans both to introduce the vines and wines of the Near East and Iranica into their own countries, and to take their own vines into cultivation. If they did not do so it can only have been because there was a cultural resistance; they did not, as it were, see the point of Dionysus.

I dealt in the Prologue with those limitations, climatic and other, which have prevented the spread of vine-growing and *V. vinifera* literally all over the world: and I claimed that one of these limitations was not a matter of viticulture, but of culture *tout court*. The aim of this chapter is to show how and when the vine and wine were introduced to the countries of the Far East, above all to China; how they showed themselves perfectly well able to flourish there; how certain regions of China, India and even Japan are rich in country which would make some of the most perfect vineyard land in the world; how nevertheless our vine and our wine simply did not 'take'. It is almost as if there were, between Mediterranean man and the grape-vine, a symbiosis so that the vine cannot flourish without Mediterranean man; and perhaps Mediterranean man is equally unable to establish himself permanently where the vine does not grow.

Until the learning and industry of Berthold Laufer, formerly curator of the Field Museum of Natural History, Chicago, put an end to the legend, it was held by scholars and social historians that all the important introductions of economic plants from Iran to China occurred during the Han Dynasty's rule over that Empire; and furthermore that a single man, General Chan K'ien, was responsible for nearly all of them. In historical fact, however, the General introduced only two plants to Chinese agriculture:[3] one was the incomparable fodder-plant *Medicago sativa*, alfalfa; the other was an Iranian cultivar of *Vitis vinifera*. The first was adopted with enthusiasm and spread swiftly to millions of acres of Chinese pasture; the second was regarded with mild interest, cultivated here and there as a curiosity, but, on the whole, rejected.

The Chinese of the second century B.C. had small knowledge of the West and on the whole held it to be simply barbarous—a point of view they persisted in until late in the eighteenth century. But they had contacts of trade with the Iranian lands, to whose civilization they had made important contributions and from which they were, in the next several centuries, to receive valuable plants and techniques. About 128 B.C. the Emperor Wu of the Han sent an envoy, General Chan K'ien, to Iran with instructions to seek out a people called the Yūe-chi and to make an alliance between them and the Chinese Empire against the troublesome Turkish people called the Hiun-mi. In the course of his mission General Chan found himself, at various times, in several countries of Iranian culture, chiefly Sogdiana, Fergana and Bactria, in all of which viticulture had been established for centuries and wine was a staple. These countries were not unknown to the Chinese, but they were more or less unvisited by them. Trade relations had been established with Fergana, and even with Parthia, the central Iranian land, for a particular reason. The reason was that Chinese army officers and horse-copers had recognized the very great superiority of Iranian thoroughbred horses over the Mongolian ponies which the Chinese had had to make do with: the Chinese government was in the market for them.

Chan K'ien spent two years in Fergana, Sogdiana and Bactria. In 128 B.C. he reported to his government that the people of Fergana, whom he calls Ta-yūan, and also the An-si, that is Parthians, 'have wine made of grapes'. He must have sent more details, for in the *Shi-ki* it is written that in Fergana the rich stored wine in quantities up to ten thousand gallons, and kept it for several decades without risk of deterioration. Seeds of the Fergana wine-vine were sent to the Emperor Wu, and these were planted, as was alfalfa, in Crown lands near the Imperial Palace. There they flourished, and the vine-yard was soon being noted by foreign ambassadors.

Now here there is an interesting point quite overlooked by Laufer, Bretschneider and other sinologues: the Fergana vines were certainly culti-vars of ancient origin; they must have been the product of centuries of selection and vegetative propagation. Their seeds would not, then, have 'come true'. As anyone knows who has cultivated vines in number, and has propagated them by various means, not one per cent, perhaps not one-tenth of one per cent, of the seedlings of a cultivated vine are worth growing: a very great many of the vines springing from the Fergana seeds must have been quite worthless, and thus the first introduction of the vine may well have been somewhat discouraging. There were no doubt enough vines of some merit in the batch to persuade the Emperor's gardeners to give them a trial; but their vineyard would have been nothing like an Iranian one.

This then was the first introduction of 'the vine of history'—and of reli-gion and poetry—from the West to China. What use did the Chinese make of it? From notices of the vine and wine collected by Laufer from many and diverse Chinese documents during the succeeding centuries, it seems clear that they remained on very unfamiliar terms with this plant and its product; they continued, for over a thousand years, to write of it as a curious and strange foreign thing which they had only just heard of and were not very interested in. In the Annals of the Tsin Dynasty it is noted that Sogdiana has grapes, that the wine made of them is abundant there, and that a rich man may have as much as a thousand gallons of it in his cellar; also, that this same wine is a favourite drink in Tashkend. The Emperor Yuan of the Liang Dynasty was a man of letters and he wrote a book called *Kin lou tse*. He reigned for only two years, A.D. 552–5. It is from him that we learn that the Scythians had vine and wine: 'The people in the country of the Great Yūe-chi are clever in making wine from grapes, flowers and leaves. Sometimes they also use roots and vegetable juice which they cause to ferment . . . in the eighth month when the storm blows over the leaves [? of vines] they are so much damaged and torn that they resemble silk rags; hence people speak of the grape-storm . . .'[4]

In the T'ang period the Chinese had contacts with Syria and the culture of the vine was again brought to their attention; it is recorded by T'ang observers[5] that in Arabia some of the grapes are as big as hens' eggs; which may possibly have been true, though I doubt it. And so on: there are many other instances of such notices.

If, then, China had the vine and wine of the grape from Iran, what of the rule—for it can fairly be called a rule—stated and exemplified elsewhere in this book, that with any new introduction of an economic plant comes its name in the country of immediate provenance? The Chinese word for grape, brought back by Chan K'ien, was *budō*: it is still current, as also in Japan. But the language of Fergana in the second century B.C. is a lost one. Here is what Laufer has to say about it:

'Since Chan K'ien made the acquaintance of the grape in Ta-yüan and took its seeds along from there to China, it is certain that he also learned the word in Fergana. Hence we are compelled to assume that *bu-daw* is Ferganian . . . which in my opinion may be connected with New Persian *bāda* (wine) and Old Persian βατιάκη (wine-vessel).'[6]

An interesting suggestion made by Laufer is that the Chinese seem to have paid no attention to their native vines, and indeed hardly knew that they were there, as it were, until their interest in the genus had been stimulated by the introduction of *Vitis vinifera*. The argument for this is philological: a work called the *Pie Lu*, a *materia medica* published long after the introduction of the vine from Iran, referring to wild vines in Kan-su, probably *V. bryoniae-folia*, uses not some native Chinese name, but the Ferganian loan-word: thus, the Chinese did not even have a name for a plant which was nevertheless native, and in several different species. (The Ferganian word evolved or was modified to *p'u-t'-ao*.) This does look as if the introduction of the Eurasian vine was what turned Chinese attention to vines in general. Later other, indigenous names are applied to the wild vines of China, and Chinese herbalists and others writing about the vines were perfectly clear as to the difference between the wild and the alien cultivated *Vites*. One such writer, Yen Shi-ku, writing about A.D. 500, '. . . ironically remarks that regarding the *yiñ-yü* [a Chinese wild vine] . . . as a grape is like comparing the *ci* of Northern China (*Poncirus trifoliatus*) with an orange; that the *yin-yü*, although a kind of *p'u-t'-ao* is widely different from the latter . . .'[7]

Of course, not all the *V. vinifera* vines subsequently in China were derived from Chan K'ien's original introduction of seeds and name from Fergana. More introductions were made from Turkestan and elsewhere. The gifted Uighur people had vineyards and made wine, and, as the administrators of the two Mongol empires of the early and late Middle Ages were recruited in their ranks, they may have communicated a taste for wine to their barbarous masters; at all events the Mongol khans were importers of wine, though they never grew their own. Once again, the method of later introductions is always stated as being by means of seed. One cannot help wondering whether this is an assumption made by Chinese historians or our own sinologues with little knowledge of horticulture or of genetics and a vague idea that the seed always gives rise to the desired plant; or whether, on the other hand, seed is specifically named and meant in the Chinese texts. If indeed seed was always used, then the vine populations of China would have been peculiar to that country, a mixed lot of seedlings of varying merit, and not reproducing the qualities to be found in the Iranian vineyards of their parent vines.

A work entitled *Kwan-chi* (*c.* A.D. 500) names three kinds of grape as being well established in gardens or vineyards: yellow, black and white. An author called Li Shi-chen mentions four varieties: one with round grapes is called 'vegetable dragon-pearls', another 'crystal grapes'. There is no mention of wine, no question of these grapes being vinified. A little later the number of varieties is greater, and seedless grapes are being grown; the fruit of the variety *so-so* is said to be as big as that of a climbing plant identified as *Schizandra chinensis*—in other words, very small, the berries of that plant being about a quarter of an inch in diameter. The *so-so* was perhaps the type of grape used for making currants, and coming from Corinth or from Zante.

A thousand years later the Chinese were still re-introducing the grape-vine, cultivating small vineyards in certain provinces but still making wine only rarely, locally, and on a very small scale, as a curiosity. The Emperor K'an-hi (1662–1722) caused three new varieties to be introduced from Hami in Turkestan; they are described as: one red or greenish and long, like mare's nipples; one not very large but of agreeable taste and aroma; and one no larger than a pea but most delicate, sweet and aromatic. This viticultural Emperor observes—and it is worth noting that his observations are very sound ampelography—that these three varieties degenerate when planted in the southern provinces where they lose their aroma, but persist well in the north if planted in dry and stony soil: which is the true nature of *V. vinifera*. 'I would', wrote K'an-hi, 'procure for my subjects a novel kind of fruit or grain rather than build a hundred porcelain kilns.'[8]

There are many accounts and reports by Chinese officials and travellers of the grapes of Chinese Turkestan. But always the reference is to the quality of the grapes as fresh fruit or for the making of raisins, and, at least in South China, there is never any mention of wine. The following is translated from the French of an eighteenth-century Jesuit missionary's account of the grapes of a place which he calls Hoai-lai-hien: 'We speak according to the evidence of our own eyes: the berries of these bunches of grapes are as large as purple damsons, and the bunch long and broad in proportion. The climate may be responsible; but if the books speak the truth, it is due in the first place to the fact that the vines were grafted upon jujube trees; and the thickness of the skin of these grapes would incline us to believe it.'

Nonsense, of course; but it was widely believed in Europe also until early in the nineteenth century that one genus could be grafted upon another totally unrelated one, though how this absurd belief persisted when any trial would have disproved it is hard to understand.

Yunan had become well known for its raisins by the ninth century,[9] but Pekin seems rather to have imported its raisins from Hami in Turkestan. In 851 an Arab merchant named Soleiman, who left an account of his travels and trading in China, wrote: '. . . the wine taken by the Chinese is made from rice. They do not make wine from grapes; nor is it brought to them from abroad; accordingly they do not know it and make no use of it.'[10] Laufer, who quotes this passage, says that it was doubtless true of South China where the Arabs traded. It was not quite true of the North. But the reason for this was not climatic, and it would be as easy to make a sweet, heavy wine in South China as in Madeira or southern California.

The earliest account of wine of the grape being made in North China is found in a history of the T'ang Dynasty. In A.D. 647 a spectacular kind of grape was sent to the Emperor T'ai Tsun by a Turkish people called the Yagbu. These grapes were called 'mare's nipple grapes' (see above), *mazhu p'u t'ao*, the fruit being purple and the bunches two feet long.[11] Following the account of this prodigy, which had first been accomplished in Syria and was later to be repeated, under glass, by William Speechley in England, comes: '[Grape] wine is used in western countries, and under former dynasties it was sometimes sent as tribute, but only after the destruction of Kao-ch'an, when mare's nipple grapes cultivated in plantations were received, also the method of making wine was simultaneously introduced into China [A.D. 640]. T'ai Tsun experienced both its beneficial and injurious effects. Grape-wine when ready shines in all colours, is fragrant, very fiery, and tastes like the finest oil. The Emperor bestowed it on his officials and then for the first time they had a taste of it in the capital.'

Either this practice of paying tribute in wine was long remembered, or it was resumed, for in the eighth century the poet Li Po refers in his *Pen ts'ao yen i* to the fact that 'The Hu people annually offered grape-wine.' There is another poem, devoted entirely to wine (grape wine) in this case, by a Tsin Dynasty poet of Tiu-hwan, Chan Hun-mao by name, now lost but referred to in a historical work. The point of this is that Tiu-hwan was on the great main road to Turkestan, where viticulture was seriously practised and not, as in China proper, just toyed with as an amusing but alien culture.

'The curious point is that the Chinese, while they received the grape in the era of the Han from an Iranian nation, and observed the habit of wine-drinking among Iranians at large, acquired the art of wine-making as late as the T'ang from a Turkish tribe in Turkestan. The Turks of the Han period knew nothing of grapes or wine, quite naturally as they were then restricted to what is now Mongolia, where soil and climatic conditions exclude this plant. [They do not, of course, but the rest is true.] Vine-growing as a matter of course is compatible solely with a sedentary mode of life; and only after settling in Turkestan where they usurped the heritage of their Iranian predecessors [end of fourth century A.D.], did the Turks become acquainted with the grape and wine as a gift of the Iranians. The Turkish word for the grape, Uigur *özüm* [other dialects *üzüm*], proves nothing along the line of historical facts . . . It is even doubtful whether the word in question originally had the meaning grape; on the contrary, it merely seems to have signified any berry, as it still refers to the berries and seeds of various plants. The Turks were simply epigones and usurpers, and added nothing new to the business of vine culture.

'In accordance with the introduction of the manufacture of grape-wine into China, we find this product duly noted in the *Pen ts'ao* of the T'ang [*Chen lei pen ts'ao*], published about the middle of the seventh century, and in the *Pen ts'ao shi i* by Chen Ts'an-K'i who wrote in the K'ai-yuan period (713–741). The *T'an pen ts'ao* also refers to the manufacture of vinegar from grapes. The *Pen ts'ao yen i*, published in 1116, likewise enumerates grape-wine among the numerous alcoholic beverages.' [Laufer]

Turning from China proper to the surrounding semi-barbarous peoples, it has already been made clear that peoples of Turkish stock from Mongolia, having conquered and settled in formerly Iranian territory by the end of the fourth century, had acquired the arts of viticulture and wine-making. But these arts, as Laufer says, were necessarily confined to those folk among the Mongols, Tartars, Huns and so forth who had settled down to a sedentary, farming way of life. Among the nomadic horsemen who continued to issue from Mongolia and Central Asia in hordes and hurl themselves against the great settled empires of both east and west, vineyards could not be cultivated; but wine could be and was imported by them, or exacted from their tributaries. A Chinese account of an embassy to the Tartars in the first half of the thirteenth century is of interest in this connection, for it establishes the use of glass wine-bottles more than a century before they came into use in Europe (see Chapter V). The ambassador was Sü-T'in, his master was Li Tsun of the southern Sung, and his embassy to the Great Khan Ogdai or Ogotai, heir to the empire of Jenghiz. Sü says that at the Great Khan's headquarters he was offered grape wine. It was not, he adds, made by the Tartars, but sent to them in glass bottles by Moslem tributary countries. One bottle contained about ten small cups. Sü says that in colour this wine resembled the juice of the southern Chinese persimmon. The juice of that fruit is, it seems, claret-red. Sü was warned by his hosts that if he drank too much of it, it might make him drunk. He does not say how he liked it: as usual among Chinese, it is treated simply as a curiosity.

It has been suggested elsewhere in this book that—making due allowance for the length-of-day factor (some plants being extremely sensitive in the matter of their ration of daylight at particular seasons)—temperate-zone plants can be cultivated at low latitudes where it is possible to set them at high altitudes, in other words, give them the climate they prefer by taking them up a mountain. Tibet, then, must be able to accommodate the vine in some parts of the country. It has unfortunately proved impossible to discover more than the bare fact that wine was not unknown there in the Middle Ages. In connection with the passage quoted above touching the bottled wine offered to a Chinese envoy visiting a Mongol horde, Laufer says: 'Naturally, it was a rare article in Mongolia, and for this reason we hear but little about it. Likewise in Tibet grape-wine was scarcely used, being restricted to religious offerings in the temples.'[12] Once again, then, the wine of the grape is to be found as an element of a religious rite. And it seems that, scarce though the wine might be, it was not imported for the temples, but grown in Tibet: for (see below), of the imported wines used in the capital of China during the Yuan, the Tibetan was evidently regarded as second only to that of the Qarā-Khoja.

One of the places visited by Marco Polo in his extraordinary journeys to and in China between 1271 and 1294 was Tai-yüan-fu, capital of Shan-si province. Among other splendid qualities—for this was a very great city—it had its vineyards, and this Marco Polo specifically recognizes as unique, thus: 'Vineyards are numerous, supplying a great abundance of wine; and although within all the jurisdiction of Ta-in-fu no other vines are found than those in the district immediately surrounding the capital, there is yet a sufficient supply for the whole province.' I have modified both the translation of this passage given by Yule and Cordier, which is in conformity with the principal edition of Ramusio, and that of the widely-read *Everyman* edition. Ramusio and Yule have 'wine'; Ernest Rhys, editor of the *Everyman* edition, has 'grapes', on the ground that the people made no wine and that Marco Polo must have been misunderstood at this point. I think he is wrong: for it is apparent from contemporary or near-contemporary Chinese sources that wine was made at this time, thus confirming the original reading.

# The Far East: Dionysus Rejected

86 *A bronze mirror back from the T'ang period (seventh century* A.D.*) is decorated with a Hellenistic vine motif which reached China by way of Persia. At this time Chinese attention was once again being drawn to the vine by contacts with Syria, but as usual, without lasting result.*

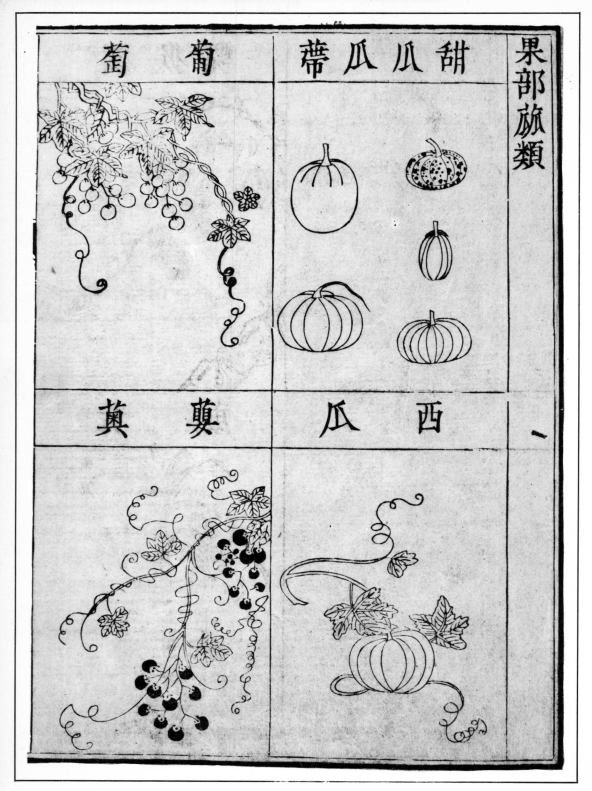

果部蔬類

葡萄　蒂瓜瓜甜

蕒蕢　瓜西

*A page from a sixteenth-century Chinese herbal, left, shows native vines (87).*
*Right (88), the vine forms the sides of a brush-pot from Korea.*
*Below (89) is a vine native to both China and Japan, Vitis thunbergii. In Japan the leaves are eaten as a vegetable, and formerly a parasite grub of the vine was baked and given to children as a remedy against convulsions.*

88

89

90 *A frieze on the Armenian church at Acht'amar, on Lake Van.*

*Detail of a frieze on the same church.*

*Armenia is geographically and viticulturally central to the Old World. The stone frieze (90, 91) and the Gospel illustration (92) are evidence of the vine's importance in this region, yet all the diffusion of the vine-and-wine culture was westward, and the introduction of the vine to the Far East was late and abortive.*

92　*A miniature from a fourteenth-century gospel shows Abraham entertaining angels under a vine.*

93 *The vine motif as it appears in northern India: the figure is faintly Indian but the composition is still Greek.*

*On the silver dish from the Punjab (94) the sinuous vine is part of a thoroughly Indian scene. Third or fourth century* A.D.

94

95   *In the late sixteenth century under the Emperor Akbar many vines were planted in the northern provinces. A painting made for the Emperor shows a Mughul vine-trellis.*

96

97

The Mughul Emperor Jahangir, though a
Moslem, was a notorious drinker. He had
himself portrayed on gold coins with a wine
cup in his hand (96) thus ignoring two pre-
cepts of Islam, and he owned fifty cups of
precious stone, such as this outstanding piece
of dark green jade (97). A verse inlaid in gold
reads: 'From King Jahangir the world obtained order./ The age was illuminated by
the ray of his justice./ From the reflection of
red wine may the colour of the jade cup
always resemble that of the ruby.'
A white jade cup combining the forms of
flower and ibex (98) was made for his son,
Shah Jahan.

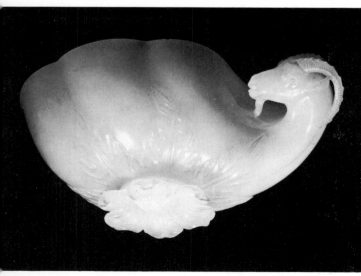

98

The fact appears in the Statutes of the Yüan Dynasty; moreover, 'The *Yin Shan Chen yao* written in 1331 by Ho Se-hwi contains this account: "There are numerous brands of wine; that coming from Qarā-Khoja (Ha-lo-hwo) is very strong, that coming from Tibet ranks next. Also the wines from P'in-yan and T'ai-yüan take the second rank. According to some statements grapes, when stored for a long time, will develop into wine through a natural process. The wine is fragrant, sweet, and exceedingly strong; this is the genuine grape-wine." The *Ts'ao mu tse*, written in 1378 by Ye Tse-k'i, contains the following information: "Under the Yüan dynasty grape-wine was manufactured in Ki-nin and other circuits of Shan-si Province [Marco Polo's San-si]. In the eighth month they went to the T'ai-han Mountain in order to test the genuine and adulterated brands: the genuine kind, when water is poured on it, will float; the adulterated sort, when thus treated, will freeze. In wine which has been long stored, there is a certain portion which even in extreme cold will never freeze, while all the remainder is frozen: this is the spirit and fluid secretion of wine. If this is drunk the essence will penetrate into a man's arm-pits, and he will die. Wine kept for two or three years develops great poison." '

Laufer, from whom I quote this passage, could make nothing of it: we can do a little better. First, if you freeze wine the alcohol does remain unfrozen, and some such method has been used in Canada, instead of distillation, to make apple-spirit, or, in Normandy, *calvados*, although I do not know exactly how it is done. As to the wine 'floating' on water, can it be that this wine was, in fact, brandy? It does not seem to me impossible that by the time of this dynasty the art of distillation may have reached the Chinese. Even so, the spirit would only float as the water began to sink as it froze.

The bit about armpits is the sort of nonsense which Chinese medicine abounds in. But as to wine developing poison with keeping, one cannot help thinking, again, of distillation. Inefficient distillation may result in the presence of poisonous alcohols, for example, fusil oil; long, still keeping will allow this to accumulate at the top of the bottle or jar, and it might well poison the drinker of the first glass from it. I recall that when I was a boy my father always inverted and shook a bottle of whisky before he opened it, 'to mix up the fusil oil'. I daresay that was nonsense, but he must have got the idea from some wine-merchant. I by no means insist that these 'wines' were, in fact, brandies. I merely suggest that it is not impossible. (See page 225 on distillation at about this time.)

In 1373 the first Ming Emperor agreed to accept the tribute of Tai-yüan in the form of grape wine. But—here again is the typical Chinese reaction to this wine—an order was made that tribute in that form was not to be offered again.

Although still more evidence could be offered for local viticulture and wine-making on a rather modest scale in some provinces of China—and even, in the sixteenth century (earlier documents are questionable or obscure), for distillation of brandy from grape wine before this new addition to the art was applied to the native rice wine—there is really no point in giving it; for it all amounts to the same thing: that many cultivars of *V. vinifera* were introduced to China, time after time, from *c.* 128 B.C. to modern times; that vineyards were planted; that they flourished; that the Chinese learned to make wine from the vintages; but that this art never assumed the slightest social or commercial importance, never 'took'. And that the only really satisfactory reason one can find for this is, to borrow from the myth, that Dionysus was incapable of a Chinese epiphany.

For India there is nothing much among the ancients. Theophrastus mentions the vine as growing there in the north; it may be he had heard of a native *Vitis*, or it may be that *V. vinifera* had been introduced. Strabo says that in Sindh there was a wild vine, and that wine was made from its grapes; this, also, could be true; but there is no reason to think that the Indian species were ever taken into cultivation. But one has to remember that the ancient Bactria was in part the modern Afghanistan; and that Bactria was one of the most ancient vinelands, and for many centuries an exporter of wine. It would be surprising if the vine had never spread into the neighbouring north Indian countries. And the more surprising fact, in support of the theme that viticulture and culture *tout court* are closely connected, is that although the cultivation of the vine did in fact, as Strabo notes, spread into parts of India, and although the high mountains of the north provide suitable country for vineyards even at that rather low latitude, it is certain that viticulture never really 'took' in India, any more than in China.

Climatically, there is no reason why vineyards should not do very well indeed in the mountainous region of the whole of northern India, if planted at suitable altitudes. The only satisfactory reason one can put forward to explain why Indians do not grow wine is that, like the Chinese, they do not want to; it is not proper for them. That the thing can be done is clear, for under the Emperor Akbar there was considerable planting of vines in the northern provinces (*plate 95*); and it may be that wine was made, for as I have noted in another chapter, among sophisticated, urban Moslems the Koranic ban on wine is very often disregarded. The most nearly viticultural country of India was Kashmir, and Chinese records of the grape being grown there go back to the second century B.C. Granting this to be true, it is nevertheless the case that India rejects the vine and its wine as decidedly as does China. Were it otherwise there are a thousand sites in the mountainous north, even north of the 30th degree of latitude which is probably the southern limit of the 'natural' habitat of *V. vinifera*, where vineyards would do well and whence fine vintages might be coming to us. But there it is: there is no mention of wine of the grape, or even of grapes, in Vedic literature. It even seems to be the case that the word *drāksā*, grape in Sanskrit, is a loan word.[13] An occasional Chinese reference to the use of grape wine locally in India, with the possible implication that the wine was locally grown, is of no more significance to my general argument than the reference in W. Ainslie's *Materia Indica* to the fact that the French had succeeded in growing some grapes and making some wine at Pondicherry: these are simply horticultural *tours de force*.

Finally, there is the case of Japan. When Laufer wrote his *Sino-Iranica* in 1919, or rather published it, for the writing was a work of years, he asked a Dr Tanaka, a Japanese at the United States Government's Bureau of Plant Industry, to contribute a note on the case of Japan. Dr Tanaka says that the early history of *V. vinifera* in Japan is obscure. But from the notes he gives of ancient Japanese dealings with the vine, it is clear that several species are involved and that they are being confused with each other; and that later they are confused with *V. vinifera*. The native vines of Japan are several. Of *V. coignetiae*, it seems that the Japanese ate the fruit and made wine with the grapes, while the leaves were fermented and dried to be smoked. These are late practices, however. The Japanese name for this vine is *Yamo-budo*. *V. thunbergii*, *Ebi-dzuru* in Japanese, of which the leaves are cooked and eaten as a green vegetable, is host to a grub which eats the pith of the canes; this grub used to be extracted, baked and given to children as a remedy against convulsions. *V. flexuosa* bears edible fruit. Finally, there is *V. saccharifera*, *Ama-dzuru*, whose fruit is eaten and whose leaves are chewed by children for their sugar. But in the case of all these vines it seems that only the wild harvest is taken; and none is properly in cultivation as a crop plant.[14]

Some ancient records which came to light in the province of Yamashi-ken, late in the nineteenth or early in this century, and which were published in a lecture by Viscount Fukuba, a celebrated pomologist, were of singular interest. According to these, in the year 1186 a peasant named Amenomiya Kageyu discovered a stand of vines growing on Mount Kamii-wasaki, near Kōfu. They were presumably in fruit or he would perhaps not have noticed them. He took some of these vines into cultivation. (In fact, it is not clear whether there was just one vine or many, which may be of importance.) The cultivation was successful and the vines were propagated; from them, in 1197, grapes described as 'choice' were presented by the grower to the Shogun Yoritomo. There is no question of this story being mere legend, for in the sixteenth century at the time of Takeda Harunobu a sword of honour was presented to the Amenomiya family by way of reward for the excellent grapes with which they provided their lord: Fukuba saw the deed of presentation, which had been preserved in the family; it was dated the equivalent of our 1549. Dr Tanaka says: 'The descendants of this historical grape-vine are still thriving in the same locality about the original grove, widely recognized as a true *Vitis vinifera*. According to a later publication of Fukuba there is but one variety of it.'

All of which is very odd. In the first place it is virtually inconceivable that *V. vinifera* should be really indigenous to any part of Japan: it would mean that there is a single, outlying occurrence of the species, separated from the known habitat by the entire width of Asia, many thousands of miles. The reason why this is impossible is that there is, in nature, no such thing as a species; we simply group together as such those individuals within a genus with are less unlike other groups than they are unlike each other. Variation occurs to a greater extent as you get further, geographically, from the principal centre of the species. Although some species are hemisphere-wide, and a very few almost world-wide, this is so only when there is a chain of the plants, with no gaps of considerable magnitude in their continuity. Moreover, since the grapes procured from this Amenomiya vine were apparently 'choice', the vine was no wilding, but either a cultivar, or a seedling of such which happened to be a good one.

The most likely explanations are two: first, that what Amenomiya found was an old, abandoned and forgotten planting from an earlier introduction, for example from China; or second, that the seedlings had risen from seed dropped in the faeces of a bird which had flown from China—a thing not impossible, I suppose, for grape seeds pass unharmed through the intestines of birds.

There were very much later deliberate introductions of vines from Europe and America: in a recent work[15] Nagao Tsuchiya says that large-scale viticulture in Japan began with the Meiji restoration in 1867. Both the Japanese government and such private enthusiasts of means as Zenpei Ozawa introduced more than a hundred varieties of the vine during the 1870s. A generation later, Zenbei Kawakami introduced about two hundred and eighty varieties from the United States, Germany and—which is curious —Korea. Again, during the Taishô era, 1912–26, between two and three hundred varieties of grape-vines were brought into Japan from France, Italy and elsewhere. In short, in that half-century something like six hundred varieties of the vine were introduced into Japan. And at the same time Zenbei Kawakami was starting on a programme of vine-breeding to produce hybrids for Japanese conditions.

Now these facts do not vitiate, they reinforce our argument: for what was happening in Japan at that time? The country was engaged, in a manner unique in history, in deliberately and self-consciously Westernizing its whole culture, or trying to. Technologically, this programme was a tremendous success, as we know, although 'success' may be, perhaps, an odd word to use of a policy which culminated in Hiroshima. But however hard a people may work to assimilate an alien technology they always, if they have an ancient culture of their own, reject the spirit of the culture they are borrowing. For example, the Far East has adopted Western industry and science, but it has rejected Christianity; and, on the whole, it has continued to reject Dionysus.

Technically the Japanese failure with grape-vines is curious. Growers had some success with such North American hybrids as 'Delaware', 'Concord', 'Campbell Early' and other 'foxy' *Vitis labrusca* derivatives. But they had none with *V. vinifera*, always excepting the Amenomiya seedling. All attempts to establish the *plants nobles* failed, as they had failed in North America, but without reference to phylloxera. Nagao Tsuchiya makes the surprising claim that this failure was, and is, caused by the heavy rainfall of Japan. Later he tells us that in the Yamanashi province, regarded as the most suitable for viticulture, the province of the Amenomiya grape, the mean annual rainfall is eight hundred millimetres. But the mean annual rainfall of, for example, the Gironde valley is about the same, and that of Dijon not much less. In Yamanashi, however, seventy per cent of this rainfall occurs during the growing season of the vines, and Tsuchiya is of the opinion that this is too much for the European vines. At all events, he and a colleague, Shôroku Izumi, built a glass roof (not a hothouse, simply a cover) over a planting of European vines, to keep the rain off them, and the success of the vines thus sheltered from the direct impact of rainfall demonstrated that the explanation given was the correct one.

It seems that the Amenomiya vine remains the only 'true' vine which can tolerate the climate of Japan, and from it the Japanese gather both wine grapes and grapes for dessert; but in this we can by no means find a Far Eastern epiphany of Dionysus, but only one more example of the Japanese genius for borrowing from the foreigner without conceding anything to his beliefs or his tastes. No Bacchae will ever dance in manic rage upon the slopes of Fuji.

# CHAPTER IX

# *Triumph and Disaster: North America*

THE STORY OF THE EURASIAN GRAPE-VINES in North America is threefold:
it begins with success; it continues with three centuries of disastrous failure;
it concludes in triumph. Out of what happened in North America came the
greatest disaster ever suffered by the viticulture of the Old World; and, by
way of compensation, the solution to the problem created by that disaster.

One of the problems which faced the Conquistadors in their conquests
and colonizations in America was that of providing a supply of wine for the
Mass. It should not be thought of as a minor problem; to the Spaniard of
the sixteenth century it was of the very first importance; it is literally true to
say that the Catholic European could not live his life with anything like
peace of mind in the total absence of *Vitis vinifera*. It was quite as important
to the sixteenth-century Spaniards as it ever was to the sectaries of Dionysus
or Flufluns. Hernán Cortés in particular was a man of fanatical piety who
had to be restrained by his own chaplains from destruction of idols at
dangerously inexpedient moments, and from mass-conversions of Aztec
and other natives of Anahuac, which his religious advisers knew to be
worthless.[1]

The ships from Spain carried a provision of wine, of course. It does not
seem (see below) that there were plantings of the vine in Hispaniola or
Cuba, the first parts of the Americas to be colonized. Most of the ships
coming from Spain brought wine from the Canary Islands, where all out-
ward-bound ships and most inward-bound stopped to water. The ships
were small and few, some were lost at sea, cargo space must have been extremely valuable and wine is a bulky cargo, although one way to bring it
was as ballast. It was, in short, obvious that the sooner vines were planted in
the New World, the better.

Although the conquest, even of the relatively small area of Mexico in the
immediate neighbourhood of the city, was not really complete until 1530,

Cortés first sent to Spain for vine-cuttings in 1522, at the same time as he
sent for other useful plants. It is from the following brief reference to this
transaction that we can, I think, conclude that there were then no vines to be
had in Hispaniola or Cuba: 'De las islas del America transporta [Cortés] el
ganado mayor y menor, las canes dulces, que el immortal Colon habia llevado a las
Canarias, con otras plantas que nacen en aquellos climas calientes. De España
[llevo] las vides, morales, peros y manzanos.'[2]

It is obvious that had Cortés been able to get his vines from the islands,
with that sugar-cane which 'the immortal Columbus had brought from the
Canaries', he would have done so. As it was, he had to fetch his cuttings, with
apples, pears and mulberries, from Spain. His agent there was his father
Martin Cortés. But the Conquistador did not stop at that; as soon as he
began the building of the new Mexico City, near the site of the great Venice-
style water-city of Tenochtitlán which he had more or less destroyed, he
advised the new Governor, who had been sent out from Spain because the
Council of the Indies did not trust him, to require all ships entering the port
of Vera Cruz from Spain to bring with them a quota of plants and seeds.[3]
But the only plant which he specifically ruled must be planted, while he
himself still had control of New Spain, was the vine. For he made *reparti-
mientos*, that is, grants of land and Indians as slaves to work it, conditional on
the planting of a quota of vines. This regulation was one of the by-laws of
the new Mexico City municipality, drawn up while that city was still building, in 1524.[4] For every hundred Indians of the *repartimiento*, a thousand
vines had to be planted, and they must, moreover, be the best obtainable.
Whether the planter had to fetch these from Spain or the Canaries, or
whether the authorities established a vine-nursery, does not appear.

Very curious is the attitude of the Conquerors to the native *Vites* of the
land they had conquered. Although the presence of these wild grape-vines
did suggest to them that the Old World vine would flourish in the new
country, they seem hardly to have considered taking them into cultivation.
The plenty and the great size of these wild vines is described by Toribio de
Motolinia in his *Historia de los Indios de Nueva España*. He was much struck
with their immense ramifications and vast root system; the grapes, he says,
are green; and he adds that some Spaniards made vinegar with them, and
others wine, but it was poor stuff. What were these vines? One can hardly
be sure, but certainly more than one species was native to the country. The

point is the extremely interesting use which the Spaniards did make of them. As far as I can discover no former writer on this subject has pointed out that, three centuries before the North Americans suggested grafting the European vine on to native vine-stocks as a means of combating phylloxera, the Spaniards in Mexico were using grafting as a means of increasing the new vineyards quickly; and were, in fact, under a legal obligation to do so. This is made quite clear by the promulgation of a municipal order by Cortés in 1524, immediately following the one I have already quoted (see note 4): '*Item. Que habiendo en la tierra plantas de vides de las de España en cantidad que se pueda hacer, sean obligados a engerir las cepas que tuvieren de la planta de la tierra, o de plantarlo de nuevo, so las dichas penas.*'

Motolina confirms that this order was widely obeyed, and that the usual method of propagating the European vine in Mexico, during the first years following conquest, was to graft them on to the native vines. It so happens that the same author enables us to say with precision when the first vineyard of such grafted vines was established: he wrote his account of the country in 1536. He describes the vineyard in question as being 'four leagues from this city'—that is, Pueblo de los Angeles—at a place called Val de Cristo. Pueblo de los Angeles was founded in 1530. By 1541 vineyards were established in Michoacan. Raphael Heliodoro Valle in his *Historia del Vino en Mexico* says, moreover, that in 1593 one Captain Francisco de Urdinola established the first *bodegas vinicolas* in New Spain, at the Hacienda de Santa Maria de las Parras. And by the beginning of the seventeenth century vineyards and bodegas were also established in Tehuacan, where '*dánse muchas y buenas uvas*'.

It is at least possible that Cortés' order that the Spanish vines should be grafted into the native wild vines saved the Mexicans from the failures and disaster which followed attempts further north in the United States to establish the Old World vine. Whether the range of *Phylloxera vastatrix* ever extended as far south, I am not sure. But if it did, the Spaniards had stumbled upon the right way to deal with that aphis.

Although in Mexico, as in Greece some thousands of years earlier, the reason for the first planting of the vine was a religious one, yet the planters were laymen, and the Dominican, Franciscan and Jesuit clergy could get their Mass-wine from their flock. Between 1522 and the end of the century vineyards, which were all of them small, were planted wherever possible in

the provinces of Mexico City, Puebla, Vera Cruz, Guadalajara, and the
present-day Morelia. No difficulties of the kind which were to thwart the
Old World vines in the north seem ever to have been met with. But when
it came to extending vine-planting to the remoter parts of the country in the
west, the missionaries, the pioneers in the task of opening up and settling
those parts, had to do their own planting: thus the trail of expanding Christianity in Mexico is also the trail of *Vitis vinifera*; there, as in Hellas, the plant
travelled with the cult. The principal agents of the work in Mexico were
the Jesuits. Father Burrus, S.J., of the Istituto Storico della Compagnia di
Gesu, writes:[5] 'The Jesuits in Mexico established their first missions among
the Indians in 1590. This was in a region that constitutes the present state of
Sinaloa. As it was several hundred miles from Mexico City where they
would have been able to secure Mass-wine, they were forced to plant their
own vines. This is evident from all the mission reports from this date to the
year of expulsion of the Jesuits from Mexico, namely 1767.'

The direction in which the Jesuits moved in establishing their chain of
missions across the wild country was north-west, and a small vineyard was
planted at each establishment. We should not visualize a field-type vineyard
such as we are familiar with; a few vines, trained on the mission buildings or
on a fence, and allowed to grow large, is more like it. By 1683 the Jesuits
had reached the west coast and crossed to Baja California: the apostle of the
Lower Californians was Father Kino and in his account of his mission to headquarters he writes: 'On the 21st [November 1683] . . . they brought us
grape-cuttings, small pomegranate and quince trees, which they requested
from Father Marquina and which we have planted in the hope that this land
of California will produce wine for the Mass.'[6]

This attempt at settlement failed; a second, in 1697, succeeded, and it
must have been after this date that Father Uguarte established the vine firmly
in Lower California, a little later than the date given by Guadalupe Vallejo
(see below). Thereafter the colonization of Lower California by the vine
carried by the missionaries proceeded as it had done in Mexico, until in
1769, this time in the hands of Franciscans, it reached Upper California (see
below).[7]

Such was the first phase, a success, in the introduction of the vine to
North America; it may also be assumed that in so far as it was also planted in
Central America, the case there was the same. Further north, however, in

the parts of America colonized by the English and French, the case was very different and far more complicated by difficulties.

The colonists who brought civilization from Asia to barbaric Greece, and their successors who carried it to Italy and France while the hellenized Carthaginians were doing a like office for Sicily, Spain and North Africa, had met with no natural obstacle to check their planting of the vine. *Vitis vinifera* was native to many of the regions they planted—that is, the native vine was of the same species as that from which the Asiatic cultivars derived, and subject, therefore, to the same evolutionary influences, including pests and diseases to which, consequently, both native wildings and alien cultivars had much the same resistance. The wild vines of Europe were hosts to many insects and fungi, but to none, probably, which were new to the cultivated vines of eastern Europe and south-west Asia, so that the new cultivated vines brought to the West by the Greeks and Carthaginians were adapted to resist such parasites.

Very different was the case of the European vines in North America, north of Arizona and east of the Rockies. There are, in that country, between the 30th and 50th parallels, about thirty species of the genus *Vitis* (see Appendix). Some of them were less evolved than the Old World vines, and especially than *V. vinifera*; others were very like it and capable of cross-breeding with it. But the point of greatest importance here is that the American native vines supported a number of parasitic organisms, of which three were important, quite unknown to Eurasia. They are an oidium, *Uncinula necator*, which colonizes the leaves and soft stems of the vine; a mildew, *Plasmopara viticola*, which does likewise and also attacks the berries; and an aphis, *Phylloxera vastatrix*, which in one of its life-phases attacks the leaves, in another the roots, of the vines. The point of importance is this: the American *Vites*, or most of them, having evolved in company with these three creatures during millions of years, had adapted themselves to tolerate them: the aphis and the two fungi were parasites, but did not become pathogens of the American wild grape-vines. The Eurasian vines had their parasites, too, such as the fungus called Grey Rot, and at least two members of the lepidoptera,[8] and to these they, too, could offer resistance and so tolerate them in the way that a dog tolerates its fleas, or a man his body lice in those countries where washing is not usual. But they had, of course, no resistance whatever to the vine parasites of the New World. It was the opinion of A. M. Negrul that since the vines of Eurasia and of North America sprang from a common ancestor, resistance to the oidium, mildew and phylloxera of the vine should be genetically potential in *V. vinifera*, and that if populations of that species were submitted for a sufficient time and in sufficient number to attacks by the three American parasites, then resistant individuals would emerge from which resistant strains could be propagated. This, however, would be a very long-term undertaking; nor is it certain that Negrul was right.[9]

Vines introduced to North America, north of Arizona and east of California, by colonists from Europe were sooner or later attacked by one or more of the American vine parasites, and died. It took about two-and-a-half centuries to convince the Americans that this was so, because they did not really know what was happening, they knew only that the vines would not flourish.

But the existence of wild, fruitful native American vines affected the introduction of viticulture in another way. It meant that while some settlers, usually of the higher social class, continued to believe that only the old Eurasian cultivars would be worth growing, and that the native grapes were not much more valuable than blackberries, other, more practical and less, as it were, literary men thought that it would be both easier and more profitable to domesticate wild native vines than to teach the Eurasian ones to live and bear fruit in America. If, as I believe, this difference of opinion was, with very important exceptions, roughly along 'class' lines, there is good reason for it: the settlers from northern Europe, of farming stock, or of peasant stock, or even from the towns, were not accustomed to drink wine anyway and did not know good from bad; those from southern Europe, being of the lower orders, were used to drinking wine, but of the roughest kind, and were not fastidious. On the other hand, settlers of gentle breeding found, and rightly found, the wine of the wild native grapes very nasty indeed; they not only wanted wine as good as they were accustomed to drink, they wanted it, I think, as one of the attributes of a civilization, of a classicism, for which, in their promised but still primitive and wild land, they were homesick. The mystique of wine as an attribute of ancient order and sophistication is as powerful as that of the ancient tongues or the ancient rules of architecture.

Of the many American *vites* there were two—not the two which subsequently became of importance to Europe in saving the vineyards from phylloxera—which made the greatest impression by their beauty and their spectacular fruitfulness, evidence of that bounty of God which settlers had expected in the New World; they were *Vitis labrusca* (*plate VIII*), most northerly of the wild vines with the possible exception of the Asiatic *V. amurensis*; and *V. rotundifolia*, which became known in the vernacular as the Scuppernong grape, a more southerly species especially plentiful and prosperous in the region of Maryland. The first European discoverer of America was an Icelander, Leif Ericsson the Lucky, whose voyage to what is now part of New England is recounted in the *Saga of Wineland the Good*, a poem which, without any doubt in my opinion, is a record of a real adventure and not a work of the imagination. The voyage took place in about A.D. 1000, and the most striking feature of America which was noted by Leif and his crew was the great plenty and fruitfulness of grape-vines. It is likely that these vines, for which the Vikings named the country they had found, and of whose grapes they shipped a cargo, were *V. labrusca*, unless the landfall was made much further south than Americanists believe to have been the case. The grapes of this species are, in the wild, small, growing on bunches of good form and medium size; in cultivation the grapes may be purplish-red and even white, for among cultivars grown in isolation recessive characters often receive the opportunity to emerge. These grapes are sweet and juicy, but they are marred for most palates by a kind of mustiness, or 'foxiness' (*gout de fox*), as it is called. This flavour, often modified to be less offensive, occurs in the cultivated derivatives of this vine, such as Noah, Isabella, Strawberry Grape, Framboise, and many others, both strains and hybrids too; for the character is a dominant.

The Scuppernong grape makes an enormous plant, bearing vast quantities of fruit, clambering through and over even large trees. The first written account of the impression made by the species on Europeans appears to be that of two members of the ill-fated party sent by Walter Raleigh to settle Roanoke Island and the vicinity (*plate 99*). Their names were Amidas and Barlow and the date 1558, and it was their impression that, '. . . in all the world the like abundance is not to be found'.

Even before this date, however, it seems that the European vine had been planted on North American soil. It is remarkable evidence of the hold that wine and vine had on the European imagination (for there are, after all, other means to the mere slaking of thirst, as there are many other intoxicants) that the first idea of party after party of arriving colonists was to plant vineyards, like Noah after the Flood. It is, perhaps, not surprising: for five or six thousand years wine had been of religious significance to all the peoples of Eurasia. Such a tradition cannot have failed to mark the soul of the European; but it is curious that it should have been as powerful in its influence on Swedes as on Italians.

We cannot know for certain who was the very first European to plant a vine from the Old World in North America; but the first on record was a Spaniard and no doubt his plants came by way of Mexico where, as we have seen, the vine was already established. In 1566, a Spanish captain named Menendez destroyed the Huguenot colonies which had been settled on the coast of what is now Florida, killing men, women and children as was the amiable custom of his countrymen. He then founded the Spanish colony of Augustine, really no more than a mission with satellite missions up and down the coast. From one of these, Santa Elena, the commanding official wrote a letter to the King of Spain on the progress of the settlement; his name was Bartolomé Martinez and among other things he claimed: '. . . I planted with my own hands grape-vines . . . etc. . . .' To me it seems likely that since the massacred Huguenots had been French from La Rochelle, they had already planted their vine; but neither their plantings, nor those of the Spanish, had any consequences and no doubt the vines perished.[10]

From the earliest times of settlement there were, as I have said, men who thought that the wise policy for the provision of wine would be to domesticate the native grapes. John Hawkins, the navigator, ship-builder and slaver, was one of the first to suggest this. Lord Delaware, first official backer of viticulture in North America, was of the same opinion: writing to the Board of the Virginia Company in London, from James Towne, in 1616, he said: 'In every brake and hedge, and not far from our pallisade gates, we have thousands of goodly vines, running along and cleaving to every tree, which yield a plentiful grape in their kind. Let me appeal then, to knowledge if these natural vines were planted, dressed and ordered by skilled vinearoons whether we might not make a perfect grape and fruitful vintage in short time.'[11]

This interesting suggestion was not adopted by the Company, which instead sent to Virginia, in 1619, a party of French *vignerons* and a collection of French vine varieties; it was a sensible thing to do at the time; nobody could possibly foresee the difficulties which were to be encountered, and other Old World plants were flourishing like mad in America. Vineyards were planted, some of them of considerable size, up to ten acres probably. The vines soon began to wilt and perish; the English settlers quarrelled with the French; there were several seasons of bad weather, the surviving vines were attacked by fungus diseases. What was left of this experiment was totally destroyed, with the experimenters, in the Indian massacre of 1622.

But the Virginians did not give up; seventeen years after the massacre the Assembly of the Colony passed the following Act: 'All workers upon cane and tobacco shall this spring plant five vyne plants per pol, and next year before the first day of March, 20 per pol, upon penaltie to forfeit one barrel of corne for every one that shall make default.'

Passing, a couple of decades later, from punishments to rewards, the same Assembly offered a bonus of ten thousand pounds of tobacco for every two tuns of wine made from grapes grown in Virginia. But not only were the difficulties discouraging; wine-growing offered little prospect of profit in the face of competition from cheap, imported Madeira which one colonial historian calls 'a noble strong drink'.

Another determined attempt to establish viticulture in America was made in 1710 by the then Governor, Alexander Spotswood. He planted a colony of German Rhinelanders, to whom land was freely given in Spotsylvania County on condition that they cultivate grapes and make wine, which they did, perhaps with European vines, although the point is not clear and they may have planted *V. rotundifolia*. At all events, these Germans met with some success for: 'The Governor's "red and white Rapidan" became well known and graced his table so often that "his dinners were pleasing to all his friends".'[12]

In other parts of the North American colonies attempts were being made to cultivate the native grapes. The first Dutch settlers in New Jersey do not seem to have planted vines. But the Swedes, who founded a colony at Wilmington in about 1630, although they planted no European grapes, regularly vinified the harvest of wild native vines, making their wine much as the ancient people of what is now Soviet Armenia must have done it some six or seven thousand years before. But the policy was a stop-gap; as soon as the apple-trees which the Swedes had planted were bearing, they went over to cider.

In due course, too, the Dutch of what later became New York made an attempt or several attempts to establish vineyards. Two Dutch visitors, Jacob Dankaerts and Peter Sluyter, noted in 1679:[13] 'Although they have several times attempted to plant vineyards and have not immediately succeeded, they nevertheless have not abandoned hope of doing so by and by, for there is always some encouragement although they have not as yet discovered the cause of failure.' And the English, when they took control of the province and called it New York, ignored Dutch experience and again set about trying to grow vines. In 1664 Governor Nicholls, the first English Governor, using typically English seventeenth-century economic methods, gave a monopoly (or perhaps, rather, sold it) to one Paul Richards, to grow grapes and make wine which would be free of excise. Richards was given the privilege of himself taxing any other settler who planted vines, at the rate of five shillings per annum per acre. Once again, the vines failed: unknown to the vinearoons, as Lord Delaware called them, the phylloxera, the vine-louse, was busy consuming the roots of the vines as fast as they were planted.

At the outbreak of the Revolution there were only a few, very small, private garden vines left in the province.

What, then, was the 'some encouragement' mentioned by Dankaerts and Sluyter, and which must have been the explanation of why the vinearoons kept trying again and again? Since there are some soils in which the vine-louse cannot survive; since in any case it does not rise to pandemic proportions excepting in the presence of dense populations of *V. vinifera*; since cultivars vary a little in their resistance to the louse; since the fairly near neighbourhood of wild American vines was necessary to communicate the infestation—for these reasons there were, here and there and from time to time, successes with the European vine which made would-be vinearoons believe that what other men could do, they could do, and that it was all a matter of soil, local climate, skill, variety.

It must have been such small and local successes which blinded the settlers and colonists to the real trouble, for they were usually experienced farmers or gardeners.

# Triumph and Disaster: North America

99 'The Arrival of the Englishmen in Virginia'. A sixteenth-century map of the Roanoke area, showing native vines growing on the mainland (upper right). An observer wrote that '. . . in all the world the like abundance is not to be found'.

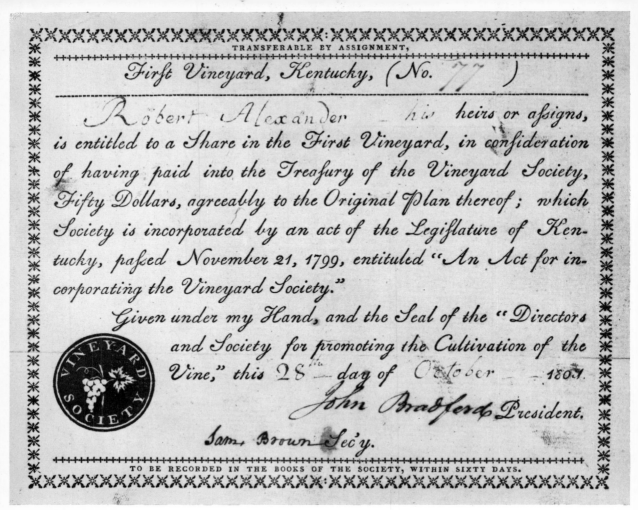

First Vineyard, Kentucky, (No. 77 )

Robert Alexander — his heirs or assigns, is entitled to a Share in the First Vineyard, in consideration of having paid into the Treasury of the Vineyard Society, Fifty Dollars, agreeably to the Original Plan thereof; which Society is incorporated by an act of the Legislature of Kentucky, passed November 21, 1799, entitled "An Act for incorporating the Vineyard Society."

Given under my Hand, and the Seal of the "Directors and Society for promoting the Cultivation of the Vine," this 28th day of October 1801.

John Bradford President.

Sam. Brown Sec'y.

TO BE RECORDED IN THE BOOKS OF THE SOCIETY, WITHIN SIXTY DAYS.

100

The wine yielded by the native north American vines was not good, and attempts were made again and again to introduce European varieties. In eastern and central areas at least, all these attempts mysteriously failed. One such attempt was made by the Kentucky Wine Society (100), founded in 1798 by a Swiss named Dufour who believed, strangely, that wine 'promoted temperance'. During the nineteenth century the defeated wine-growers turned again to the native varieties. Nicholas Longworth had transformed reaches of the Ohio River into 'the Rhine of America' (101), and after his fifteen hundred European plants had died, like everyone's else's, he tried what proved to be the first good native cultivar: Catawba. By 1859 there were two thousand acres of vineyard about Cincinnati, and a poem by Longfellow celebrated 'Catawba Wine' (102). This solution was not the final one: the problem of the parasite phylloxera was to be overcome at last by the grafting of Old World vines on New World rootstocks and by the breeding of resistant hybrids (see Epilogue).

101

102

The early colonists of California were Spanish-Mexican Jesuit missionaries, and the first European vines were trained around mission houses. The Franciscan Junipero Serra (103) planted Old World vines at the San Diego Mission in 1769, and found that they flourished exceedingly. The oldest winery in California is the small building behind the San Gabriel Mission (104), dating from 1771. Here the grapes were pressed by Indians on a stone floor, and the juice drained through a hole in the wall into an open pool of adobe (to the right of the building) whence it was carried to the fermenting tanks in leather bags.

103

104

*General Vallejo (105), founder of the
towns of Sonoma and Santa Rosa, last
Mexican commandant of California
and first senator elect from Sonoma
County. Vallejo revived wine growing
at Sonoma Mission in 1836, and in
1851 he established his fine vineyard-
estate of Lachryma Montis (106). His
prosperous vineyards attracted other
growers to the region.*

105

106

## 107

*The father of Californian viticulture was a close friend of Vallejo: Count Agoston Haraszthy (108). At his Buena Vista vineyard at Sonoma (107, 109) Haraszthy introduced the best vine varieties from Europe, and revolutionized Californian viticultural techniques, opening the way for the extraordinary success of California as a wine and vine land. Above, the grape harvest, with Haraszthy's large white house in the centre background.*

108

109 'Champagne' corking at Haraszthy's Buena Vista vineyard in the early 1870s. The wicker baskets in the foreground were woven by Chinese employees of the vineyard society. The building at the rear is the brandy distillery.

110  *The century-old Trinity grape-vine at San Gabriel, California, one of the largest in the world.*

An interesting and valuable source of information about early American viticulture is to be found in the writings of William Penn. Penn, whose colonies were the best managed, the most quickly and completely successful, advertised the good work in Britain by writing a series of pamphlets to encourage emigration. In his *Letter from William Penn to the Committee of the Society of Free Traders* (1683), he describes some of the native grapes, for instance, 'the great Red grape called by ignorance the Fox Grape; also a white kind of Muskatel'.[14] And again, 'a little black Grape like the cluster-Grape of England'. The red grape I cannot identify; the white must have been one of the muscadines, perhaps *V. rotundifolia*, introduced from further south or growing north of its chief habitat; the little black grape could have been one of a dozen species but was perhaps *V. labrusca*; or there are other vines native to Pennsylvania.

Penn had with him a Frenchman named André Doz who had some knowledge of viticulture, and in 1683 he planted a vineyard on the east bank of the Schuylkill River, in what was called the Manor of Springettsbury (later Lemon Hill, Fairmount Park in Philadelphia). Apparently he planted two hundred acres before he came to grief. By way of rent for the land he paid 'One hundred vine cuttings yearly on demand.'

Penn was not sure whether: '. . . it were better to fall to Fining the Fruits of the country, especially the Grape, by the care and skill of Art, or send for foreign stems and sets'. And he declared that if God gave him life he would try both and hope that: 'the consequences would be as good wine as any European countries of the same latitude do yield'.[15]

This intention was not realized: he let Doz over-persuade him to plant French vines and ignore the natives. Anyone who has tasted wine of the American wild vines will not blame Doz; he was after all not French for nothing. He knew nothing of the local diseases of the vine nor of its pests. He could see wherever he went that such other Old World fruits as the peach were flourishing, so that even the Indian settlements had a glut of peaches. The consequence was, as usual, failure; the vines slowly but surely perished.

There is no real need to pile up more instances, although further attempts to establish the Eurasian vines will be noticed below. By 1700 it should have been clear that while the attempt to introduce wine as a local product could succeed if the native vines were cultivated, the attempt to establish the vines of France, Germany, Italy and Spain had failed and would continue to fail.

In the southern states, as they were to be, the story was much the same. And it is at least possible that in the Deep South there was an added difficulty. *Vitis vinifera* is a deciduous plant. As explained in the Prologue, where the winter temperature fails to fall below about 45 degrees Fahrenheit, the whole cycle of life is disturbed. Leaf-fall may not occur properly, dormancy may be imperfect, axillary buds may start into growth. In the Deep South, and especially if the vines introduced were of northern European strains and not those which had already been acclimatized to Mexico and had in any case come from southern Europe or from the Canary Islands, would-be vinearoons may well have encountered the difficulties of growing a temperate-zone woody, deciduous plant in sub-tropical or near-tropical conditions.

The first English settlement in Georgia was made in 1733 at what is now Savannah and among the first European plants to be imported were grape-vines. Probably with due regard to the climate, they were imported from Zante—possibly with the idea of making currants rather than wine, at all events the Zante grape was a currant-grape. Within four years it was clear that these vines had failed, but it is possible that this was at least in part owing to want of care, for the colony was much disturbed by internecine strife and the gardens were neglected. A few years later two of the greatest men in American history were trying to solve the problem. George Washington, who was landscape-gardening Mount Vernon in the English manner of the times—in fact he was among the earliest (for Hoare's masterpiece at Stourhead was not finished until late in the 'forties)—took a great interest in all kinds of fruit-trees and planted timber and ornamental trees in considerable number. One of his difficulties was that his slaves were not to be trusted excepting under the master's eye, and when he was not there they neglected the watering of newly-planted specimens with fatal consequences. On 16th December 1771 Washington wrote in his diary: 'Finished planting the Grape Cuttings in the Inclosure below the Garden—the first twenty-nine rows of which, reckoning from the side next the Spring, are the Winter Grape, the other five are the Summer Grape of tolerable good taste and Ripening in October.'

These vines were probably natives. Thomas Jefferson, at Monticello, was likewise a great 'improver', in fact his mania for improving together with a general carelessness in matters of business was to ruin him and leave him poor in his old age. He planted vineyards and he made wine from his grapes. Like so many other Americans of education—that is, under the spell of the ancient classical traditions—he turned his attention to the vines of the Old World, and he brought his vine-dressers and the vine-cuttings from Tuscany. Vine-cuttings taken in late autumn and correctly packed will live for six months if they are kept cool and damp, and probably much longer, so that there was no difficulty in transporting them. Vineyards were planted on a hillside near Charlottesville. Failure was so soon obvious that no wine was ever made from these Tuscan vines, nor is this surprising, for the place was surrounded by wild native vines every one of which was probably a source of phylloxera and fungus disease. With the failure of the Tuscan grapes the Italian vinearoons were turned on to making wine from the harvest of wild grapes. It seems that some of this was sent to friends as the product of Jefferson's own vintage but, as Hedrick[15] remarks dryly, 'he continued to stock his own cellar with French wines'.

Jefferson's last contribution to the viticulture of his country was to recommend, in a letter to one of the three greatest American pioneers of the vine (see below), John Adlum, the planting of a variety which is of great interest as being almost certainly the first, fortuitous, hybrid between an American species and *V. vinifera*. It was not recognized at the time, although by 1808 (see below) at least one expert had spotted the fact. This variety was called 'Alexander', or sometimes 'Tasker's Grape': 'I think', Jefferson wrote, 'it will be as well to push the culture of that grape without losing time and efforts in search of foreign grapes which it will take centuries to adapt to our soil and climate.' Jefferson is also reported to have said that the wine of the Catawba grape (see below) was 'worthy of the best vineyards of France'. This grape was to make Ohio viticulture so prosperous that a century later that state was even exporting wine to California, although by then Californian viticulture was producing very considerable quantities of good wine from European vines. If Jefferson said anything of the kind, then it demonstrates either an excess of patriotism or the decline of his taste.

This brings us into the nineteenth century, and to the date when most of the men interested in the subject had at last come to the conclusion that it was a waste of time and money to persist in trying to establish the European vines in North America. However, a final official effort was made in the third decade of the century by the State Legislature of Maryland. It is fairly obvious that men accustomed to drink the wines of France, Germany, Spain and Italy could not relish the native American wines. A Society for the Promotion of the Vine having been started in Maryland, it was given incorporation rights in 1828. Its object was '. . . to carry on experiments in the cultivation of both European and native grapes'. By 1831 there were as a result numerous vineyards about Baltimore, with plantings of both *V. vinifera* cultivars and natives. That the former failed is quite certain. For whereas, for example, the greatest of the American hardy-plant nurseries— that of William Prince, himself a great planter of vines and author of *A Treatise on the Vine*—began by concentrating on European varieties in both nursery beds and catalogue, the nursery ended by offering chiefly two native cultivars, Isabella and Catawba, both of which appear to be *V. labrusca* derivatives, although I am myself familiar only with Isabella. It does not appear that the European varieties were altogether dropped from the commerce of this nursery, and they were still being offered in newspaper advertisements long after it must have been clear that they were bound to fail. Prince doubtless had stocks to get rid of; and in any case, as I have already said, it is likely that here and there and from time to time gardeners had a success with them.

Nor is this the only evidence of final failure. A Belgian settler named André Parmentier had set up as a nurseryman on the Hudson and offered European vines for sale. Parmentier's influence on American horticulture was to be very considerable; and he, too, gave up his European vines and ended by selling only or chiefly the two native cultivars, Isabella and Catawba. One of his principal customers was a man named Robert Underhill. He was persuaded to plant a vineyard of European grapes at Croton Point on the Hudson. All these vines died, yet as he had by then become an enthusiast, he replanted, but this time with Catawbas and Isabellas, and after a few years had seventy-five acres under these vines—the first large and wholly successful vineyard in the United States. Underhill's wine was sold in New York City; it was almost certainly 'foxy', and more or less disagreeable to the educated palate.

In 1818 a German named Eichelberger began viticulture near York, Pennsylvania, and succeeded so well that according to Hedrick, York became a considerable viticulture centre in the following decades. With what appears to have been shrewdness rather than strict honesty, Eichelberger called the vine variety which he cultivated Black Madeira, a name which had the glamour of the Old World vine; and, later, York Madeira. But Prince, the greatest of American nurserymen and by far the most competent ampelographist of his day on that side of the Atlantic, identified the plant as Alexander, the hybrid variety which Jefferson had commended.

It is a singular tribute to the great prestige of the Old World vine that even centuries of failure with it could not entirely discourage new attempts to grow it. Partly, as I have said, this was owing to the inferior quality of the native grapes and their wines; but the mystique of wine had a lot to do with it. The most expert of unfavourable opinions could not quite discourage nurserymen and planters. In about 1770 a French-Canadian settler in Orange County, New York, a man later responsible for major advances in American horticulture and in the study of the American flora (among other things, he brought the great botanist André Michaux to America), writing of the various home-made drinks which farmers provided for their families in his part of the country—cider, country wines, brandies of peach and other fruits—roundly declared that wine could not be made unless from the wild grapes of the woods. Yet still men went on trying.

Until the second decade of the nineteenth century the planting of the native vines was, as it were, a negative operation: men turned to them because the European vines had failed them. The first man to take a positive line with the natives was John Adlum, who was responsible for the discovery, propagation and wise planting of the first really good native cultivar, the Catawba vine already mentioned. Adlum was a Pennsylvanian by birth but he lived at Georgetown, D.C. Although Hedrick gives him credit for *discovering* this vine, he did so only in the sense that an impresario *discovers* a great artist; that is, having planted it among others in an experimental vineyard in the second decade of the century, he distinguished it as superior and brought it to the notice of the horticultural world. It is supposed that this vine came, in fact, from the Catawba River country in North Carolina. A number of species are native to that country, outstanding being *V. rotundifolia*. In Salley's *Narratives of Early Carolina 1655–1708* there is a passage by Thomas Ashe which runs: 'Vines of diverse rank bearing both black and grey grapes, grow climbing their highest trees, running and overspreading their lower branches; five kinds they have already distinguished, three of which by transplantation and if well cultivated they own, will make very good wine; some of which has been transported for England which by the best Pallates was well approved of and more is daily expected, 'tis not doubted, if the planters as industriously prosecute the Propagation of Vine-yards as they have begun, but Carolina will in a little time prove a magazine and a staple for wines to the whole West Indies; and to enrich their Variety, some of the Proprietors and Planters have sent them the Noblest and Excel-lentest Vines of Europe, *viz* the Rhenish, Clarret, the Muscadel and Canary, etc., His Majesty, to improve so hopeful a Design, gave those French we carried over their Passages free for themselves, Wives, Children, goods and Servants, they being most of them well experienced in the nature of the Vine, from which direction doubtless the English have received and made considerable advantages in their improvements.'[16]

This account is confirmed by that of Samuel Wilson (*An Account of the Province of Carolina*, London, 1682) who to the above information and a reference to the suitably sandy nature of the soil adds: '. . . and further from the sea, rock and gravel on which very good grapes grow naturally, ripen well, and together, and very lushious in taste, insomuch as the French Protestants who are there, and are skilled in wine, do no way doubt of pro-ducing great quantities and very good.'[17]

Here, then, we have a province rich in native *vites* and at the same time planted with several of the *cépages nobles* which, although they cannot have long survived the near neighbourhood of the natives, might have flowered sufficiently often to give and receive pollen, thus giving rise to one or more hybrid seedlings. To the best of my knowledge the American parent cannot have been *V. rotundifolia*; it must have been one of the *Euvites* with $n = 20$ chromosomes. But from some such chance cross might have come Catawba, if, indeed, it is a hybrid and not rather a 'phenotypical' variant of an American species.

One of the pioneers of viticulture to whom Adlum sent Catawba was Nicholas Longworth, who was born in New Jersey but had settled (1803) in Cincinnati, which at that time was a village of log-houses with eight hundred inhabitants. He was a lawyer, but he made a large fortune by buying land which became valuable. (The appreciation of value was, in fact, astounding: it seems that every five dollars invested in land was fifteen hundred dollars twenty years later, and Longworth was a multi-millionaire when such monsters were rare.) In 1828 Longworth retired from business and proceeded to turn local reaches of the Ohio river into the 'Rhine of

America' (*plate 101*). Like so many others he started his vineyards with European grapes, importing twenty varieties. All fifteen hundred imported plants were soon dead and he turned to planting Catawba. By 1859 he and his imitators had two thousand acres of vineyards about Cincinnati to their credit, not to mention Longfellow's poem 'Catawba Wine' which, like the beverage it celebrates, is not of the highest excellence. The point is, however, that the right solution had been found; or at all events, one of them: the prosecution of viticulture with plants naturally resistant to the native parasites of the vine.

A more advanced and ultimately better solution was of course to cross-breed some of the best natives with *V. vinifera* vines of high quality, in the hope of producing a hybrid more resistant than the European parent and bearing better fruit than the American parent. It had taken thousands of years to produce the best Old World wine varieties; by such cross-breeding the Americans could get at least some of the advantages of that long labour of skill and time. Adlum completed the good work which he had started by writing in 1823 his *The Cultivation of the Vine*, a handbook on the correct planting of the natives and on the vinification of their fruit. But the credit for taking the first steps towards the final solution, the production of good hybrids, was another's; or rather it belongs to several others.

The Alexander vine already mentioned (and commended by Thomas Jefferson as early as 1798) was found in the wild by a gardener named John Alexander and first cultivated in the garden of his employer, Governor John Penn. This vine had morphological characters which make it certain that one of its parents was a *vinifera* and the other *V. labrusca*. Its fruit was 'foxy', as was that of all subsequent *labrusca* derivatives; but it was a step in the right direction, taken by Nature herself, as it were, by way of example to man. Alexander was the only one of such hybrids to be found and recognized at the time; it is possible that there were others in existence. At all events, in 1808, Bernard M'Mahon, a well-known and clever horticulturist who published *The American Gardeners Callendar*, described in that work fifty-five varieties of the European grapes, and four American of which three were, he says, *vinifera* × *labrusca* seedlings.

M'Mahon was not only the first to advocate hybridization of grape-vines as the right policy for American viticulture; he has an even greater title to fame and to the respect of all wine-lovers. Not much less than a century before the millions of acres of ancient and new vineyards in the whole zone of Old World viticulture were threatened with extermination by the phylloxera which had been unwittingly carried across the Atlantic (see Epilogue), M'Mahon was writing that, as a means to cultivating the fine Old World grapes in America: 'I would suggest the idea of grafting some of the best European kinds on our most vigorous vines which no doubt would answer a very good purpose.'[18] Whether he tried it does not appear: probably not, or we should have heard about it; nor is it clear whether he had actually examined the roots of *vinifera* vines which had perished in American soil and found, not, perhaps, the cause of the trouble, that is the aphis—but at least the immediate cause of death—that is the damage done by the aphis.

The first hybrids to be produced by deliberate crossing were the work of Dr W. W. Valk of Flushing, who, in 1845, successfully crossed Black Hamburgh with the *labrusca* derivative Isabella. Two things should be made clear: first, he was not the first ever to cross grape-vines deliberately; during the eighteenth century several head gardeners of great English estates had done so, most notably William Speechley, author of an excellent *Treatise on the Vine*.[19] Secondly, the technique now used for this work had not yet been attempted: only modern vine-breeders have overcome the difficulties, inherent in the extreme smallness of the vine flower, of removing the corolla, castrating the flower, and leaving only the stigma intact, to receive a chosen alien pollen and be covered against chance pollination. The method used by Valk was more likely that of twining the two vines to be crossed together, perhaps under glass, and getting the pollen clouds thoroughly mixed, so that cross-pollination might occur. It was very chancy but there were usually a few successes. More important than Valk in the same field, and very little behind him in time, was F. S. Rogers of Salem, Massachusetts. Rogers worked with a *labrusca* cultivar called Carter as the seed-bearing parent; and with Black Hamburgh and Chasselas doré as the pollen parents: he was probably the first man ever to use the scientific method described above. His first crosses were made in 1851 and they gave rise to forty-five hybrid seedlings of which no fewer than thirteen were judged worthy of introduction to commerce, an astonishing figure; several of these are still in cultivation. It is odd that Rogers was never able to repeat this success. His seedlings are not good by European, nor by modern American, standards; but he had shown what could be done. It took a surprisingly long time, however, for

breeders to learn to eschew *V. labrusca* as a parent; it never fails to communicate its 'foxiness' to its offspring. Rogers' example was followed, and by
1900 there were about two thousand hybrid vine varieties in cultivation in
the United States.

It is a curious and perhaps rather mortifying fact that many, and perhaps
most, of the finest fruit plants produced by hybridization have been the result
of chance and not design. The strawberries are exceptional, but cases in point
are the apples Cox's Orange and Granny Smith and the pear Doyenné du
Comice. The Concord vine, for long and perhaps still the most important
variety commercially in North America, was another of this category of
chance hybrids. A seedling vine which sprang up in the garden of E. W.
Bull of Concord, Massachusetts, bore fruit in 1843. Seeds from its grapes
were planted; one of the seedlings was Concord, as it was named when put
into commerce, and in the past century more Concord vines have been
planted in North America than all other native varieties together; and more
wine made from its grapes. In a sense the final solution to the problem of
viticulture in America was found with this grape; but it is not altogether
final—no solution is—since it is being replaced in American vineyards by
new American, and by the very good modern French, hybrids.

Before coming to the very different tale of California, something should
be said of the diffusion of viticulture in others of the eastern and middle
states. The first vineyard ever planted west of the Allegheny mountains was
that of Colonel George Morgan, a noted gardener and pomologist of New
Jersey, who in 1796 moved to western Pennsylvania and planted there, among
other things, a vineyard with 3,480 cuttings of European vines, from Bordeaux, Burgundy, Champagne and the Cape. Presumably they failed; there
is no record. In western New York grape-growing on a commercial scale
was started about 1853 by a German named Reisinger, but it did not develop
into an industry of importance until after the Civil War. Only native vines
were planted: the wine made was, and still is, a sparkling white sold as
'champagne'—which is not regarded by the law as a fraudulent practice in
either Great Britain or the United States (though United States law does
require that the bottle bear on the label the place of origin).

One of the most curious incidents in the history of American viticulture
was the Kentucky/Indiana enterprise of a Swiss do-gooder named Jean-
Jacques Dufour. This worthy man had read, in the Swiss newspapers,

accounts of the fighting in the Revolutionary war. And what struck him most was the complaints of French officers enlisted under the Marquis de La Fayette that there was no wine to be had in America. In his later-written *The Vine-dresser's Guide* he says that he reasoned that grape-growing must be possible at latitudes in America equivalent to those of the principal European centres of viticulture; and that he believed the drinking of wine to be the best promoter of temperance by reducing the drinking of spirits.[20]

Dufour went to America, landing there shortly after the founding of the United States. He spent about three years looking for suitable vineyard sites and not finding what he wanted. He says that vineyards of European vines had all perished and gone back to bush; and that he hardly saw a dozen healthy *viniferas* in the country. At last he did find a small plantation of healthy European vines, the property of a Frenchman named Legaux at Spring Mill on the Schuylkill river. Apparently the vines had been imported from South Africa. And with some of these Dufour began his vineyard in the Great Bend of the Kentucky river, about twenty miles from Lexington. In 1798 he founded the Kentucky Wine Society (*plate 100*), and a year later in Philadelphia he bought 10,000 cuttings in 34 varieties, all European. In 1801 seventeen members of his family joined him, to found a colony.

As usual the vines failed: their lingering death implies that the roots had been attacked by phylloxera. Fungus diseases may also have played a part. But, also as usual, soil and climate were blamed, and the whole colony shifted to a new situation on the Ohio, in Indiana, later the town of Vevay. Here, too, the vines failed, excepting some plants of Alexander, and the Cape vines. It is extraordinary that no experienced fruit-grower suggested grafting: after all, the practice of grafting fruit plants was by then about four thousand years old. But as I have noted, that was first suggested by M'Mahon six years after the final failure of the Dufour experiment, the only case in history, as far as I am aware, of a vineyard being planted as a means to the promotion of temperance.

By 1800, then, the failure to establish *V. vinifera* culture in eastern and middle America had become clear. By 1850, after three centuries of trial and failure, attempts had been abandoned; and viticulture had been successfully established by the domestication, hybridization and large-scale planting of the native American vines. Meanwhile the European vines were flourishing extravagantly in California.

The aphis *Phylloxera vastatrix* is confined by its nature to the temperate zones, to certain kinds of soil, and geographically is checked in its extension by certain features of country, for example by high mountains or by swamps. Finally, it must have a *Vitis* species to live on. Its life-cycle is extremely complex: in one phase it reproduces its kind sexually; in another, parthenogenetically. Again, in one phase it lives upon the leaves, in galls which it forms by burrowing; and in another, on the roots where similar galls are formed. For reasons we need not enter into, its principal 'attack' in the case of the American vines is on the leaves; and in the case of the Old World vines, on the roots. These roots have not developed the power to cicatrize the wounds made in the course of forming the galls; consequently, when attacked by the aphis, they rot.

The two principal fungus diseases of the vine, native to America, require moisture in which to propagate themselves and grow; and they are not active below a certain minimum temperature. In perfectly dry conditions they cannot flourish, for there must be a film of water on the leaves of the vines. Thus in very dry summers the incidence of these diseases in the vineyards of Europe is low, as it is in very cool summers; in warm, moist summers, it is high, sometimes catastrophically high.

California—or at least many parts of California—has little or no summer rainfall; rainfall is not absolutely necessary, for the fungi can propagate themselves in conditions of heavy dew, and, above all, of fog; the coast to the north of San Francisco is subject to much fog, a condition which, incidentally, makes the large-leaved rhododendrons such as *R. sinogrande* flourish there as hardly anywhere else. This fog makes the littoral difficult for the vine. But in many parts of this state the two fungus diseases so deadly to the European vine cannot flourish; or at least, cannot so flourish that they are difficult to control.

The native *Vites* of California, for instance *V. californica*, being protected by the Rocky Mountains, seem not to have become hosts to the phylloxera. Parts of California were, in short—although the fact was not of course realized—the only part of the northern temperate zone in America to which *V. vinifera* could safely be introduced, provided that the plants had not already become contaminated by contact with the native American vines east of the Rockies. Chance operated in favour of viticulture: the European vines were introduced to California not from the east, but from the south, that is from Mexico, which had no phylloxera until it was introduced there.

The introduction of the European vine to Mexico has been discussed already. The earliest colonists of California were Mexican, that is, Spanish-Mexican, Jesuit missionaries, who were established in Baja California, the southern part of the province, by 1669. One of the earliest of the Spanish settler families which Europeanized the country was that of General Vallejo (*plate 105*), a planter and gardener of note and one of the first wine-growers in the Napa valley (see below). In 1891 the General's niece, Guadalupe Vallejo, wrote some reminiscences called *Ranch and Mission Days in Alta California*. In these she says that the Jesuit missionaries had vineyards in Baja California in the early 1670s. Father Juan Uguarte was probably the first planter on any scale, but Father Kino had planted a few vines even before his time. These vines were, as we have said, brought from Mexico. Guadalupe Vallejo says also that: 'The first grapevines were brought from Lower California in 1769 and were soon planted at all the Missions except Dolores, where the climate was not suitable.'[21]

This introduction coincides with the establishment of the San Diego Mission by the Franciscan Junipero Serra (*plate 103*), whose Order was taking over the older, Jesuit missions in western North America. These Franciscans introduced most of the European economic plants to California by way of Mexico. The task of getting these new introductions properly cared for, propagated and popularized was not by any means an easy one: the Indians, with great plenty of game, fish and wild vegetable foods, could see no reason why they should toil away at horticulture and agriculture: they were still in paradise and objected to being evicted and made to get their bread in the sweat of their faces. Yet the northward movement of the vine was quite rapid and by 1823 it had reached and was established at Sonoma.

There was, of course, no question of commercial wine-growing in this early phase. The truth is that the Mission vineyards of eighteenth-century California were planted for precisely the same reason as were the temple vineyards of Sumeria and Babylonia and the temple vineyards of pre-Dynastic and early Dynastic Egypt: for the provision of sacramental wine, although there was a surplus of wine for secular drinking and for distillation. And again precisely as in the case of Egypt some four or five thousand years earlier, the culture of the vine was slowly (but in the Californian case much less slowly) secularized until vineyards ceased to be found solely as ecclesiastical glebes, became first parts of the estates of wealthy gentlemen, and finally commercial undertakings to provide wine as a drink for the upper classes and even for the common people.

It is not now possible to identify with assurance the vine variety—the same throughout the province—which was planted by the Spanish Fathers. It is certain only that it was a pure-bred *vinifera* and that it came from Mexico. Its ancestor had been brought from Spain, even possibly from Italy. According to George A. Pettit of the University of California College of Agriculture,[22] the vine in question was a seedling of Monica, a vine much cultivated in the monastery gardens of South Europe in the eighteenth century. Whatever its antecedents it became known as the Mission grape and as such it was long in cultivation. It still is: in 1960 there were still more than 9,000 acres of it. It rendered one very major service, for it clearly demonstrated that *V. vinifera* cultivars would flourish in California.

And flourish is the word: never, excepting perhaps in Morocco and in Syria, did *V. vinifera* find itself in more congenial conditions than in California. In an earlier chapter I mentioned Strabo's reference to Syrian vines with a girth two men could not embrace and with clusters of grapes two feet or more long. Similar enormous bunches of grapes of the variety *mazhu p'u t'ao* (see Chapter VIII) were sent to the T'ang Emperor by Turki tributaries in A.D. 647. This kind of growth was reproduced in California. A single instance will suffice to demonstrate the almost fabulous difference between the behaviour of this species in California and its wretched performance east of the Rockies: at some time after the middle of the eighteenth century Mission vines were planted in the vicinity of Santa Barbara, and at the end of the nineteenth they had for some—probably bad—reason to be cut down and grubbed up. All had attained an immense size: the largest measured eight feet round the base of the trunk, divided into fourteen main branches at about ten feet from the ground, and had, in 1895, yielded by itself a crop which weighed nine tons, equivalent at a conservative estimate to about nine thousand bottles of wine.[23]

Not until the 1830s did viticulture become secularized in California. In 1831 there were about one hundred thousand vines in the near neighbourhood of Los Angeles and considerable production of wine for sale: but the business was still almost entirely in the hands of the regular clergy of the San Gabriel (*plate 104*) and San Fernando Missions.

Although the soil, climate and relative freedom from the worst vine-diseases of southern California were all favourable to the rank growth and heavy cropping of the Old World vines, the climate, as far north as Los Angeles, was and is not favourable to the production of fine table wines. There is too much sun; temperatures are too high, the wine if not modified is naturally very strong, sweet and heady. Skill can modify these faults, but not easily and not enough. The chemistry of the matter is roughly as follows: the several species of yeast present in the bloom of all grapes vary in their efficiency as converters of sugar into alcohol: the best of them will continue at work, increasing and turning sugar into alcohol in the process, until the ambient fluid is between sixteen and seventeen per cent alcohol by volume; the worst of them ceases work when the alcohol element in the fluid reaches about six per cent. It was Louis Pasteur who first distinguished and isolated these yeasts. Of the best yeast there are very many strains, in fact each viticultural region seems to have one specific to it. Since Pasteur's time it has been possible first to sterilize the must entirely, killing all the yeasts; then to inoculate the pasteurized must with a strain of the best yeast, and so ensure that all the sugar in the must is at the disposal of this one, efficient yeast, and not partly consumed by other, less efficient, yeasts in competition with it. This is not an argument in favour of this course; for although the practice is almost universal in the production of ordinary wine, it is at least possible that the very finest wines are produced in the old, 'natural' way, perhaps because not all alcohols are the same by any means, and a balance of different alcohols may be aesthetically desirable. But the point here is this: that, fermenting their must by the ancient method, the Californian growers were bound to get a wine which, though very alcoholic, still contained a great deal of sugar, for grapes grown in the conditions there obtaining, as in those of Morocco, Algeria, Syria, and so on, may, when fully ripe, contain over thirty-five per cent of sugar by volume. (Roughly, two per cent of sugar in the must becomes one per cent of alcohol in the wine, where fermentation is scientifically efficient.)

It is a curious fact that it very rarely occurred to wine-growers that the solution of their problem was in their own hands. For the simplest way to deal with this business is to pick and vinify the grapes before they are quite ripe, at a moment when the sugar content and acid content are just what they should be for the best result. It is true, however, that means of measuring these attributes were not readily available until the late nineteenth century. At all events, although California could grow much better wine than any other province of North America at that time, the production of fine vintages was not possible until viticulture had moved first north, into a more temperate climate, and then into the highlands. Before coming to this improving migration of the vine it will be as well to say something more touching the developments in the region of Los Angeles.

As early as 1824, one Joseph Chapman had planted 4,000 vines in Los Angeles and by 1831 the *pueblo*, as it then was, had 100 acres of vineyard, about 100,000 vines. In 1829 Jean Louis Vignes—propitious name!—a native of Cadillac and therefore almost a Bordelais, arrived at Monterey in California from, of all places, the Sandwich Islands. Two years later he settled in Los Angeles. He bought about a hundred acres of land, subsequently the site of the Los Angeles Union Station, and there was on this land a big *aliso* (alder) tree from which he called the ranch El Aliso; he thus came to be known to his fellow-townsmen as Don Luis Aliso, or del Aliso.

Don Luis' vines came to him as cuttings from France, skilfully packed by experts for the journey round Cape Horn. He made his first vintage in about 1837 and thereafter both wine and brandy in increasing quantity every year. He was joined first by one nephew, then another, and then more of his kin from France. He was from the first a good and active citizen, joining the volunteer police (*vigilantes*) and taking public office. His enterprise flourished.

Vignes was not really a *vigneron* by trade, but a cooper, and this fact came in very handy. He was able to build maturing-vats into his cellars, using local oak; and thus to hold his vintages until they were properly mature. These vintages got larger, for by 1840 he had forty thousand vines bearing heavily. Moreover, this introduction of coopering brought about a revolution in Californian wine-handling which repeated that which had occurred in France and Italy some sixteen centuries earlier: the Spanish Fathers had used roughly-made Indian earthenware vessels for their wine and had transported it in leather bottles after the very ancient manner. Vignes did for California what the Allobroges and their *cuparii* did for Burgundy and the other great French centres of wine-growing.

Having barrels, then, Don Luis could turn shipper of wine, and in partnership with one of his nephews, Pierre Sansevain, founder of the later great firm of Californian wine-merchants, he began to send his wines by coasting vessels (that importance of water-transport once again) to other parts of California. Moreover, imitating the European device for maturing heavy wines, he took to sending them as ballast round the Horn to Boston and back. One curious fact emerges from an account of some of Don Luis' wine, written by a visiting United States Army officer, Brevet Major W. H. Emory, in 1846: 'We drank today wine of the country manufactured by Don Luis Vignes, a Frenchman. It was truly delicious, resembling more the best description of hock than any other wine. Many bottles were drunk, leaving no headaches or acidity on the stomach.'[24] One would not expect a wine like hock to be produced in the climate of Los Angeles; the skill of the Vignes family must have been of the highest order; or Major Emory's standards of comparison very imperfect. But Vignes may have discovered the desirability of picking his grapes early in the season.

Vignes' example was followed by others, notably by William Wolfskill, a German-Irish Kentuckian, a trapper by trade who drifted into California, turned vinearoon and made a great success of that and of horticulture in general. As early as 1855 a planter called G. C. Yount had been growing grapes in the Nappa valley to the north, and in 1842 Wolfskill obtained a grant of land there from Governor Juan Bautista Alvarado. Some of the finest American vintages were to come, and still do come, from the Nappa County, but Wolfskill's vineyards seem to have been for the production of table grapes for the San Francisco market.

Throughout the 'forties and 'fifties cultivars of *V. vinifera* continued their steady colonization of California, for Vignes and Wolfskill had many imitators and the great Gold Rush of 1849 gave a tremendous stimulus to the demand for wine and for the spirits distilled from it, the Californian brandy long known by the Spanish name, *aguardiente*. By mid-century the vines were firmly established in Sonoma, and the conquest of California was virtually complete.

But apart from the relatively large undertakings of Vignes and Wolfskill and their associates and successors, viticulture in California a hundred years ago was largely what, in Europe, would have been called a 'peasant' industry: each grower had a small vineyard, made his own wine more or less well, drank some of it, sold the surplus as best he could. Equipment for pressing, for *cuvage*, for cellarage, was primitive; there was not a bottle factory in the whole province. Moreover few wines were properly matured before sale, because growers had neither the cellars, cellar equipment, nor capital to make it possible to hold their vintages for the anything from three to ten years which may be necessary, or at least desirable. This state of affairs was shortly to be changed by one of the most remarkable and admirable men in the whole immensely long history of viticulture.

Agoston Haraszthy de Mokesa (*plate 108*) was a Hungarian nobleman born at Futtak in the *comitat* of Backsa, now for some reason part of Yugo-slavia; this country had been rich in vines and in wine since about the first century B.C. At the time of that famous edict of Domitian discussed in Chapter V—of which Apollonius, referring to the banning of the practice of making eunuchs promulgated at the same time, had said that the Emperor spared men but castrated the earth—the viticulture of this region was spared by the intervention of a special embassy. The year of Haraszthy's birth was that *annus mirabilis* of the great Reaction, 1812. As country gentry his family were wine-growers. But Haraszthy read law in Vienna, entered the Imperial Army, and as a member of the Royal Hungarian Bodyguard, attained the rank of colonel while still in his early twenties. He transferred from the Army to the Civil Service and was appointed Prefect, if that is the right word, of Bacska, with the title of Count. Later he served as Secretary to the Viceroy of Hungary. Despite his Imperial Service he was a Hungarian nationalist, a friend of the patriot Kossuth, and a liberal of the romantic and even poetic type then fashionable. Being naturally wanting in discretion, for that is not an aristocratic attribute, his careless talk got him the name of a dangerous revolutionary in Vienna, and he was obliged to flee the country in disguise, going first to Hamburg, then to London, and thence to New York where he landed in 1840, still only twenty-eight years old. He seems to have been of the type of liberal aristocrat first incarnate in the Marquis de La Fayette, but unlike the Frenchman he had a sense of humour and a rael will to get down to the brass tacks of social improvement while leaving the politics to men who preferred political to material dirt on their hands.

While negotiations to enable his family to join him were in train, he travelled the whole United States in company with General Lewis Cass, United States Army, and as a result he wrote a book on the resources of the country, designed to encourage immigration from Hungary. His friendship with Cass was of use, for without some kind of strong pressure on Vienna, it would have been fatal for Haraszthy to return to Hungary, and the Imperial government was refusing to let his family go. The United States Government obtained a pledge from Vienna that Haraszthy should be allowed to return to Hungary and collect his family and take them all back with him to America; and having a well-founded contempt for the promises of Habsburgs and other royalties, it meanwhile held some important State papers required by Vienna until Haraszthy should be back in the United States. The Count's estates were confiscated, but in 1842 he, his wife and three sons, father and mother, arrived in America and settled in Wisconsin. It is doubtful whether the United States ever received more valuable immigrants.

Haraszthy made roads, built bridges, founded new settlements which flourished, experimented in farming; he also planted his first vineyard, using European vines, which failed as usual. He was a public-spirited man and he served on committees and associations for the promotion of immigration and other causes. In 1848, the year which shook every throne in Europe, he collected money and arms for his friend Kossuth and the Hungarian revolutionaries and was of very real service to them. In the same year, suffering badly from asthma, he moved his whole family to San Diego in California. In those days the journey—they took the southern route—was long, hard and dangerous, and a report was received in Wisconsin that the entire party had been massacred by Indians. There was nothing unusual in that, therefore it was believed; and Haraszthy's agent proceeded to sell up his property and estates. Haraszthy learned of this when he arrived in California. Presumably the money raised was invested in his new home and ventures and he was soon active in local affairs, being elected sheriff of San Diego in 1850. He imported cuttings of Hungarian vines, which were and are among the best in Europe, while Hungarian ampelographists and vinea-roons have always been in the first rank (in our own times Count Teleki, for example). His first vineyards were at San Francisco, but he later planted at Crystal Springs and finally, in 1858, in the Sonoma valley (*plates 107, 108*). The vine variety of his introduction which became of the first importance was Zinfandel. Meanwhile he was founding a commercial nursery, its principal business being in young vines. He did not neglect his public life: he served in the State legislature, he became Assayer of the United States Mint during the presidency of Franklin Pierce, and he occupied other public offices of importance. Like Pericles he was charged with making away with some of the State's gold; of this unfounded charge he was in due course acquitted.

Haraszthy's first Sonoma vineyard was planted because he had found that the fogs of San Francisco were harmful to the vines. Attila Haraszthy, Agoston's son, was made manager there and in about 1868 nearly half-a-million vines were planted, either in the vineyards themselves, or in the vine nursery. One hundred and sixty-five different varieties were imported from Europe. Haraszthy made extensive use of cheap Chinese labour; he attracted more immigrants from viticultural countries in Europe; he cut deep cellars out of his stony hillsides; and one way and another sent land values at Sonoma up from six dollars to one hundred and fifty dollars per acre within a very few years. He used his own judgment as to the manner in which the vines should be cultivated: for example, he found that Californian growers irrigated their vines, decided that this was altogether unnecessary, refused to adopt the practice thereby lowering his production costs, and ultimately convinced the whole state that he was right. From his growing nurseries went out not only such noble varieties as Traminer, Riesling and Tokay, but also sound advice which was increasingly followed. It was Haraszthy who persuaded Californian vinearoons to plant hillsides rather than flat, rich land; and he it was who, when local oak ran out, first turned to redwood as material for casks.

The Count, turned journalist to put forward his ideas, wrote a very good book on the proper culture of the grape and the correct making of wine, forced the inferior though hitherto serviceable Mission grape out of cultivation, introduced proper cellarage, maturing and bottling, and greatly improved the wine of the whole state. As a result of his influence and ideas, and of the way in which the Californian press plugged them, it was proposed to exempt vine-growers from taxation to help them in enriching the state. By 1860 two hundred thousand vines a year were being planted; and because of Haraszthy's influence they were of the best varieties and they were well cultivated, in the right soils and the right situations; and the grapes they yielded were soundly vinified.

Thus by 1860 California had become, in two centuries, one of the world's greatest vine-and-wine-lands. And much of this triumph was owed to Louis Vignes and Agoston Haraszthy, than whom very few men have served Dionysus better.

# CHAPTER X

## *The Vine in the Southern Hemisphere*

IT HAS BEEN EXPLAINED, in the Mexican case, that for the Spanish conquerors of America a provision of wine was an urgent and immediate necessity of religion; the planting of the vine could not, like that of other Old World plants, be postponed until the country had been pacified and life in the new colonies become settled and peaceful. Thus Cortés, as we saw in the last chapter, was arranging to plant vines in Mexico as early as 1522; and Francisco Pizarro, although he had not his distant cousin and model's fanatical piety, was very much under the influence of the Dominican Vicente de Valverde. This brave, cruel and narrow-minded priest was not of the type who were Cortés' religious advisers; he was a bigot, with a horror of the gentle and sophisticated religion of the Incas, which led him to urge upon Pizarro just the kind of excesses of piety which the Mexican missionaries were busy checking in Cortés. Peru, moreover, was more difficult to reach by sea with supplies of Mass-wine than Mexico. The planting of vines in that country was therefore a matter of urgency.

The first phase of the conquest of the Tahuantinsuyu—Chile, Peru, Bolivia, Ecuador and small parts of other South American countries as they are now—was completed on 28th August 1533 when the Sapa Inca Atahualpa, cheated and betrayed by the Spaniard and abandoned by his own people, was baptized and then garroted in the main square of Caxamarcha, the Bath or Aix-les-Bains of his vast empire. Within twenty years at the most, vineyards were flourishing in Chile.

It has not proved feasible to establish with anything like the accuracy which was possible in the Mexican case, the date of introduction of the first vines to South America: there can be little doubt that the first countries to receive the vine were Peru (*plate 111*) and Chile, for not only did they comprise the most important part of the Inca Empire, they were also rich in ancient mountain terraces long carefully and intensively cultivated (*plate 112*) and in remarkable works of irrigation, so that the vines could readily be given ideal conditions. And as countries with a very ancient and sophisticated agriculture they were also rich in men and women who would be quick to learn to cultivate the new plant.[1]

The earliest record which I can find of vines being cultivated in Peru refers to one Bartolomé de Terrazas, a Spanish settler who had received a *repartimiento* near Cuzco, the old Inca capital, and who was there teaching his *Indios* to cultivate the vine; the date is 1550.[2] There can be no doubt that the Spaniards had realized that, altitude compensating for low latitude, the vine would flourish about Cuzco, and it is probable that the first vines were planted there before 1540. It was not long before they were followed by others. Pedro de Valdivia, in one of his letters written in 1551, only eleven years after he had led the second expedition for the conquest of the Chilean province of the Tahuantinsuyu, reports that grapes were already 'abundant' about La Serena in the north of the province, and about Santiago; and wine, he says, was being made at El Reino de Chile by 1556. Nothing could better prove the high priority given to this plant by the conquerors; it followed close upon their heels to provide the one essential commodity which the country itself did not afford them. As Valdivia fought his way south, until he was killed fighting the Araucanians across the River Maule—the same people who, alone, had successfully resisted the Incas—vineyards sprung into being in his wake. The rate of viticultural expansion was extraordinary; Chile had become a land rich in vines by 1570, and five years later their number had trebled. And this was despite the fact that although the pacified natives might cultivate the vine, even on their own account, the militant ones seem to have regarded it as a symbol of the white man's power and of the ferocious cruelty of the new religion which he brought with him. It is at least possible that, having noted the religious importance of wine, the native Chileans thought that by striking at the sacred plant they would be making war on that merciless Christian God in whose name they were being massacred, enslaved and even burnt alive, an atrocity beyond their experience. It is, at all events, a fact that when the people of Concepción rose under their *cacique* Antecul, they destroyed every vineyard they could reach and clearly made a dead set at the grape-vines.

Although it was necessary, in the first phase of the conquest, that vines be planted for Mass-wine, once ships were regularly reaching the new

Spanish empire from Europe, the case became very different. Once it was obvious that, from the Maule in the south to Bolivia in the north, the Old World vines were perfectly at home and were spreading at such a rate that there must soon be far more wine than the land could absorb even if the natives took to drinking it, the Spanish government became alarmed. It was important for Spain and Portugal, poor countries both but with an abundance of wine, to check the production in the growing colonies of a commodity which they could export to the colonists, at an inflated price, in exchange for the silver, gold and such enduring riches as the enslavement of the Indians would create. An attempt was therefore made to prevent, by absolute prohibition of vine-planting, the production of wine in Peru and Chile, and indeed throughout the whole Spanish empire in the Americas.

Now this kind of legislation has never been enforceable: it has already been noted that the prohibition of planting which the Romans included in their treaties with the Celts and which Cicero condemned, did not prevent the vine from crossing the Alps; that Domitian's anti-viticultural edict of A.D. 92 could not be applied and had to be, at least in part, withdrawn; that the French government had again and again to renew the laws restricting vine-planting and is still at it; and that only in the single instance of the Marquis of Pombal's anti-viticultural legislation did the law take effect in Portugal, and this was among a people who were right under the ruler's hand. The Royal Cedula promulgated in Madrid on 1st June 1654 made it necessary for any landowner wishing to plant a vineyard to obtain special permission from the authorities; the implication of its language was that such permission would not be granted; when it *was* granted the new vineyard was burdened by the same regulation with a heavy tax, perhaps heavy enough to cripple it.

But the colonists understood very well that this was a protectionist measure favouring Spanish wine-growers and perhaps obtained by their intervention. And if the case of Chile can be taken as representative of what happened in Peru and elsewhere in the empire, the Royal Cedula was simply ignored. At all events, vineyard planting continued steadily, and wine output rose, until in 1767 new legislation in Madrid again attempted, and again failed, to check them. So that while the market for wine in South America grew rapidly, so did the supply of wine, and the hopes of the Spanish wine-exporters were never realized: they were defeated by the flourishing growth and abundant fruitfulness of their own vines transplanted to the Andes.

Chile, receiving the grape-vine from Peru, passed it on to that part of the country which was to become Argentina. Once again the Jesuit missions were the 'vectors' of the sacred plant in its attempt to conquer the world. The Jesuit mission in the neighbourhood of Cordoba was the first to have a vineyard within the present frontiers of the Argentine republic; thence the vines, no doubt of the Mission variety which was being planted in Mexico, travelled with the clergy; god and plant moved, as in the remote Hellenic past, together, first to Tucuman, to the valleys of Salta, Jujuy and Catamarca, and so throughout the whole Andean region of the Argentine.

As in Mexico, Peru and Chile, the development of viticulture from an aspect of the cult into an industry was checked by restraining laws promulgated from Madrid. In Argentina this check seems to have been more nearly effective than in Chile, for although, between the sixteenth and nineteenth centuries, vineyards were established on a commercial footing, and by the eighteenth century wine-growing was one of Argentina's industries, it remained insignificant until one or two enthusiasts took a hand. Perhaps their most important contribution to the improvement of the art was the introduction of French cultivars. This viticultural revolution, centred in the province of Mendoza, began about 1870 and continued until the aspect of Argentinian vitiviniculture, as it is called in that country, was transformed.

The, as it were, Agoston Haraszthy of Argentina was Don Tiburcio Benegas; there are, in fact, curious likenesses between the two men; both took the lead in confused communities where leadership was wanting; both had distinguished careers in local politics on the grand scale; both were men of education, good sense and great energy, taking an interest in all the activities of their worlds; and, by the way, both were led to settle, each in his particular corner of the world, by the need to relieve the sufferings of asthma.

Benegas was born in Rosario de Santa Fe in July 1844, and moved to Mendoza in 1865 on the invitation of his elder brother. There was much work for everyone, for the town had been totally destroyed in the disastrous earthquake of 1861. Not long after his arrival Benegas noted that business activity in the province was much hampered by the want of banking facilities: manufacturing, agricultural or commercial undertakings were financed by the rich landowners who lent their money reluctantly and at a ruinous rate of interest; and as for depositing money in safety, apparently the only way was to bury it. Benegas, who was then twenty-five, decided to found a bank.

His powers of persuasion must have been considerable for he united the rich men of the province into a company under the chairmanship of Don Exequiel Tabanera, and founded his bank. It was an immediate success but was, nevertheless, soon in difficulties, owing to the fact that its largest client, the Provincial Governor, would not or could not repay the interest and principle of the large loans he had obtained from it. At the time of this crisis Tiburcio had returned to Rosario to manage the Banco Nacional branch there. He asked to be transferred back to Mendoza, took over the management, formed a new company, acquired the assets and liabilities of the old one, settled the matter of the Governor's debt, put the new company on a sound footing, and sold it back to the Banco Nacional.

In 1870 Benegas married Lubina Blanco, and it was this marriage which gave rise to his interest in viticulture, for his father-in-law had long been an enthusiast of the vine and in 1872 published a pamphlet on the subject, *Vinas y vino en Mendoza*.

In 1883 Benegas bought a property of 250 hectares called 'El Trapiche' in the province of San Vicente (then called Godoy Cruz). There was a vine-yard of old provincial vines (see below), but much of the estate was so wild that *guanacos*, wild animals of the llama genus, not to mention 'ostriches', used to come wandering in from the mountains. Benegas' first care was to extend the vineyard, and not with the local vines, but with French *cépages* imported first from Chile and later directly from Europe. A new bodega was built and it was equipped with the most modern winery devices and machinery from France. The undertaking suffered setbacks and difficulties: Benegas' sons were still too young to be really useful auxiliaries on his great plantings; and Benegas himself was so deeply involved in the big business and politics of his province that he could give only part of his time to the work. He was much concerned with bringing the railway to Mendoza —the first train steamed into the city in 1885—and in 1886 he was elected Governor of Mendoza province. The fact remains that his pioneering work did transform the industry in his country, and that he found time to write a useful little handbook on the correct choice of varieties for the production of fine wines; the preparation of the land, the cultivation of the vineyards, and on correct vinification.

Before Benegas set to work on them, all the vineyards of Argentina were planted with *criollas*, which we may render 'colonials'; moreover these old vines were not eliminated by his work. They were of some ampelographical interest: derived from cuttings and perhaps seedlings of vines originally brought to the country from Spain by way of Peru and Chile, they had come to differ so considerably from the ancestral type as to require separate classification. These changes must have come about as a result of three centuries of selection, a selection which had created local cultivars, different from those in the next parish, some of which were doubtless true clones derived from some single, outstandingly fruitful or otherwise desirable variant. It is of interest that these changes had come about within so short a time as three centuries. And it explains, in a modern and well-documented example, what must have happened to *Vitis vinifera* in ancient Armenia, Egypt, Canaan, Greece and Italy, a process which has given us the several thousand modern cultivars of the one species, with an enormous range of morphological variation and variation of habit and character.[3]

Cobos, in his *Historia del Nuevo Mundo*, gives the credit for the first wide distribution of the Spanish vines through what are now Peru, Chile and Argentina to one Hernán or Hernando de Montenegro, apparently early in the seventeenth century. It seems possible that some of the original cuttings planted in Argentina survived into the twentieth century. For example, in 1910 Professor Alazraqui, in the course of a survey of certain provinces of Argentina, examined and described vines in La Rioja which he conservatively estimated as one hundred and fifty years old. In Mendoza and in San Juan he found vines measuring, at the base of the trunk, about a metre in *diameter*, that is to say over ten feet in circumference. In some cases the ramification of a single plant covered an area thirty yards in diameter. In La Rioja a large number of vines had trunks eighteen inches in diameter. Some of these *criollas* must certainly have been planted very early in the eighteenth century, and perhaps even earlier.

But as a result of the example set by Benegas, and of the fine work done by Leopoldo Suarez (see Note 5), by 1910 the more advanced vineyards were planted with *plants nobles*, either as extensions to the *criollas* plantations, or in their room. *Criollas* were retained where the wine was wanted for domestic consumption and for subsistence viticulture. The *plants nobles* were known, whatever their origin, as *francescas*, possibly because Benegas had concentrated on French cultivars, and although many of the vines were of Italian or Spanish derivation. Argentinian viticulture received a second great boost into the modern age of viticulture when Suarez imported, from every major viticultural region of the Old World (he was, at the time, Director of the National School of Vitiviniculture), over six hundred varieties new to the country, including the more important rootstock hybrids bred in France, for grafting.

To return to Chile, the country which, viticulturally speaking, was to be the most important in South America. Not only did the vine cared for in vineyards continue to flourish but it showed a marked tendency to naturalize itself. Molina[4] reports that by the mid-eighteenth century wild vines were to be found growing in the woods in the region of Curico in northern Chile; he describes them as black 'moscatel' grapes. There is no question of these having been anything but vineyard escapes, for there is no *Vitis* native to South America and the nearest thing to it, a *Cissus*, cannot be mistaken for a grape-vine. Meanwhile, however, Chilean vinearoons were becoming dissatisfied with the old Spanish vines: historians of the vine in Chile say that whereas in the early epoch the vines brought from Spain yielded a wine of good quality in great abundance, '*a lo largo de los años, se denaturalizaron y no se obtenian de ellas caldos de la calidad requarida por cientos viños . . .*'[5] How, and in what manner, these old vines became 'denatured' is not clear; I know of no other such case in the history of *Vitis vinifera*, apart from the occurrence of disease, which is not here the case. There is a theory that long-continued vegetative propagation of a plant ends in its degeneration, possibly caused by a virus disease which is propagated and intensified by this means. The remedy is to make new 'crosses' and begin again with seedlings. At all events, either the quality and quantity of the wine made in Chile did really decline, perhaps because of incorrect pruning of old vines or perhaps for some physiological reason; or else the taste of the Chileans grew more sophisticated, so that wines which had once satisfied them no longer did so. For whichever cause, inspired and aided by a Frenchman named Bertrand, Don Silvestre Ochagavia Echazareta, well known as one of the most progressive Chilean agriculturists of his day, began a movement in 1851 for the replanting of the Chilean vineyards, the new *encépagement* to be with vines of the great French vineyards which had by then entered upon their golden age. These French varieties made such an improvement in the quality of the Chilean wines that Ochagavia's example was followed by all the principal wine-growers. With the consequent improvement came another innovation, the maturing and bottling of wines on the *demas viticoltores*, the wine-growing estates; and with that, an export trade in wine began, first to the countries of the American Pacific coast. Domestic exports were followed by foreign exports: in 1877 a grower, Macario Ossa, actually exported wine to Bordeaux, and there sold it, moreover, for a satisfactory price, a remarkable instance of coals to Newcastle, although really explained by the fact that Bordeaux is an emporium for wines as well as a centre of production. Ten years later Chilean wines were beginning to compete with those of the ancient wine countries, attention being first called to them by their appearance at the Vienna Exhibition of 1873, though, as early as 1855, several Chilean wines had taken Gold Medals at the Liverpool Exhibition of that year. The quality of these wines, products of French vines transplanted to the Andes, was confirmed at the Paris Exhibition of 1889 where Chilean wine-growers were awarded, jointly, a First Class Award and, severally, six Gold Medals.

Although, long before this time, all the South American republics other than the extreme tropical ones had their vineyards, none perhaps could offer the vine such favourable conditions as Chile. Not only was Chile good to the vine; it was good to the vinearoon; Chilean viticulture is, socially, of the most desirable kind, in that its one hundred and ten thousand hectares of vineyard are ordered and worked by no less than thirty thousand vineyard proprietors. Seventeen thousand owners have vineyards of less than one hectare, less, that is, than two-and-a-half acres or five jugera. Nine thousand of the vineyards are between one and five hectares; fourteen hundred are between five and ten hectares. Only two hundred and fifty owners have more than one hundred acres of vineyard and only eighty-six more than two hundred acres. Thus by far the greatest part of the vineyard acreage is in smallholdings, and provided that a holding be not so small that the cultivator is in want, and that a ready market is available, the smallholder is the happiest and most independent of mankind. The present condition of Chilean viticulture is reminiscent of that of Italy before 100 B.C., before the industry was exploited by big capital and slave labour. It is calculated that every hectare provides one hundred man-days of work per annum, and the great interest of this statistic lies in the fact that the Chilean vine-dresser evidently works exactly as hard as his Italian predecessor of two thousand years ago: that is, one man can manage to look after seven jugera of vines. Chilean viticulture provides a livelihood for about fifty thousand workers and their families.

Not since the vines were introduced to Italy has any country been able to offer them the advantages which they enjoy in Chile—the climate, the soil and the servants are all just what they need. It is, therefore, possible that if there is ever to be another epoch of really great wines, an epoch to be compared with that of the Lesbian and Chian wines of the fifth century B.C.; of the Campanian wines of the first century B.C.; of the Ports of the early nineteenth, the Bordeaux and Burgundies of the middle to late nineteenth century A.D.—it may well be a golden age of Chilean wines. The *encépagement* has been *noble* for nearly a century now, but it must be remembered that it has in the past taken more than five centuries to reach the oinological peaks. In the hot north of the country sweet and heavy wines are grown; in the more temperate centre, dry wines of substance; in the cool south, light wines of delicacy. Chile, in short, is a new Oenotria.

For the great wines of the possibly coming golden age we shall have to look to the riverside *côtes* of the Aconcagua, Maipo, Mapocho and Cachapoal. The vineyards lie on the rivers not so much, this time, for reasons of transport, as for reasons of irrigation. Chilean *viticoltores* claim that the quality of the water fed to their vines has much to do with the quality of the wine; it is very possible, for river water carries plant nutrients in solution or suspension. For the red wines of these riverine vineyards, the dominant vine varieties are Cabernet, Merlot and Malbec, vines of the Gironde estuary, of Médoc, St Estephe and St Julien, whose ancestors perhaps came from Campania and ultimately from Lydia. For the whites, the *cépages* are equally impeccable, with Sémillon and Sauvignon dominant. And of an importance which cannot be exaggerated is the fact that *Phylloxera vastatrix* has failed to establish itself in these vineyards. If there is any substance in the claim that the post-phylloxera wines from grafted vines are inferior to the pre-phylloxera wines, then again Chile has an enormous advantage, since the vines are not grafted, but self-rooted.

The northernmost province of Chile which favours good wine is Coquimbo; north of that the vines are still the old Spanish ones, like the *criollas* of Mendoza, and the wine is of inferior quality. The best reds at present come from the O'Higgins and Colchagua vineyards of the Valle

Central, where Pinot Noir, the great vine of Burgundy and of Champagne, is added to the *cépages* already named. At higher altitudes of the same region the Riesling is cultivated. In the extreme south, as in the extreme north, the old Spanish vines are still grown for the daily wine of the people.

The remarkably early and rapid establishment of the vine in South America, and the three centuries of struggle described in Chapter IX to establish it in North America, demonstrate very clearly the manner in which the peoples of the vine cling to a plant and to what is still almost a cult. Even if we regard alcoholic liquor as a necessity, the vine is not essential excepting in a cultural sense, since any fruit will yield wine of a kind.

This same very characteristic attachment to the vine and its wine is manifest in two other cases in which people of the Mediterranean culture, although not of Mediterranean 'race', established new colonies of European-ism in the Southern Hemisphere. It does seem that Europeans could no more feel that they had created the environment proper to them, in the new lands of the west and far south, until they had planted vineyards where this was possible, than they could feel at home until they had re-created the social institutions and the architectural styles, albeit modified by local conditions and rapidly growing new traditions, in the new lands. Mere economic considerations, though no doubt important, do not sufficiently explain the often costly persistence by colonists who were as determined to have the company of the vine in their new homes in Africa and Australasia as were the Greeks of the eighth and seventh centuries B.C. to have it with them in their new African, Spanish and Italian colonies. In the case of Spanish America there was, it is true, a special reason for the haste to establish the vine; as we have seen, it was the churchmen, there as in sixth-century England, who were so anxious to get vineyards started. It was as important to them to have a source of sacramental wine at hand for their rites as it was for the Thracian and Lydian sectaries of the Vine in the Greece of 1000 B.C. or thereabouts. But this special motive is of much less importance in the case of South Africa, next to be considered.

At some time shortly after 1640 the Dutch East India Company found it necessary to establish a major watering and victualling station for their East Indiamen on the way to Batavia and back. It was decided that no place would be more suitable for this purpose than that cape which the Portuguese navigator Bartholomew Diaz had called Cape of Storms when contrary winds prevented him from rounding it in 1486; and which his patron Prince Henry, introducer of the vine to Madeira and thus patron of one of the world's great wines, had renamed Cape of Good Hope. By great good fortune, or perhaps good judgment, the man chosen by the Company to be first Commandant of the Cape settlement was a gentleman of parts, able, intelligent and cultured: this was Jan van Riebeck.

Van Riebeck made his first call at the Cape in 1648; but it was not until 1652 that he landed in Table Bay with his party of settlers, and at once began building a fort and a house. His second task was the laying out and planting of gardens and a farm for the production of vegetables and wheat for his people; and while the land was being broken and planted, he was arranging to import fruit-trees and grape-vines. The planting of the first garden in the Cape, in a soil and a climate unsurpassed anywhere in the world, could not have been in better hands at that time: in the mid-seventeenth century the Dutch were far ahead of any other European people in the arts of horticulture. English gardeners were learning fast and were, in due course, to surpass their masters in some elements of the art, but in 1652 it would have been quite impossible to find better gardeners than the Dutch, unless perhaps in China and Japan.

Riebeck's biographer, Godee-Molsbergen, says that during the 'fifties the Commandant was importing grape-vines in variety for trial in the new settlement. He seems first to have planted some kind of muscadel or muscatel grape, from Spain or, more probably, the Canary Islands or Madeira: the vine is called *Hanepoot* in Dutch, and there was another called *Steen*. It is at least certain that within a remarkably short time (see below) the Cape was exporting 'Cape Madeira' wine, and it is more likely that the name was taken from the vine rather than simply from the similarity of the Cape wine to that of Madeira. Godee-Molsbergen sets something of a puzzle, however, with his list of the places from which Riebeck imported vines for trial: St Helena, Persia, Spain, Italy, Germany and France, indeed, all make excellent sense: all but St Helena were ancient lands of the vine, and the Commandant had to find out which kind of vines would be suited by the South African climate. But apparently he also had vines from Batavia, Amboina, Mauritius, Madagascar and even Japan. It seems to me that this list of place names throws a faint, but surprising, light on the obstinacy with which Europeans insisted upon taking their vine wherever they went; it is entirely possible that in the seventeenth-century explosion of Europeanism all over the world, comparable with the seventh-century-B.C. explosion of Hellenism all over the then known world, vines would at least be given a trial even in the most unsuitable climates. The traders and colonists might know that it was useless to plant vines in the colder countries; but not that the tropics were even less propitious for the plant. As to how there came to be any vines to try in such places, either the Omanis or the Portuguese might have caused vines to be planted in Madagascar; the climate of its high plateaux would be at least as suitable for viticulture as the mountains of Dhofar or Grand Canary. The Portuguese pioneers of the great European expansion were also masters of Mauritius from 1505 to 1598, and could, therefore, have been responsible for the planting of the vine in that island. In both places the conditions for the vine were by no means impossible and some success may early have been met with. In neither island did viticulture become of any importance. As for Batavia and Amboina, it is again the case that the Portuguese were the forerunners of the Dutch, and any vines to be found there must have been planted by them: the plants can hardly have prospered in that climate, unless at a great altitude. As for vines from Japan, this makes no sense at all, unless Riebeck had the idea of trying Far Eastern species, species other than *V. vinifera*, in South Africa. Even this is in the highest degree improbable, for (see Chapter VIII) the Japanese, while they used fruit, leaves and parasitic grubs from three native *Vites*, did not cultivate them, or at least not seriously. It is true that from the twelfth century there was some cultivation of *vinifera* vines in one part of Japan (see Chapter VIII) but it was hardly likely to have been known to Riebeck.

By 1657 Riebeck had a small vintage. The quality of the single cask of wine made in 1658 was promising, and a first vineyard was planted in the same year, twelve hundred vines at Bishop's Court, or Protea. (Protea is from the name of a genus of shrubs with spectacular flowers, peculiar to South Africa.) He asked the company for a piece of land for a more extensive planting: this was Bosheuvel, near the present Wynberg, and three thousand gulden were spent on maintaining the vineyard during its first, unproductive years. The first considerable vintage from this was made in 1665, the quantity of wine being one-and-a-half leaguers, that is, about one hundred and ninety gallons: the quality, especially the bouquet, was good.

111   *The vine was introduced into South America after the conquest by the Spanish Catholic missionaries, whose urgent need was for a supply of Mass wine. On the church at Juli in Peru native sculptors have carved the vine alongside indigenous motifs such as death's heads.*

# The Southern Hemisphere

112

The Spaniards found Inca stone terraces such as those at Machu Picchu (112) excellently adapted to viticulture. The vine yielded abundantly in South America, and particularly in Chile, where the vineyards were replanted after 1851 with vines from the great French vineyards. The soil and climate are just what the vine needs, and it may be that the really great vintages of the future will come from the Andes in the golden age of Chilean wine.

113

*Viticulture in South Africa dates from the 1650s when the first commandant of the Cape settlement, Jan van Riebeck, sent for vine cuttings from countries all over the world. Above, a Cape vineyard; right, African labourers pruning.*

114

116

It happened that at the time when the vine was enriching planters in South Africa, Dutch domestic architecture was at its zenith, and the older vineyards of the country have buildings as beautiful as any in Europe. Left (115), the wine cellar at Groot Constantia near Cape Town, a vineyard first planted in the 1680s by Governor van der Stel. Vineyards near Stellenbosch, Cape Province (116) were planted by the end of the seventeenth century.

117

The vine's triumphant conquest of the world was completed with its introduction into Australia and New Zealand. Captain Arthur Phillip, first Governor of New South Wales, brought vine cuttings with him when he landed in Australia in 1788. In 1830 James Busby (117) travelled through France to select cuttings and study viticultural methods, which he then applied successfully in his vineyards in New South Wales. His textbook on viticulture (118) was the first to appear in the Southern Hemisphere.

118

A

# MANUAL

OF

# PLAIN DIRECTIONS

FOR

PLANTING AND CULTIVATING

## VINEYARDS,

AND FOR

# MAKING WINE,

IN

NEW SOUTH WALES.

BY JAMES BUSBY.

𝔖𝔶𝔡𝔫𝔢𝔶:

PRINTED BY R. MANSFIELD, FOR THE EXECUTORS OF R. HOWE.

1830.

119 *Scenes at the Château Tahbilk vineyard in Victoria around 1870.*

120 *The entrance to the old winery at Château Tahbilk, Victoria. The name, like the vineyards themselves, combines the old and new nations of the vine.*

The Cape wine which was to make a name in Europe during the next hundred years (later to vanish, alas!) was the product of another Governor's enthusiasm for the vine: that of Simon van der Stel, who was Governor of the Cape from 1679 to 1699.

Van der Stel either came out to his post with an interest in viticulture, or he inherited that interest from Riebeck. Jane Austenites will recall that when Marianne Dashwood, in *Sense and Sensibility*, has had her heart broken by Willoughby's villainous conduct, the kind and vulgar Mrs Jennings has a recipe for mending it which she proposes to Elinor Dashwood: 'My dear . . . I have just recollected that I have some of the finest old Constantia wine in the house that was ever tasted . . . so I have brought a glass of it for your sister. My poor husband! How fond he was of it! Whenever he had a touch of his old cholicky gout, he said it did him more good than anything else in the world. Do take it to your sister . . .' That must have been about the year 1800: the wine came from one of two vineyards, Groot Constantia (*plate 115*) or Klein Constantia, planted by van der Stel as his personal property and for his own pleasure, near Cape Town and in what is, perhaps, pomologically the richest valley in the world, at the back of Table Mountain. The planting was made in the 1680s. Groot Constantia was planted, either from the first or at a later replanting, with Muscat de Frontignan, a French grape, though anciently of probably Syrian provenance;[6] and a Red Muscatel, possibly Spanish or Portuguese. The vintage of Groot Constantia was a dessert wine, strong but delicate, and with what is described as something singularly pleasant in its bouquet: it was fortified with a small addition of locally distilled brandy. The vineyard never yielded more than sixty leaguers; it is, and for thousands of years has been, a sore trial to wine-growers that wines of a particular quality, product of a combination of *cépages*, soil, climate, aspect and vinification, cannot be produced in boundless quantity, for the exact conditions cannot be reproduced elsewhere, often not even in the near neighbourhood of the vineyard. Such, for example, is the case of the famous *Romanée Conti* vineyard, and of the Montrachets. But there are many other instances.

The wine-merchant, however, is under no such dicffiulties as the wine-grower: he had his methods; and it is a fact that far more Constantia was sold in London alone, let alone Amsterdam, than both vineyards could have produced.

Klein Constantia, yielding a white wine from *Hanepoot* and a White Muscatel, produced ninety leaguers in a good year, never more and usually less. It, too, may have been fortified.

In 1688 the arrival at the Cape of French Huguenot immigrants seems to have given a marked stimulus to more extensive planting; it is apparently the case that many of these were from some of the major viticultural regions of France. The effect of this immigration—and no doubt of the Governor's success with Constantia which was quickly apparent—was striking; by the end of the century very considerable vineyards were established at Stellenbosch (*plate 116*), that of Paarl among others, while the Governor's son and successor in office, William Adrian van der Stel, was planting upwards of a quarter of a million vines at his own estate of Vergelegen. Its eems, in fact, that his extravagant private investment in viticulture was one of the causes of his getting into financial and other difficulties, which resulted in his recall by the Company.

Although clearly the quantity of wine being produced by the first decades of the eighteenth century made export of wine quite possible, it was not officially encouraged at first, possibly because the Company's ships had more profitable uses for their limited cargo-space. As early as 1691, less than ten years after van der Stel had made his plantings and less than three after the arrival of the first party of French vinearoons, William Dampier was able to sample local wines at the Cape in the course of his voyage round the world:

'The chief fruits are grapes. These thrive well and the country is of later years so well stokt with vineyards that they made abundance of wine, of which they have enough and to spare; and do sell great quantities to the ships that touch here. The wine is like a French High Country wine, but of a pale yellowish colour; it is sweet, very pleasant, and strong.'[7]

Although the reputation of Constantia was established even abroad by 1715, and despite what Dampier says about the vast quantity of wine sold to ships, when in 1743 Governor-General Baron von Imhoff left the Cape for Batavia he instructed the Governor and Director of the Council at the Cape, Hendrik Swellengrebel, among other things, that the: 'Export of wine is not permissible except where the Company has no other cargo for its ships. Wine can only be stowed in the hold and not between decks . . .'[8] From the same source, it is clear that the Baron was not satisfied with the quality of South African wines and thought that the vinearoons could do better: 'Further, the making and treatment of wine has in my opinion not by a long way reached that stage of perfection which is possible and I shall therefore request the Directors to send out a few viticulturalists from the Rhine and also a few from France, if they are procurable, in order to instruct the settlers in the proper way of making wine.'[9]

In mid-century the Company itself was buying the entire output of the Great and Little Constantia, giving it away to foreign governments and to private persons whom it wished to distinguish, and selling what it did not give away. Thirty-six leaguers appeared on the Amsterdam market in 1762, fetching an average of about £150 a leaguer, about a guinea a gallon, for the white; and for the red, as much as £333 a leaguer, a fabulous price for wine for it means, if we take this highest figure, that it was costing the merchant eight shillings and ninepence gold per bottle, equivalent to something like £3 a bottle in our money. It can hardly have reached the retail market at less than a golden sovereign per bottle. There were, then, people in Holland and England at the time who were willing to pay, in present-day values, £6 or £7 a bottle for the wine of Groot Constantia. There is another side to this coin, however.

From as early as we can find records until this present year, it has been the case that, excepting where the grower could himself control the sale of his wine, as in the case of the great châteaux vineyards of the Médoc, St Emilion and the neighbouring parishes, the grower and maker of the wine have been wretchedly underpaid, while the merchant has enriched himself. And it is instructive to glance, in this connection, at the by no means exceptional case of the Cape vinearoons. For the leaguer of White Constantia which the Company was selling in Europe for between £120 and £190, the grower and maker received £12. For the Red Constantia selling to the merchant at up to £333 in Amsterdam, the grower and maker received £16. For the ordinary wine, which by this time was coming from Stellenbosch, Paarl, Fransch hoek, Tulbagh and other vineyards, the price paid the grower and maker was about 24 rixdollars the leaguer, that is about £4 16s. gold. Much of this ordinary wine went to the pursers of ships calling at the Cape which had run short of the Spanish or Madeira normally carried; and also in exports to the Company's settlements in Batavia where, even though van Riebeck had apparently obtained some of his vines for trial, clearly no serious planting had been done.

As well as making a very nice profit on the Constantia sold in Europe, the Company got revenue from the Cape vineyards by putting an excise duty of one shilling and eightpence per leaguer on all the wine pressed in the colony, which, by the Assyrian or Egyptian standards of round about 1000 B.C., and by the standards of the British governments of our own time, was extremely reasonable and could hurt nobody. Moreover, a very valuable consolation, wine alone was freed of the tithe levied on all other crops to support the clergy in the comforts and luxuries which men of their condition are accustomed to. Other sources of wine revenue to the Company were licences sold to the retail wine-shops which became a feature of the colony's social life: this tax was yielding £5,000 gold per annum by mid-eighteenth century, and the licensees were restricted by law to a profit of not more than one hundred per cent.[10]

During the following hundred years no other South African vineyard became world-famous after the manner of the Groot and the Klein Constantia. But more and more were planted. It was the old story: reluctant vinearoons at first, South African farmers became increasingly attached to the vine, until eventually there were far too many vineyards, as there had been in Italy from late Roman republican times and in France from as early as about A.D. 1400. The wines produced were of every kind, but those best known were of the dessert variety—Cape Madeira and Cape Malaga, for example—and were perhaps slightly fortified rather than natural wines. But good natural wines, mostly named simply for the vine of their origin, were abundant also. Critics were not wanting to point out that good though the best South African wines might be, the ordinary wines were worse than they had been. Again, the old story: as quantity rose quality declined.

A 'General Return of Products', drawn up for the Dutch government in 1802, shows that the vine population had risen enormously since van Riebeck's first planting in 1652. At the Cape proper there were 863,000 vines planted; at Stellenbosch, which included at that time not only Stellenbosch itself but the vineyards of Caledon, Paarl, Malmesbury, Piquetberg, Tulbagh and Worcester, there were in all 907,300 vines growing. The vineyards were yielding an annual average of 5,784 leaguers of wine.

I should not trouble the reader with such figures, of little interest excepting to the rural economist, if there were not a special reason for doing so. When I was considering the progress of the vine as it colonized Europe in antiquity, as it overspread North Africa, as it crept outwards from ancient Armenia to engross all ancient Iranica, one could gain only the haziest idea of how long it took this plant to begin to exercise an important influence over the economic and social life of the communities in question. But South Africa would provide the historical economist with a means of measuring much more ancient cases by comparative study. For, and this is perhaps worth emphasizing, there was no significant progress in the arts of cultivating the vine and making its wine between about 1000 B.C. and the mid nineteenth century A.D.; or let us say, respecting the work of Mago the Carthaginian and his Italian emulators, that there had been some improvement in techniques and management about 250 B.C., although chiefly in details. In the planting, manuring, irrigation, pruning of vines; in the pressing of grapes; in the method of fermentation; in all that is comprehended in the word *cuvage*, the Cape of Good Hope vinearoon of A.D. 1800 knew neither more nor less than the Punic vinearoon at the other end of the same continent in 180 B.C., or than Columella could have taught him in the reign of Tiberius Caesar. His wine-press, indeed, might be a little more ingenious, with more blacksmith's work in it and less carpenter's work; but no considerable step forward was taken in viticulture proper until the work of Dr Jules Guyot was published in about 1850; or in oinology until the work of Louis Pasteur. And just as Mago's work had been translated for the benefit of Italian wine-growers in the second century B.C., so Guyot's work was to be translated and published not, indeed, in Cape Town, but in Melbourne (see below). Nor, until the hydraulic wine-press came into use, was there any significant change in that tool unless we go back to the revolution which replaced the giant 'tammy-cloth' of the Egyptians first with the lever-press and then with the screw-press as we know it. So that the Cape growers were developing their industry by very much the same means as the vinearoons of Campania in the century before and the century after the First Punic War, even to the extent of having labour which if not actually slave-labour, was probably quite as cheap. Dedicating relatively few hands and few acres to the vine, the Cape growers raised wine production from nil to 650,000 gallons a year in something over a century, creating a new industry, marginal in its demands on raw material and soil, worth £50,000 gold a year to their country.

As we have seen, the first initiative in establishing the vine in South Africa was taken by van Riebeck; and the first great impulse to expansion was given by van der Stel and by the arrival of French immigrants. The second great stimulus was also of French origin: the Napoleonic Wars caused further expansion of the vineyards in the Cape, until the vine was occupying as much territory as, and perhaps rather more than, could properly be afforded it.

Cut off from her ancient sources of wine by the fact of being at war with all Europe, Britain turned to the Cape. The Governor, Sir John Craddock, evidently nervous lest his constituents' product be found unworthy, appointed a Wine-Taster, on 25th December 1811, to ensure that the wines exported were only the good ones: this official was to make certain that all wine exported was sound and not less than eighteen months old. He had also to inspect the casks, either passing them as good, or condemning them as unsound or foul; when he condemned a cask he was to stamp it 'condemned'. Any grower trying to use foul or unsound casks for export of wine could be fined one hundred rixdollars; and if a grower tried to slip through a consignment in a cask which had already been condemned once, the fine might be five hundred rixdollars and six months in prison. There was apparently a good deal of trouble about casks, for official tables of correct sizes had to be published, and the number of imperial gallons to a cask fixed by law. The official Wine-Taster's office lasted until 1826, when it was abolished.

Britain's interest in Cape wine gave South African viticulture that final push which it needed to complete the conquest of the new territory of the vine.

In 1811 export of wine to Britain amounted to only sixty leaguers: it was all Cape Madeira; presumably the Constantia was still going to Amsterdam or it was being kept at home. Only one year later, in 1812, the figure rose to 2,281 leaguers, most of it 'Madeira' but some of it table wine. By 1815 the exports had risen to 3,647 leaguers. These four years of more or less enforced drinking of Cape wines had performed the useful office of teaching the English to like them; for the exports continued to rise and by 1824 the figure was 8,000 leaguers. However, the readiness with which wine-importers in England accepted Cape wines had a pernicious effect; after the abolition of the Wine-Taster's office growers began sending poor wines, immature wines, in short any kind of wine they happened to have in cask. The reputation of South African wines began to suffer; and in due course the damage done was so great that the good name which Cape wines had established was lost for a century, and was only re-established by a deliberate policy of withholding all wine from the English market for some years, while standards were raised and steps taken to ensure that the higher new standard was respected.

Thus the colonization of those parts of South Africa most suitable for viticulture, by the *cépages nobles* and other ancient and famous cultivated varieties of the vine, was completed in about two hundred years, between mid seventeenth and mid eighteenth century. Among its side-effects was one which probably not even the great van Riebeck had foreseen: the endowment of the vineyard regions with very beautiful houses. From Punic and Roman republican times, because large-scale viticulture attracted big capital and the proprietors of the great vineyards were often very rich men; and because, also, viticulture was a branch of commerce in which a gentleman could engage without social disgrace, vineyard owners were often men of taste; for these reasons villas and châteaux of great beauty were frequently associated with vineyard estates. Such was the case along the banks of the Garonne, the Loire and the Moselle, for example. It happened most fortunately that at the time when the vine was enriching its planters in South Africa, Dutch domestic architecture was at its superb zenith; thus the older vineyards of the country are blessed with houses as beautiful as any in Europe.

We come now to the last and most recent triumph of the vine; the conquest of the far southern part of the Southern Hemisphere. As a symbol of the completion of that conquest, and therefore of the conquest of the whole world, I have taken (see below) the publication in Melbourne in 1865 of a translation of Dr Jules Guyot's magisterial treatise on vitiviniculture. In that work Guyot put forward certain arguments in favour of vineyard planting which were of particular relevance and worth to the peoples of newly-colonized lands. He did not, of course, have them in mind: like most Frenchmen he was almost incapable of taking seriously any country beyond the French frontiers; and what he had in mind were the bad-lands of France itself, the wastelands of the Landes for example, and the naked chalk of Champagne. But it will be obvious from the passage quoted below, in the language of Guyot's Australian translator, that the arguments applied even better to the new lands overseas. Moreover, the passage would be worth quoting for the light which it throws on the economic influence of the vine in the past, on its power to people unpromising land with human beings as well as with its own kind by supporting far more of them (this is probably no longer true today) than the land it occupied could have fed if planted to bread grains or to grass.

'The raw products of poor soils, which realize the highest prices, are the best adapted for the development of any colony, because by the culture of such products the colonist is certain to ensure the cultivation of all the others. The capitalist, that powerful agent of progress, will not waste his means in furthering the cultivation of inferior products. He will soon discover that one acre of the Château-Lafitte or of the Clos-Vougeot, gives more wealth for the public than one hundred acres of poor wastes planted with a forest or turned into an ordinary farm. To speak more precisely, in poor soils the production of bread and meat will not create wealth, whereas wealth will always produce bread and meat . . .'[11]

Here two things must be pointed out: first, that the soils of Australia were not poor; but they were new—they had to be cleared and cleaned—so that the cost, for example in labour, made them 'poor' from the economic point of view for some years. The second thing is that what was true enough in 1860 is far from true a century later: the overwhelming rise in world population has entirely changed the picture; and it is probable that within one more century, bread and meat will have to be produced absolutely regardless of cost. The argument from capitalism, sound enough in 1860, is utterly unsound in a state of affairs where what matters is not profit in money per man-hour-machine-acre, but volume of food produced per man-hour-machine-acre. Guyot continues—and one must remember that we are reading him in Melbourne in 1865—'Never will the cultivation of corn or artificial prairies [pastures] . . . people the deserts . . . without a subsidy, and that subsidy can only be permanent for products of high cultivation such as the vine . . . which always realized a gross price from three to eight times as much as the products of farms of the same acreage . . .'[12]

What Guyot has in mind is to make the vine, with its high cash return, finance the growing of necessary but low-cash-return crops. He goes on to point out that in 1857 the average gross return on an acre of vineyard was £60, on an acre of wheat, £12. And, having cited more figures, he concludes: '. . . in the present circumstances the vine employs and gives food to from three to eight times the number of persons and affords, besides, net profits in the same proportion . . .'[13] In short, that the colonizing power of the vine was that much greater than the colonizing power of subsistence crops. Of course, the problem of enabling the Landes and other wastes to support a population was by no means the same as that of enabling Australia to do so. But there is a close parallel: for in both cases capital and a high income from it was needed, to finance the growing of necessities and the establishment of other cash or industrial crop cultivations. But above all, it was important for the new lands to attract and to support people as soon and as numerously as possible. And Guyot says: 'But to convince the most sceptical that it [that is, the advantage of the vineyard over the farm] is not an arithmetical paradox, it will be sufficient to ask him to compare the populations of the vine and farming districts. In the latter he will see immense plains, dotted here and there with small oases: in the former rich villages are crowded together in every valley.'[14] And he then goes on to show, again from figures in his notebooks, that, comparing labour costs, the vineyard is shown to be nourishing from five to eight times as many workers as the ordinary farm.

It was, however, simply a personal taste for the vine and wine, rather than such arguments as these, which led Captain Arthur Phillip, first Governor of New South Wales, to bring vine-cuttings with him among the tools and materials which he carried and landed in Australia in 1788. The cuttings had been taken at Rio de Janeiro and at the Cape; and they were planted, perhaps the very first European plants of all, at a place called Farm Cove after clearance of trees and undergrowth. The south-west of New South Wales is a part of the world famous among botanists for the richness of its flora, favoured by both warmth and high humidity. These conditions led to excessive growth of the vines with the usual consequence that the fruit was abundant and of poor quality, and the first wine made from it disappointing.

But in Captain Phillip we have another instance of the European's persistence in having his vineyard and his wine. In 1791 he shifted his vineyard to Parramatta, fifteen miles inland. There results were more promising, good enough to make the Governor ask London to send him out some expert help. Two French prisoners-of-war were sent; they seem to have been picked at random on the principle that all Frenchmen were vinearoons; Phillip's pair were nothing of the kind and did nothing to advance the career of the vine in Australia.

During the first decades of the settlement the colonists were pinned to the coast by their inability to make their way through and over the very wild country of the Blue Mountain range. But in 1813 three adventurous explorers, including a man named Gregory Blaxland, managed the crossing, and thus opened up the interior. Blaxland cut himself a farm out of the wild at what is now Ermington, on the Parramatta river, and there in 1816 he planted a vineyard. Six years later a quarter pipe of his wine was sent to London and there awarded a Silver Medal by the Society for the Encouragement of the Arts, Manufactures and Commerce (now the Royal Society of Arts); a subsequent consignment of three-and-a-half pipes received the Gold Ceres Medal. But one has a feeling in reading of these events that the awards were made for the initiative and skill of growing wine at all in the new colony, rather than in recognition of the quality of the wine.

Such were the pioneer-amateurs, the usual beginners, in Australian viticulture. The first man to approach the business in a professional spirit was one John Macarthur, revered by wool-men as the pioneer of the Merino sheep in New South Wales. Macarthur had had an appalling row with the Governor, Bligh of H.M.S. *Bounty* fame, and from 1809 to 1815 was unable to live in Australia at all owing to the implacable hostility of that extraordinary man. He spent the year of Waterloo in wandering about France, visiting vineyards and making notes on viticultural techniques, chiefly in Burgundy until he crossed into Switzerland and, at Montreux, met and talked with a Swiss farmer who had had experience of trying to plant the European vine in America. He then returned to France, moving slowly from vineyard to vineyard in the south. He was back in England in 1816 and sailed for Sydney with a cargo of French vine-cuttings with which he planted a vineyard about forty miles from Sydney, at Camden. He also took up and cleared twenty acres of land near Penrith on the western slopes of the Nepean river. They were planted to vines and in 1827 Australia had her first commercial vintage, twenty thousand gallons of wine.

But more important than the two first amateurs, and than Macarthur, to the establishment of healthy growth of viticulture in New South Wales, and ultimately in the other states, was a remarkable young man named James Busby. Busby was an original: vineyards have been planted and cultivated by free men, by Negro and Indian and native slaves, by debtor bondsmen, by female labour; Busby used orphans, but one should hasten to add that it was benevolently done. He went out from England in 1824 to be school-master at an orphanage of which, presumably, he became the principal, for he seems to have been in charge of it. It was at Cabramatta. In 1830 he planted his first vineyard in the Hunter valley and introduced viticulture into the orphanage curriculum. The idea was that the profits of viticulture should help to support the orphanage and should at the same time give the orphans a trade. This whole manifestation of nineteenth-century liberalism in the tradition of enlightened self-interest was successful, at least as far as the establishment of the vineyards was concerned; we hear no more of the orphans. Perhaps they all became rich vinearoons. By 1850 there were 760 acres of vines in the Hunter valley, certainly sufficient to give a livelihood to a couple of thousand men and their families. Busby, meanwhile, had pub-lished the first textbook on viticulture to appear in the Southern Hemisphere, and he had been back to Europe for better vines; both events belong to 1829/30.

Like Macarthur before him, he toured the French vineyards, whose owners were generous with help and advice; only in our own time have the French vine-growers been forced by the ferocity of modern life to try keeping their knowledge and their noble vines to themselves; in the past they gave plants and knowledge freely to the potential rivals who were establishing themselves in the new lands: and if modern French wine-growers have lost business to those of the Cape and Australia they must blame those of their ancestors who gave help to men like James Busby. At the request of the British government and with the help of the French, Busby collected twenty thousand cuttings of *cépages nobles*. (Today, the export of cuttings of these incomparable old vines is forbidden by law.) And at Montpellier he was given one cutting from each vine in the national collection of the best varieties of the world, three hundred and sixty-five vines from Persia, Arabia, Hungary and the rest of Europe. He returned to Australia in 1832, and there continued to plant vines and to bully and cajole other planters such as Macarthur and Blaxland to give away their own sur-plus cuttings to new settlers wishing to plant vineyards.

The establishment of viticulture in New South Wales was firmly assured by 1850, then. Busby, however, was no longer there to see the results of

his labour.  He was, as will appear, in New Zealand.  Some of the vines he
personally planted were still bearing grapes a century later.  His greatest
service to his country was, no doubt, that by his foresight he not only made
certain that sound methods should be used from the beginning by writing
and publishing his *The Culture of the Vine and Art of Wine-making*, but that
he ensured the high quality of the Australian *encépagement*: it was Busby
who was responsible for the fact that the Pinots (of Burgundy and Champagne) and the Shiraz vines were planted for red wines; and, for the whites,
the Sémillon, Ugni Blanc, Blanquette and Verdhelo.

In the following decades not only did viticulture expand swiftly in New
South Wales, it spread to all the other states, almost as soon as they were
founded, excepting only the climatically unsuitable Northern Territory.  It
was of small importance in Queensland and in Western Australia, but very
important in South Australia and Victoria.  Some idea of growth rate can
be obtained from the example of the vineyards planted by William Ryrie in
the Lilydale district thirty miles from Melbourne, in 1838; the few acres
first planted had expanded to one hundred by 1848, to three thousand twenty
years later.  This was owing to two Swiss immigrants, the brothers de
Castella, who bought Ryrie's vineyards and established two wineries on the
Burgundian model.  One of their neighbours, the Baron de Pury, was equally
successful.  The wines which became known as Lilydale Yerings were, for
about twenty years, between about 1890 and 1910, almost certainly among
the world's great vintages.  It is a thousand pities that the subtopian sprawl
of Melbourne, and the growth of the dairying industry, have since overwhelmed and exterminated vineyards which bade fair to rival those of the
Gironde and the Burgundian *côtes*.  As if butter and milk could not be
produced almost anywhere in the world, whereas the best wines . . . However, there it is.

The recruitment of vinearoons was much assisted by the Gold Rush of
the 'fifties.  Disappointed prospectors from all over the world turned to
wine-growing in the region of Ratherglen and generally in the state of
Victoria, when they had no luck at the diggings; important among these
were the Blampieds, brother and sister, teenagers from Lorraine who found
no gold but who established and succeeded with the St Peter's vineyards
between Ararat and Stawell.  There were others.  But there were also
French Protestant immigrants who came from the viticultural parts of

France and who were able to plant their vineyards and build their wineries *en pleine connaissance de cause*.

The most important of the Australian wine-states today is South Australia. Viticulture began there, about the city of Adelaide, in 1838. During the subsequent expansion when the vine colonized the suitable soils of the whole region, plantings—once again thanks to Busby's influence—were confined to *cépages nobles*. The principal varieties were Cabernet, from the Bordeaux region; Riesling, from the Rhineland; Malbec, Grenache and Carignan, also from the great French vineyards; Mataro and Verdhelo from Portugal; and the vine of Tokay in Hungary. The principal vineyard region is the Barossa valley, fifteen miles of admirable *côtes* with a variety of suitable soils. The immense population of vines is served by a people whose feeling for their trade goes back far beyond their century-and-a-half of Australian experience, for they derive in great part from Protestant immigrants who came to Australia from the viticultural but oppressively Catholic parts of Europe.

The vine's conquest of Australia took less than a century. Exports of wine began in 1854. They now exceed one-and-a-half million gallons a year. Their quality, although certainly high, is not as high as one might hope for; it seems clear that the Lilydale Yering wines proved beyond doubt that certain parts of Australia could produce great vintages, comparable with the wines of France's golden age. But this triumph has not been repeated. Why? There are self-evident reasons. The wine is being produced in great quantity and has to be up to a standard set, as it were, by the industry's advertising agents; that is to say, the grower and wine-maker have to produce a standard product in great quantity. The best wine has never been, and can never be, produced in that way. The methods described and perfected by Dr Jules Guyot in 1860 have not been and probably cannot be bettered, if what you aim to do is to produce great vintages. But, using those methods, you will rigorously limit the crop of grapes, you will pick the fruit almost berry by berry, you will vinify in quantities not exceeding fifty gallons at a time. In short, you will be confined to practices which preclude the production of vast quantities of a standardized product. And, of course, the Australian growers are perfectly right: they must live in their time; the times demand quantity production and standardized products. We can, however, hope that there are, or that there will be, small growers aiming to produce great wines, and that here and there in viticultural Australia wines equal to the great vintages of early Imperial Rome or Second Imperial France will be made.

The last province to be added to the commonwealth of viticulture was New Zealand. The first introduction of vines occurred in 1818 and the settler who made it was one Samuel Marsden whose cuttings came from New South Wales. Nothing much seems to be known about this. He was an amateur, planting on a merely domestic scale; a forerunner. Chronologically the second introduction was to South Island: French settlers at Akaroa either brought cuttings with them from France, or they obtained them when their ship called at one of the ports of New South Wales. Curiously enough, this introduction seems to have had no future. It should have done. Apart from other parts of the island, the foothills of the Southern Alps must provide soil, climate and site conditions suitable for the growth of fine wines, more suitable than the actual vineyards region which is, in fact, in North Island.

A brief digression on the use of vine-cuttings in our whole history of the vine's diffusion will not be out of place here. The spread of viticulture from prehistoric to modern times, from its ancient first home in western Asia to every suitable soil and climate in the world, has depended, to a considerable extent, on the long persistence of life in a short length of ripe vine-wood. Vine-cuttings, suitably packed, remain viable for six months and sometimes more, although at high temperatures they will begin to grow, without forming roots, in the packing. They survive long sea-voyages perfectly well. Of course, there were often great losses: for example, when in 1866 settlers in Queensland, Australia, decided to start a vineyard on the western slopes of the Darling Downs, near the town of Roma, they had to bring the cuttings as part of a wagon cargo drawn by oxen from Toowoomba. The distance is only two hundred miles; but it was over appalling country and the journey was made in conditions of blazing heat and drought; the oxen could make only between three and four miles a day, so the journey took two months. Only three hundred of the original thousand cuttings were still alive. But the importance of this persistence of life in vine-cuttings is not to be exaggerated: the alternative means of creating new vineyards was by seed. But this would, as has already been explained, have entailed the loss of the qualities of the old and proved varieties, and taking a very long chance indeed on getting a seedling as good.

The first effective introduction of the vine to New Zealand was due to the indefatigable James Busby (*plate 117*) who was sent there as British Resident in 1833. He planted vines in the Bay of Islands region where he had his headquarters. The vineyard is said to have been on a 'domestic' scale, but apparently he sold part of his wine to augment his income. The commercial vineyards of New Zealand are all in the same part of the country, so that it is clear that the sites were not chosen for suitability, but because Busby happened to be obliged to set up his home in the Bay of Islands. It is true that the climate of Auckland and Hakeos Bay and their surrounding country is comparable with that of some southern French vineyards; but winters are very mild, probably too mild, for the very best results.

The *encépagement* of New Zealand vineyards is, on the other hand, impeccable. There has recently been some planting of new hybrids.

As has been shown, one of the great improvements in viticulture between 5000 B.C. and our own time was the outcome of a book, of that part of Mago the Carthaginian's great treatise which dealt with the subject of wine-growing. There were, between the publication of that work in Latin and Greek after the Third Punic War, and the nineteenth century of our era, innumerable books published on the subject. But none which had such important effects until the publication of the treatise by Dr Jules Guyot in 1860. Guyot had already been recognized as both the boldest innovator and the soundest authority on the subject. I have quoted some of his economic arguments. But in his book he described the methods of pruning, protecting and manuring the vine, and the correct handling of the vintage, to which we probably owe the golden age of the clarets and sauternes which followed.

The publication of this treatise, in Marie's translation, in Melbourne in 1865, completed, with satisfying neatness, the conquest of the world by European man's most ancient partner in the diffusion of his civilization and manners. Since that event, the scientific study of the vine and its cultivation, the chemistry of wine, and the industrialization of the processes of the vintage have progressed. We understand more about the nature of *Vitis vinifera* and its wine than did Mago or Haraszthy or Guyot. But we cannot yet grow a better wine; nor, but by following their advice, one as good.

# EPILOGUE

'A NEW ENEMY OF THE VINE, worse than the Oidium, threatens to destroy the vineyards bordering the Rhône . . .'[1] This was the dramatic opening sentence of a report, submitted by three distinguished scientists to the French Académie des Sciences, in the year 1868. The Oidium they referred to was that Powdery Mildew of the vine which had arrived from America a decade earlier and had been checked by the discovery of a preventive treatment of the vines, based on sulphur. As for this new enemy, Messrs Bazille, Planchon and Sahut, the *rapporteurs* in question, were not yet sure what manner of creature it was, but their ignorance did not last long. It is curious, and aesthetically satisfying, that the first phylloxera attack on the vineyards occurred in the most ancient province of French viticulture, the Allobrogican; but this was not its first appearance in Europe; Britain had been the stepping-stone between the homeland of the new enemy in America and the great viticultural centres of the Old World. A vine-grower in Hammersmith, near London, sent some vine-leaves to the Oxford University botanist Professor I. O. Westwood in the summer of 1863; there was something wrong with them, they were covered with galls. Westwood discovered that the galls were formed by an aphid. Unfortunately, Westwood published nothing about the matter at the time, and it was not until 1869 that he wrote an account of this event in the *Gardener's Chronicle*.[2]

We have already noted in Chapter IX how it had proved impossible to establish the Old World vines in North America: planted time after time, they perished in almost every case. But it does not seem that any serious attempt was ever made to discover why this happened; or why, for example, no such difficulty was encountered in Mexico or in California. Until the middle of the nineteenth century the creature which had now appeared in Hammersmith and in Provence had contented itself with defending its home territory against the invading European vines, and with great success. Its invasion of Europe was almost certainly brought about by the importing of some American native vines (*plate VIII*), either as ornamentals, for their magnificent autumn foliage; or for the peculiar flavour of their grapes, 'foxiness' refined, in some cultivars, to the musky taste of such grapes as Framboise and the Strawberry Grape.

It is typical of politicians in general and of imperial politicians in particular that, faced with two enemies to the prosperity of their people, they attack the wrong one: thus, while the new pest of the vine was spreading with appalling swiftness through the French vineyards, Louis Napoleon turned against the far less dangerous Prussians, thereby making certain that France would be defeated both on the battlefield and in the vineyards. The latter of these two defeats was by far the more costly.

Planchon and Signoret succeeded in identifying the new enemy to the extent of referring it to a genus of aphids which had been named, by Fonscolombe, *Phylloxera*; it was subsequently given the appropriate specific name of *vastatrix*. Something must now be said about the nature of this devastator of the vineyards. In America it is parasitic on and has evolved with certain *Vites* which have developed a toughness of the rootbark. The root resists penetration by the aphis, which therefore confines its attention to the leaves, burrowing into them and forming galls. They do little harm and are tolerated by the vine and by vine-growers, who, until the fairly recent invention of systemic insecticides, had in any case no means of getting at a pest which was not in but under the leaf surfaces. There is no need to go into the complex details of the insect's life-cycle, which includes both parthenogenetic and sexual reproduction; but there is an autumn generation which descends to the root of the vines there to produce, in due course, the winged, sexed generation of the spring. On Old World vines the aphis found itself living on a plant with tender roots, which it could penetrate. On these roots the gall-forming substance secreted by the aphis caused open wounds, as a consequence of which the roots soon began to rot and the vines to die. In Europe, moreover, the aphis found immense, densely crowded populations of vines, that is to say conditions favouring its swifter and swifter increase. And the very fact that the roots these creatures were living on died, forced them to move on and find another host.

The speed with which the phylloxera spread throughout Europe, but particularly in France, is almost incredible: the creature made its first appearance in Hammersmith in 1863, in Provence in 1865. Twenty years later the French wine industry lay in ruins and thousands of wine-growing landowners, small peasants, large firms or great noblemen, had been brought to bankruptcy: 'The fantastic social change caused by the disease [*sic*] can be seen in the economic facts: out of 2·5 million hectares of vines, 1·5 million were destroyed by the insects. In 1875 83·6 million hectolitres of wine worth 545 million francs were produced; in 1889 only 23 million hectolitres worth 8 million francs were pressed. Vast sums were spent on importing wine— 545 million francs in 1887. Vineyards which sold at one time for 12,000 francs the hectare were making 600 francs as cornlands. Wages fell from 3 francs to 1·50 and distress and alarm grew everywhere . . .'[3]

The government was not inactive; they did what they could to stop the spread of phylloxera and to destroy it. Among the steps which they took to encourage scientific study of the problem was the false one of offering a large money prize for a cure, which brought in a large entry of worthless and often idiotic suggestions which scientific workers, who would have been better engaged on serious research, had to examine. Among the entries were remedies lifted from Pliny and such old wives' nonsense as watering the vines with wine. Not all the worthless suggestions came from fools and laymen; some put forward by men who should have known better show very clearly that the basic work, that of discovering the life-cycle of the insect, had simply not been done. Ordish (see Note 3) points out that Prosper de Lafitte's insistence that all one had to do was to destroy the over-wintering eggs of the phylloxera was nonsense since the adult insects were, in Europe, over-wintering in the roots. And that this did not prevent Lafitte from publishing a book on his idea, and thereby seriously holding-up the discovery of an effective remedy or control.

Two treatments suggested by science were reasonably effective in checking the aphis: flooding the vineyard, where that was physically possible; and injecting the soil in which the roots were growing with carbon bisulphide, which was extremely costly; it was, moreover, dangerous, especially when large traction-engine/steam-pumps were used for the work, for carbon bisulphide is very inflammable and the heavy gas which it gives off is explosive. And in those cases where this treatment did succeed, it was very soon followed by reinfection of the vineyard. Meanwhile some growers had, *la mort dans l'âme*, gone over to the planting of resistant American vines.

The correct solution to this tremendous problem was first suggested by M. Laliman to M. Cornu in 1875, but was not seriously taken up until at least a decade later: this was, of course, to graft the Old World vines, and particularly the *cépages nobles*, on to phylloxera-resistant American rootstocks. Cornu, while he accepted this, uttered a warning: if millions of American rootstocks were brought in and planted, it was very likely that with them would come *Plasmopara (Peronospora) viticola*, the Downy Mildew of the American *Vites*. He was right; that is what happened and it accounts for the fact that we now have to spray the vines with copper fungicides several times every summer. But it is not clear that, even had Cornu's warning been heeded, anything could have been done at that time to prevent this third disaster.

But by far the most curious aspect of this whole business of finding a remedy for the phylloxera devastation has never, as far as I am aware, been remarked on. The grafting method of coping with the problem was seriously adopted in the 'eighties and 'nineties.[4] This means that no less than three hundred and fifty years had passed since the Mexicans had started to graft European vines on to American rootstocks, following the Order in Council promulgated by Cortés in 1524 (see Chapter IX). For three-and-a-half centuries, then, the Mexicans had been experienced in this technique; yet the French, casting desperately and clamorously about for a remedy, seem never to have heard of this—and what is even more extraordinary, nor had the Spaniards, although the phylloxera was soon devastating Spanish vineyards, as it was Italian, German, Central European and eastern European vineyards. Furthermore, although the classic literature of viticulture was combed for remedies, not a soul seems to have noted that Roman vinearoons were accustomed to graft vines. Nor is that all: we have seen already that more than seventy years before the great phylloxera plague in France, M'Mahon was writing, in *The American Gardeners Callendar* (1808): 'I would suggest the idea of grafting some of the best European kinds on our most vigorous vines which no doubt would answer a very good purpose.' In short, the solution to the French problem, sought with millions of money and by thousands of workers, was overlooked though it lay ready to hand; and had to be rediscovered by Laliman and Cornu, greatly assisted by the readiness to help and the knowledge of phylloxera of the American entomologist C. V. Riley, who provided not only information, but rootstocks.

By the end of the nineteenth century the grafting of all vines planted in Europe had become standard practice excepting in those few places, with

very light, sandy soils, where the phylloxera cannot survive. And the viticultural, as distinct from oinological, consequences of the crisis are by no
means over. The French were very soon engaged in cross-breeding American *Vites* to produce rootstocks with different attributes; roots which would
tolerate chalk; roots which would tolerate heavy clays; roots with varying
geotropic angles for deep or for very shallow soils. As a result, a mere by-
product of what was, in the first place, a pest-control measure, the science of
viticulture has been carried, and is being carried, a stage beyond that attained
a century ago. Today's vine-planter can match plant to soil in a way which
was not possible in the last century; on strong soils he can use a 'starving'
stock, on weak ones a stock which is capable of exploiting them. But the
phylloxera crisis has given rise to an even more important advance.

As we have already seen, cross-breeding *viniferas* with American native
*Vites* had long since been initiated, with some success, in North America.
The French, later the Italians and Germans, now took it up with a new
object before them, a purpose of enormous economic importance. Certain
American vines had resistance to the phylloxera; others to the Downy, yet
others to the Powdery, Mildew. On the other hand, the Old World vines
had oinological qualities which the American vines could not match or even
approach. Would it not be possible, given time, to produce cultivars,
hybrids, with the quality of the best European vines, the *cépages nobles*; and
the resistance to phylloxera and to the two mildews equal to that of the
American vines? At least something approaching these results might be
attained. A great many professional and some amateur vinearoons set to
work, and in the century which has passed since the beginning of the crisis,
several thousand new vines have been bred, and some hundreds passed into
commerce. Not one of them attains the ideal which the breeders have before
them; but there is probably no reason why, in due course, and with a little
luck, this ideal should not be attained.

What has been accomplished? A number of *cépages* have been produced
which, while they possess higher resistance to phylloxera than the Old
World vine, cannot safely be planted on their own roots excepting in such
places as England where phylloxera has never established itself; but this is
no longer important because the use of special rootstocks has now so many
other purposes, for example the control of plant-vigour and of cropping
capacity, that it could not now be abandoned even if the phylloxera suddenly

vanished from the face of the earth.  These plants have, however, in varying degrees, great resistance to both mildews; so great, indeed, that with many of them it has been possible to abandon sulphur treatments entirely; and to reduce copper treatments to, perhaps, a single one in a normal season.  I myself grow a number of these hybrids, and from ten years' experience of their resistance, I have entirely given up fungicide spraying, although I have to maintain it on my *viniferas*.  Now this is of enormous importance; it reduces production costs by a very great sum.  But that is not all.  The best of these new vines are, oinologically, so good that only the conservatism and prejudice of both growers and market prevents them being recognized as *nobles*; several others are at least better, again oinologically, than many *vinifera* vines as producers of ordinary wine.  All of them, without exception, are more reliably regular producers than their *vinifera* parents.  Most of them, furthermore, have one quality, inherited from the American parents, which is possessed by no *vinifera*.  If in spring the young growth of *vinifera* vines be destroyed at the burgeoning stage by frost, which happens somewhere every year and everywhere in some years, then the entire crop is destroyed *in potentia*.  For although the vines burgeon again, and grow as usual, this second growth is fruitless for that season.  But the second growth of many of the new vines is fruitful, so that whatever happens the grower will have a crop, though a reduced one.

There is a very powerful resistance to the general planting of these new vines in France, Italy and elsewhere.  It is, in the first place, aesthetic: the aesthetes of wine claim that the wine of even the best of the hybrids is inferior to that of certain ancient noble varieties of *vinifera*; this is true; despite the fact that, in blind tests, the wines of hybrids are frequently placed top of the bill, it is true that the finest qualities of certain great wines are associated quite definitely with certain *cépages*.  But nobody is suggesting that we should no longer grow these great old vines; only that, for ordinary planting, the new vines should replace viniferas which have no such claims on our taste.  Secondly, the resistance is economic and of two kinds: first, that which comes from, for example, the purveyors of fungicides and spraying machinery, who see their livelihood vanishing; the copper and sulphur 'lobbies' are very powerful in French politics.  And second, that of growers who see, in the greater fruitfulness and regularity of bearing of the new vines, a threat to wine prices, already far too low.  But it must be said here that the interests opposing the new vines are particular; in the general interest, these vines must, in the long run, replace the old ones in all but the *grands crus* vineyards; for their cultivation must mean that we can get a larger quantity of wine from a smaller area of land; and, as the population of the world continues to rise, it is land which will be scarce.

This book, then, is being published at a moment of crisis in viticulture, a new point of departure; and if, a century hence, a new historian of the vine is forthcoming, he will have to include an account of the new era in viticulture, the era of the Eurasian-American hybrids which began when, a few years ago and in the teeth of fierce and unscrupulous opposition, the French government recommended the planting of one or two of the best hybrid cultivars; and issued certificates of toleration to certain, more numerous, others.

# NOTES

## I ORIGINS AND EARLY PRACTICE OF VITICULTURE

1 *Ampelocissus, Cissus, Tetrastigma* and *Vitis*.

2 All the *Euvites* have n=20 chromosomes and are inter-fertile. The *Muscadiniae* have n=90 chromosomes and will not cross with the *Euvites*. They are all native to the Gulf of Mexico region of North America.

3 *V. islandica, V. teutonica* of Iceland and Germany respectively; and *V. sequannensis* of France, with related species of the Lower Miocene epoch found, among other places, in the British Isles.

4 Labruscoid, from Labrusca. Some confusion arises from the use of this term. Specifically it refers only to a North American vine, as described in the Appendix, *V. labrusca*. Labruscoid means having the general character of *V. labrusca*. But in Latin the word means simply 'wild vine', with the result that scholars with no botany have often used the name to describe wild vines found growing in Europe. In fact, however, such wild vines are, of course, specimens of *V. vinifera*. They may be properly wild; or they may be vineyard escapes. This use of the name is incorrect.

5 See Levadoux, E., *La sélection et l'hybridation chez la vigne*, Montpellier 1951. See also Lattin, G., *Ueber der Ursprung und die Verbreitung der Reben*, Zuchter, August 1939.

6 *Vitis vinifera silvestris* Gmel.

7 Childe, V. Gordon, *What Happened in History*.

8 Levadoux, *op. cit.*
Friedberg, L., '*Notion comparée de fluctuations et de variation dans l'amélioration des plantes*', Ann. Agro., 1942.
Bustarret, J., '*Variété et variations*', Ann. Agro., 1944.

9 Levadoux, *op. cit.*

10 For an interesting experiment with the variety Sylvaner, clone Froelich, demonstrating M. Levadoux's argument, see Sartorius, O., '*Zur Rebenselektion unter besonder Berucksichtigung der Methodik und der Ziele auf Grund von 6–14 jahringen Beobachtungenen einem Klon*', Zeitschr. f. Pflanzenzuchtung, 1926–XII–31–74.

11. Levadoux, *op. cit.* Before coming to these, however, it will be as well to say something concerning certain modifications to the individual, or even to a

whole vineyard, which have an air of permanence but which are, in fact, ephemeral. Such changes are those induced by incurable disease, notably by a virus or virus complex present in the system of the vines. This is not the place for a discussion of this phenomenon; it is enough to say here that the changes in growing habit, in leaf and stem morphology, in quantity and quality of fruit, induced by the presence in the vine of a virus complex, and the symptoms of which are known to the French as *dégénérescence infectieuse*, are permanent only because the virus cannot be 'killed' without the death of the plant. The plant viruses are, apparently, like certain crystals, between the world of the living and the inanimate; they are complex molecules, which can be obtained as crystals; they alter the morphology and destroy the health of the plant by attacking and 'consuming' certain molecules in the substance of the plant, incorporating these in their own substance and thus multiplying their number. Nevertheless, this is a disease, due to an external cause, and could the virus be destroyed without destroying the plant, the latter would resume its normal habits and shape.

12 Bustarret, *op. cit.*

13 *Cep.* hence *cépage*, *encépagement*, etc. The word is used by the French to mean a single vine, and *cépage* to mean a variety of the vine. It is from the Greek *kepos*, a vine.

14 In *Progrès Agricole et Viticole*, 1925, 2, 322.

15 Almo, H. P., 'Bud mutation in the vinifera grape. II: *Sultanina gigas*', *Am. Soc. of Hort. Proc.*, 1935.

16 Sartorius, O., noted that in hot dry conditions a cloud of pollen is formed by the abrupt dehiscence of the pollen sacs. When conditions do not favour this method, the ripe pollen must simply fall and drift on to the stigmas. Some experiments to discover to what extent pollen was windborne seemed to show that it was not, or hardly at all. The fact remains that to some extent it must be, for a row of Muscat Hamburgh in the author's vineyard, with no visible pollen, set a full crop of fruit, being about four feet from a row of another variety with hermaphrodite flowers and therefore viable pollen. We have never observed bees or any other insects working among grape flowers, but the French viticulturist Millardet has recorded the frequent presence of *Dasytes griseus*, Kuster and *Scraptiafusea* Latr. on open vine flowers, without, however, claiming that they play the role of pollinators. On the other hand many vine flowers are fragrant and produce nectar, and Messieurs Burnat and Minot have recorded the working of a small, unidentified, hymenoptera among grape flowers, able to get beneath the cap of the flower at the stage when that is lifted to detach itself, and to collect pollen.

17 This does not appear to be borne out, at least in theory, by the genetic conditions, which are as follows: the female (pistilate)×male (stamenate) cross yields females 50 per cent and males 50 per cent. Occasional fertile male flowers, self-fertilized, yield 25 per cent females and 75 per cent males. It follows that the males are heterozygous MF and the female homozygous FF. Hermaphrodite plants, which are rare, are either homozygous HH or heterozygous HF, the homozygous plants deriving from the selfing or intercrossing of heterozygous individuals. The F×H yields F 25 and H 75. The H, HF selfing yields H(HF) 50, H(HH) 25 and F 25. H(HF) × M yields H(HF) 25, M 50 and F 25. The F ×H(HH) will yield all H(HF) since all the female gametes of the pistilate FF parent contain the gene F and all male gametes of the stamenate parent contain the gene H only, so that all the eggs must contain the pair HF. H(HH) × H(HF) also yields all H individuals, half of them homozygous and the other half heterozygous. Selfing of H(HH) yields all H(HH). H(HH) × M yields H 50 and M 50.

This scheme appears to me to favour a steady increase in the number of H vines and decrease in the number of F and M. This is, in fact, what has happened in the transformation of vines from wild to cultivated plants, but only by the deliberate interference of man, for in the wild state vines remain dioecious. The H gene arises, it seems, as an allelomorphic mutation of the M gene.

18 See A. M. Negrul, *The genetical basis of grape-breeding.* Leningrad, Institute of Applied Botany. Trans. Commonwealth Bureau of Agriculture, Cambridge. Also A. M. Negrul, '*Evolution of the Cultivated Forms of Grapes*', *Comptes rendus (Doklady) de l'Académie des Sciences de l'URSS*, 1938, vol. xviii, No. 8.

19 Negrul, *ibid.*

20 Negrul, *ibid.*

21 Negrul, *op. cit.*

22 Childe, V. Gordon, *What Happened in History.*

## II THE DRUNKEN GODS

1 Campbell Thompson, R., *Babylonia in the Days of Hammurabi*, Universal History of the World.

2 Gilgamesh Epic, Tablet X, 3.

3 Lutz, H. F., *Viticulture and Brewing in the Ancient Orient*, Leipzig, New York 1922.

4 Cylinder A, xxviii, 10–11.

5 Cylinder A, xviii, 23–24.

6 The theory that *ziggurats* were planted is dismissed by some authorities, including Henri Frankfurt, but their construction with drainage arrangements seems to show that they were in fact planted and the terraces irrigated, though by what means is no longer apparent.

7 Thurean-Dangin, *Huitième campagne de Sargon*.

8 Hommel, *Grundriss*, p. 280; Cylinder Bx. 3, cited by Lutz in *op. cit.*; de Rouge, *Rev. Arch.*, 1860, p. 297.

9 Lutz, *op. cit.*

10 Toy, *Critical and Evangelical Commentary on the Book of Proverbs*.

11 Lutz, *op. cit.*

12 Spiegelberg, *Hieratic Ostraka and Papyri*, Egyptian Research Account, 1898.

13 Spiegelberg, *ibid.* Ostraka nos. 140, 162, 248, 257, 259, 262, 291, 299.

III BACCHAE IN GREECE

1 *Iliad*, XVIII.

2 *Iliad*.

3 Diodorus Siculus, Book V.

4 *Ibid.*

5 It would be absurd to consider the play as history, of course, but in our context the point must be made that it is full of anachronisms.

6 Kerényi, C., *The Gods of the Greeks*, London 1960. See also Hehn, V., *The Wanderings of Plants and Animals*, London 1888.

7 Euripides, *The Bacchae*.

8 In our time the nearest equivalent to the Bacchic uproar is the kind of hysteria provided in crowds of teenage girls by, for instance, the Beatles.

9 Hehn, V., *The Wanderings of Plants and Animals*, London 1888.

10 Hehn, *op. cit.*

11 Hehn, *op. cit.*

12 Hesiod, *Works and Days*.

13 Hehn, *op. cit.*

14 Billiard, *La Vigne dans l'Antiquité*, Lyon 1913.

15 The interested reader is referred to: Hehn, V., *The Wanderings of Plants and Animals*, London 1888; Curtel, G., *La Vigne et le vin chez les Romains*, Paris 1903; Schrader, *Strachvergleichung und Vergeschichte*; Curtis, *Grundzuge der Griesischen Etymologie*; Weise, *Die Griesischen Woerden in Latein*.

16 *De causis plantarum*.

17 M. P. Cato, *De re rustica*, Rome 154 B.C.

18 Athenaeus.

19 M. P. Cato, *op. cit.*

20 Billiard, *op. cit.*

IV ITALY: JAM VINCTAE VITES . . .

1 Bloch, R., *The Etruscans*, London 1958.

2 Curtel, *La Vigne et le vin chez les Romains*, Paris 1903; Billiard, *La Vigne dans l'Antiquité*, Lyon 1913; Scullard, *Shorter Atlas of the Classical World*, London.

3 Hehn, V., *op. cit.*

4 Aulus-Gellius.

5 Bloch, R., *op. cit.*

6 Brea, Bernabo, *The Sicilians*, London.

7 Billiard, *op. cit.*

8 Besnier, M., *Les Catacombes de Rome*, Paris 1909.

9 'The idea of the god suffering and dying for the salvation of mankind and manifesting this salvation by his own resuscitation or rebirth—the very idea that was to become a reality in the Passion and Resurrection of Christ—pervades, needless to say, the closely interrelated mysteries of Dionysus and Orpheus. But it is significant—and a like aversion to the passional can be observed in Early Christian art—that neither the horrible death of Orpheus at the hands of the maenads nor the equally horrible death of Dionysus-Zagreus at the hands of the Titans seems to occur in funerary sculpture. . . . The belief in the powers of Dionysus was expressed in reliefs depicting the ecstasy of the Bacchic *thiasos*, the god's triumphal progress through the inhabited world, or his union and reunion with Ariadne—in short, in evocations of an overpowering joy remembered by the votaries of Dionysus as a transitory experience in life and accepted by them as a promise of unending felicity after death. . . .

'While, as I said, the passion of Dionysus—originally symbolic of the death and rebirth of nature in general and of the mysterious process by which the juice of the tortured grape is changed to wine in particular—is absent from Roman funerary monuments, it is presupposed and alluded to in a peculiar type of sarcophagus which imitates wine vats and thus suggests, in non-narrative form, both the identity of the god with the plant sacred to him and the identity of the votary with the god. The idea of expressing these two equations by assimilating the shape of the vessel destined to hold a dead body to that of the vessel destined to hold the juice of the grape goes very far back. As early as the fifth century B.C. (Pherecrates the Comedian) the Greek word for wine vat, *lenos*, was used as a synonym for sarcophagus, and sarcophagi resembling wine vats in shape (narrower at the bottom than at the top and rounded at the edges) were employed in Greece long before the Roman occupation. But these Greek specimens are cheap, inconspicuous vessels, mostly made of terracotta. Roman art transformed these modest *lenoi* into objects both precious and noble: the strigilated sarcophagi, fashioned of beautiful marble and reminiscent of their humble ancestry only in their tublike form and in the presence of open-mouthed lion heads that took the place of spouts and were originally the only figural element in the decoration.'

> (From Erwin Panofsky, *Tomb Sculpture*, London 1964, pp. 33–34.)

10 Mommsen, Theodor, *History of Rome.*

11 The introduction of wooden barrels is discussed in Chapter V.

12 Weber, *Dissertatio de agro et vino Falerno*, Marburg 1855.

13 Suetonius.

14 When Aurelian proposed to seize and plant with vines the thousands of acres abandoned by ruined farmers, and make the wine-dole a permanent institution, an indignant Praetorian Praefect exclaimed, 'Before we know where we are we shall have to start giving them chickens and geese!'

15 The *dot* or dowry of a vine plant is the stake and ties required to support it.

16 Curtel, Billiard, *op. cit.*; Pliny, *Natural History.*

17 Billiard, *op. cit.*

18 Fustel de Coulanges, Allen, cited by Billiard in *op. cit.*

19 Mosella. See Chapter V.

20 Negrul, *op. cit.*

21 Viala and Vermorel, *Ampelographie.*

22 Xenophon, *Oikonomikos.*

23 Ibn-al-Arwan, *Nabbataean Agriculture.*

24 Billiard, *op. cit.*

25 A special propitiatory rite, the *rubigalia*, was instituted by Numa against this affliction.

26 *Geoponica*: An anthology of ancient writings on agriculture made in the tenth century and dedicated to Constantine Porphyrogenitus.


V THE VINE'S GREAT NATION

1 Diodorus Siculus, *History.*

2 If a 'jar' of wine means here an *amphora* of 6 gallons, about 24 *sextarii*, it can hardly have been worth more than 60 sesterces, plus as much again for carriage. But even a raw slave can hardly have been worth less than 1,000 sesterces. The margin of profit was indeed enormous.

3 Cicero, *De republica*, 3.9.16.

4 The Allobroges had some wine on the Italian market, or at least in commerce, by about A.D. 60. Martial, in his *Epigrams*, calls their country '*vienna vitifera*'. The vine of their vineyards was the *allobrogica* of Pliny's *Natural History*. It was said to be of local origin and resistant to frost.

5 Dion, Roger, *Revue des Deux Mondes*, January 1954.

6 *Columella*, 1.20.

7 This edict caused consternation in Asia Minor and its enforcement there would have been ruinous. The rhetor Scopelianus of Clazomene was, according to Philostratus, sent to remonstrate with the emperor and obtained satisfaction. Suetonius hints that Domitian may have been frightened into withdrawing the edict by a pamphlet in circulation which contained this couplet:

> *Though you eat my very roots,*
> *Yet will I bear fruit enough to make the libation for Caesar's corpse.*

8 Dion, *op. cit.*

9 Delamare, *Traité de la police*, Paris.

10 The Allobroges (see Note 4 above) submitted to the Romans in 122 B.C. after defeat by a Consular army under Gnaeus Domitius Ahenobarbus. A year later their neighbours the Arvernii likewise made their submission after defeat at Vindalium near Avignon by the Consul Q. Fabius Maximus.

11 Quoted and translated from Dion, *op. cit.*

12 *Ibid.*

13 Ausonius, *Mosella*, Loeb.

14 Dion, *op. cit.*

15 *Gargantua*, XIII.

16 Hehn, *The Wandering of Plants and Animals*.

17 Pliny, *Natural History*.


VI THE EUROPEAN PERIPHERY

1 Diodorus Siculus, *History*.

2 Warner Allen, H., *Port and Sherry*, London 1960.

3 Strabo, *Geography*.

4 Seltman, *Wine in the Ancient World*.

5 Warner Allen, H., *A History of Wine*.

6 It would be possible to show—see for instance Slicher van Bath in *op. cit.* below —the acreage under vines in Europe at any given time until about 1900 as a function of the price of bread grains.

7 The basis for this statement is a passage in Eusebius.

8 See Chapter III.

9 On whose authority, together with that of Jornandes II following Dio Chrysostomus, this story rests.

10 Reported by Jornandes II.

11 Hehn, *op. cit.*

12 Tacitus, *Agricola*.

13 Bede, *Ecclesiastical History of the English People*, c. A.D. 734.

14 This is not, of course, the earliest case: the Belgae were importing wine from Italy through Gaul in the first century B.C. It is impossible to be sure how old the trade was at the time of Caesar's invasion—perhaps a century. Saxon imports at Frisian hands, and on their own account, were perhaps much more considerable.

15 Aelfric's *Colloquy* quoted by Wilson, D. M., in *The Anglo-Saxons*, Ancient Peoples and Places series, Thames and Hudson, London 1960.

16 Wilson, *op. cit.*

17 A source of confusion is the fact that the word *amphora* was used as a measure of wine long after the vessel itself had ceased to be used.

18 See, for example, the case of Mexico in Chapter IX.

19 Wilkins, *Leges Anglo-Saxonicae*, London 1721.

20 For an idea of the yield see Chapter IV. A low figure would be 300 gallons of wine per acre.

21 William of Malmesbury, *De Pontificum Anglorum*. Billiard, in *op. cit.*, Chapter IV, anticipates the surprise of his French readers at the very idea of wine being grown in England and points out that their own country was formerly regarded by Italian experts as too wet and cold for wine-growing.

22 See also for descriptions of viticulture at this time: Alexander Neckham in *De naturis rerum*. These may have been based on what he saw about Dunstable of whose grammar school he was headmaster in the twelfth century. But he was a cosmopolitan and a Sorbonnien, and one cannot be sure that his notices of wine-growing were of English origin.

23 Of the Ely vineyards see Rhode, E. S., *The Story of the Garden*:

> *Quatuor sunt Eliae: Lanterna, Capilla, Meorial,*
> *Et Molendinum, nec con claus vinea vintum.*

24 But one cannot consider Barnabe Googe's *Foure Bookes of Good Husbandrie* reliable as a source of information about English viticulture for they are an uncritical translation of the work of Conrad Heresbach.

25 Rose, John, *The English Vineyard Vindicated*, London 1666, with an Introduction by John Evelyn signed 'Philocepos'.

26 Comparing values of mean monthly bright sunshine hours:

| Place | April | May | June | July | August | September | October |
|---|---|---|---|---|---|---|---|
| Rhine Valley | 166 | 200 | 225 | 249 | 223 | 174 | 115 |
| Douglas, Isle of Man | 176 | 203 | 215 | 193 | 172 | 152 | 100 |
| Eastbourne | 181 | 239 | 237 | 236 | 223 | 177 | 121 |
| Torquay | 181 | 214 | 236 | 227 | 207 | 164 | 116 |

Comparing mean monthly temperatures (to nearest degree F.):

| Place | April | May | June | July | August | September | October |
|---|---|---|---|---|---|---|---|
| Rhine Valley | 47 | 55 | 60 | 64 | 63 | 57 | 49 |
| Eastbourne | 47 | 53 | 58 | 61 | 59 | 52 | 50 |
| Torquay | 48 | 53 | 58 | 62 | 61 | 58 | 52 |

It will be seen that there is not much in it; other places in Britain are roughly comparable with the above. Carefully chosen sites give higher temperatures, of course.

27 Slicher van Bath, *The Agrarian History of Western Europe, A.D. 500–1850*, London 1963.

28 Backhaus, A., *Entericklung der Landwirtschaft auf den graflich Stolberg-Wernigerodischen Domanen*, 1888.

29 Slicher van Bath, *op. cit.*

30 Any reader wishing to go into this in detail will find the following helpful in some aspects:

Hausen, Karl R., *Nach den Quellen ausgearbeitete Darstellung des Weinbaues und des mit einheimischen Weinen getriebenen inund ausländischen Handels in den Marken Brandenburgs, von 1173, bis auf die gegenwärtige Zeit*, Berlin 1798.

Anon, *Versuch einer 100 jährigen Weinfechsungsgeschichte Osterreichs von 1700–1800*, Vienna 1803.

Anon, *Mittheilungen aus der ältern und neuern Geschichte über den Weinbau am Rhein, der Mosel, Nahe, etc.*, Mannheim 1826.

Gok, Carl Friedrich von, *Über den Weinbau am Bodensee, an dem oberen Neckar und der Schwabischen Alp, mit einigen hierauf sich beziehenden geschichtlichen und statistischen Notizen*. 8. Stuttgart 1834. Ex: *Correspondenzblatt des Wurttembergischen landwirtschaftlichen* (Veneins), Kohler.

Carlowitz, Georg Heinrich von, *Versuch einer Kulturgeschichte des Weinbaues, von der Urzeit bis auf unsere Zeiten, mit besonderer Beziehung auf das Konigreich Sachsen*. 8. Engelmann, Leipzig 1846.

Hoffmann, Karl Julius, *Gedrangte Darstellung der Kulturgeschichte, Chronologie und Statistik des Weinbaues im Konigreich*, Sachsen, etc., 12. Meissen 1853. Mosche.

Gatterer, Christian W. J., *Literatur des Weinbaus aller Nationen, von den*

*altesten bis auf die neuesten Zeiten, nebst Kritiken und den wichtigsten literarischen
Nachweisen.* 8. Osswald, Heidelberg 1832.

Thienemann, *Weinwissenschaft. 1. Abtheilung: Literatur,* Leipzig 1839.

31 Russel, C. J., *British Medieval Population,* 1948.

Britton, C. E., *A Meteorological Chronology to A.D. 1450,* Meteorological Office, 1937.

32 Slicher van Bath, *op. cit.*

33 *Ibid.,* citing Labrousse, C. F., Vilar, P. and Enjalbert, H.


VII THE ABODE OF ISLAM

1 Diodorus Siculus, *History,* Book I.

2 *Ibid.*

3 Anon., *The Periplus of the Erythraean Sea,* ed. W. H. Schaff, New York 1912.

4 Theophrastus, *History of Plants.*

5 Lyall, Sir C., *The Diwans of 'Abad ibn el-Abras,* Leyden 1913.

6 Columella, *De re rustica.*

7 Strabo, *Geography.*

8 Herodotus, *History.*

9 Jackson in *Grundriss der Iranische Philologie,* Vol. II.

10 Laufer, B., *Sino-Iranica.*

11 Heyd, W., *Histoire du Commerce du Levant au Moyen Age,* Amsterdam 1959.

12 Heyd, *op. cit.*

13 Schulz, *Höfisches Leben.*

14 Heyd, *op. cit.*


VIII THE FAR EAST: DIONYSUS REJECTED

1 Neumann, *Die Hellenen in Scythenland.*

2 Heyd, W., *Histoire du Commerce du Levant au Moyen Age,* Amsterdam 1959.

3 Laufer's refutation of Bretschneider and Hirth, who had canonized Chan K'ien as saint of agriculture, is convincing. It will be found in his *Sino-Iranica,* Chicago 1919.

4 Laufer, *op. cit.*

5 *T'ai p'iu hwan yü ki.*

6 Laufer, *op. cit.*

7 Laufer, *op. cit.*

8 Laufer, *op. cit.*

9 *Yün-nan ki.*

10 Reinaud, M., *Relations des voyages faits par les Arabes et les Persans dans l'Inde et la Chine.*

11 *T'an hui yao.*

12 *T'oung Pao*, 1914, p. 412.

13 Spiegel, in *Arische Periode.*

14 Umemura, *Inosokuk-wai-no-sokubutsu-si.*

15 Nagao, Tsuchiya, *New Approach to Viticulture.*

## IX TRIUMPH AND DISASTER: NORTH AMERICA

1 Prescott, *Conquest of Mexico.*

2 Cavo, Andres, *Historia de Mexico*, Mexico City 1949. The edition is that of Fr. F. J. Burrus, S.J.

3 *Paraque cada Navia traiga cierta cantidad de Plantas y que no puedo salir sin ellas, porque sera mucha causa para la poblacion y perpetuacion de ella.* Lorenzana in *Historia de Nueva España.*

4 *Item, que cualquier vecino que tubiere Indios de repartimiento sea obligado a poner en ellos en cada un año con cada cien Indios de los que tuvieren de repartimiento mil sarmientos aunque sean de la planta de su tierra, escogiendo la mejor que pudiese hallar. Ordenanzas municipales.* Unpublished manuscript quoted by Prescott in *op. cit.* It will be found in *Ordenanzas del Anno 1524 Arch. del Excmo.* Duque de terranova y Monteleone, Hospital de Jesus, Mexico.

5 In a personal communication to the author.

6 Burrus (ed.), *Kino Reports to Headquarters*, Rome 1954. The texts are in Spanish with a translation into English by the editor. The Father Marquino referred to by Kino was the head of the Jesuit Mission on the opposite, Mexican, shore of the Gulf of California.

7 Piccolo, Father F. M., S.J., *Informe del estado de la nueva cristiandad de California*, Madrid 1962.

8 See Chapter IV.

9 Negrul, *op. cit.*

10 Hedrick, U. P., *A History of Horticulture in America.* The same admirable author's *Vines of New York* and other works have been repeatedly referred to in what follows.

11 Hyams, E., *The Grapevine in England*, London.

12 Hedrick, *op. cit.*

13 Dankaerts. J., and Sluyter, P., *Journal of a Voyage to New York*, New York 1867.

14 In Hedrick, *op. cit.* and elsewhere.

15 *Ibid.*

16 Salley, A. S., *Narratives of Early Carolina, 1655–1708*, New York 1911.

17 Wilson, S., *An Account of the Province of Carolina*, London 1682.

18 Quoted by Hedrick, *op. cit.*

19 Speechley, W., *A Treatise on the Vine or Grape-tree*, York 1790.

20 Dufour, J. J., *The Vine-dresser's Guide.*

21 Vallejo, G., *The Century Magazine*, 1891.

22 Quoted by V. P. Carosso in *The California Wine Industry*, University of California Press.

23 It may well have been this vine which was already famous by the 1830s. Matthew Keller, in *Grapes and Wines of California*, writing at that time: 'A poor woman in the adjoining country . . . has but one vine. It bore last year 5,000 bunches of beautiful grapes weighing over one pound each, yielding her the handsome sum of $400. When a girl, and leaving Monterey to remove to her present home, she picked up a vine cutting to drive her mule. The cutting she planted upon her arrival, and after the lapse of seventy years such is the result.' If this good lady was of mule-driving age seventy years before the record, vines were not the only creatures to flourish in that country.

24 Hedrick, *op. cit.*


X THE VINE IN THE SOUTHERN HEMISPHERE

1 Hyams, E., and Ordish, G., *The Last of the Incas*, London and New York 1963.

2 de la Vega Inca, Garcilaso, *Commentatios Reales.*

3 The student of the subject is referred to Suarez, L., in *Contribucion a los estudios ampelograficos en la Provincia de Mendoza*, Mendoza 1912. There is no copy of this rare work in Britain, but a copy is to be found in the Library of Congress, Washington, D.C.

4 Molina, *Compendio de la historia del Reino de Chile*, 1782.

5 In a personal communication, *Associacion Nacional de Viticoltores.*

6 A typical vine of Academician Negrul's subprol. *orientalis.*

7 Dampier, W., *A Voyage round the World*, London 1697, and later editions.

8 Perrold, A. I., *The Wine Book of South Africa*, Stellenbosch 1936.

9 *Ibid.*

10 Allamand and Klockner, *Nieuweste en Beknopte Beschryving van der Kaap de Goed Hoop*, Amsterdam 1778. And also Mentzel, O. F., *Beschreibung des Vorgebirges der Guten Hoffnung*, Glagau 1787.

11 Guyot, Dr J., *The Culture of the Vine and Wine-making*, in a translation by L. Marie, Melbourne 1865.

12 *Ibid.*

13 *Ibid.*

14 *Ibid.*


EPILOGUE

1 Bazille, G., Planchon, J. E., and Sahut, F., '*Sur une maladie de la vigne actuelle-ment regnante en Provence*', Transactions of the Académie des Sciences, XXXVII, pp. 333 and 589, 1868.

2 Westwood, I. O., *The Gardener's Chronicle and Agricultural Gazette*, January 30, 1869, p. 109.

3 Ordish, G., 'The Phylloxera Story', *Land*, Spring 1963.

4 The following table is from Ordish, *ibid.*:

| Year | Thousands of hectares of vineyards treated | | | American roots |
|------|---------|-------------------|----------------------|----------------|
|      | *Flooded* | *Carbon bisulphide* | *Pot. sulpho-carbonate* | |
| 1880 | 8 | 6 | 1 | 6 |
| 1881 | 8 | 16 | 3 | 9 |
| 1882 | 13 | 17 | 3 | 17 |
| 1883 | 18 | 23 | 3 | 28 |
| 1884 | 23 | 33 | 6 | 53 |
| 1885 | 24 | 41 | 5 | 75 |
| 1886 | 24 | 47 | 4 | 111 |
| 1887 | not available | not available | not available | 166 |
| 1888 | 33 | 68 | 8 | 215 |
| 1889 | 30 | 58 | 9 | 300 |
| 1890 | 33 | 62 | 9 | 436 |
|      |   |   |   | 1,416 |

# APPENDIX

THE VITACEAE

THIS FAMILY OF PLANTS is described as follows: leaves various, mostly alternate, simple or compound. Flowers many and small, greenish and inconspicuous, variously clustered unisexual and bisexual, four- or five-merous, in some genera provided with a prominent disc about the ovary; the calyx entire or minutely toothed. Petals, either separately expanding or falling together as a cap. Stamens, usually four or five opposite the petals. Ovary superior with two or more cells with, as a rule, two axile ovules in each. One or no style. The fruit is a small berry.

There were formerly ten genera:

*Ampelocissus*, now included in *Vitis*.

*Ampelopsis*, with about twenty species, native to central and northern Asia and North America.

*Cayratia*, now included in *Vitis*.

*Cissus*, with about two hundred species, many of them tropical.

*Columella*, with about sixteen species, Asiatic and Australasian.

*Leea*, about sixty species, all tropical.

*Parthenocissus*, ten species native to North America, China and Japan.

*Pterisanthes*, four species, all tropical.

*Tetra stigma*, forty species.

*Vitis*, about sixty species.

There would be no point in giving here descriptions of those species of *Vitis* which are of no economic importance whatever, although some of those omitted may have a place in gardens as ornamentals, or in breeding programmes. Of all the species, one is overwhelmingly the most important, the vine of history:

*Vitis vinifera, Linnaeus*: a deciduous climber growing to fifty feet or more, sometimes much more where support is found; young shoots sometimes glabrous, sometimes cobwebby. Leaves usually from three to six inches wide and long; they are three- or five-lobed and coarsely toothed. When deeply lobed the sinus between the lobes is rounded and almost or quite closed by overlapping the upper part of the lobes. Upper surfaces glabrous or sometimes downy on the veins; lower surface often more or less downy and sometimes felted. The stalk is more than half as long as the blade of the leaf. Berries oval, black, with blue bloom. In the cultivars morphological variation is far greater, of course, than anything which can be covered by a general description. This species is native to southern and south-eastern Europe and south-west Asia certainly; and possibly to North Africa. Its cultivars are counted in hundreds, perhaps thousands.

*Vitis aestivalis, Michaux*: a vigorous deciduous climber probably to over one hundred feet. Native to the central and eastern United States. Branchlets round, glabrous or loosely downy. Leaves from four to twelve inches long and wide, varying from almost entire to three- or five-lobed, the lobes being toothed, the teeth broad and shallow. The base of the leaf is heart-shaped. Glabrous on the upper face, the lower face covered with red-brown floss. Flowers paniculate, the panicles being as much as ten inches long. Berries black with blue bloom. Cultivated since the seventeenth century by, among others, George Washington, the species is the progenitor of several cultivars.

*Vitis amurensis, Ruprecht*: a vigorous, deciduous vine which looks rather like *V. vinifera*. The young growth is red, the leaves from four to eight inches wide and long, with five deeply divided lobes. The leaves are downy on the lower surface. In autumn, as with American vines, the foliage turns red or purple. This native of the Amur valley, also found in northern Korea and China, has hitherto been of no economic importance. But it is now being used as a parent of hybrid vines intended for Siberian vineyards, and it may become of the utmost importance. Some of these hybrids, tried in England, have proved to be exceptionally early.

*Vitis arizonica, Engelm.*: native of west Texas, northern Mexico, Arizona and Lower California. A low, shrubby, scandent plant with angled branchlets, short internodes and very thick diaphragms. Young growth white, tomentose, leaves broadly ovate, two to four inches wide, rarely longer, Hardly, if at all, lobed, but when it is there are only three lobes, toothed with short mucronate teeth, cobwebby when young, later glabrous. The slender stalked flower panicle is short and broad. The berries are black with a blue bloom, and palatable. This may have been one of the vines used as rootstocks for Spanish cultivars as early as 1524.

*Vitis berlandieri, Planchon* (syn. *V. baileyana, Muns.*): native to Texas and Mexico, and another of the vines which may have been used by the Spanish colonists as rootstocks for their own cultivars, this is a vigorous deciduous climber to sixty feet or more. Much ramified; short internodes. Leaves ovate to orbicular-ovate, two to five inches long, cordate, toothed with small teeth, more or less distinctly three-lobed. Bright green above; greyish-green and more or less pubescent, chiefly on the veins, below. The densely packed panicles are up to four inches long. Berries black, without bloom, or very slightly bloomy. This vine was taken into cultivation late in the nineteenth century and is now of the greatest economic importance as a parent or type of rootstocks for European and other vineyards, and of new hybrid wine and table grapes.

*Vitis cinerea, Engelm.*: native to Illinois, Kansas, Texas, Mexico and northern Florida. Probably cultivated in the eighteenth century; its wild harvest was commonly gathered in the seventeenth. Its vernacular name is Sweet Winter Grape. It is a vigorous climber, with greyish-tomentose young branches and thick diaphragms. The broadly ovate leaves are from three to eight inches long and wide, three-lobed and toothed with short, broad teeth, the apex drawn out to a point. Dull, dark green above, but grey with cobwebby pubescence on the lower surface. The irregular panicle can be as much as a foot long and the berries are relatively large, sometimes a half-inch in diameter, black, with some bloom. The grapes are said to become sweet only after frost. This is a parent of some rootstocks.

*Vitis candicans, Engelm.*: native of Oklahoma, Arkansas and Texas. Of economic importance as a parent of rootstocks and of some new hybrid wine-vines. Vernacular name: Mustang Grape. Source of wild harvest in the seventeenth and eighteenth centuries. Cultivated at least since 1860. A strong and high-climbing deciduous plant with white-tomentose young shoots and very thick diaphragms. Leaves broad-ovate to ovate-reniform, two-and-a-half to five inches broad, are hardly lobed on ordinary shoots, but quite distinctly five-lobed on very vigorous shoots, shallowly toothed. White-tomentose on both faces when young, at maturity the leaves are bright green above, white, woolly tomentose on the lower surface, and the three-inch petiole is also white woolly. The large fruit, up to an inch in diameter, is purple, with a tough skin and a very foxy taste.

*Vitis cordifolia, Lam.* (syn. *V. vulpina, L.*): the Frost Grape; sometimes also known as the Fox Grape. Used in the breeding of rootstocks, it has been dropped from the breeding programme of hybrid wine-grape growers owing to the dominance of its very powerful 'fox' or musty taste. It is a very strong climber, capable of attaining a diameter of two feet through the main stem at ground level. The broadly ovate leaves are from three to six inches long, not so wide. They are cordate with a long, narrow sinus, very indistinctly lobed or not lobed but coarsely serrate with acute teeth. The under side of the leaves is pubescent excepting on the veins; otherwise glabrous. Panicles up to a foot long. Berries round, half-inch across, black. Native to Pennsylvania, Florida, East Kansas and Texas. In cultivation at least since 1806, probably earlier.

*Vitis labrusca, Linn.*: native to New England, parts of Canada, and south to

Indiana. This was probably the first American vine to be seen by Europeans (see the *Saga of Wineland the Good*) in *c.* A.D. 1001. It has long been important as the type or parent of many cultivars; and was formerly important in the breeding of hybrid wine-vines, but has largely been dropped by European breeders owing to its extremely 'foxy' taste, which is a dominant. But several of its offspring have importance in the market for table grapes, *e.g.* Framboise, Strawberry Grape, Isabella, and others; and others for vineyard planting in Canada. It is illegal to plant its hybrids in European vineyards. The species is a very strong and high-climbing vine with either inflorescences or tendrils at every joint. Leaves orbicular-ovate or broad-ovate. (Bailey, in *Vines of New York*, says cordate-ovate to deltoid-ovate.) Three to eight inches wide, basal sinus open, three-lobed, shallowly toothed, dark green above, tomentose beneath. Panicles up to four inches or more. Berries rather large, black with a thick skin. It is a pity that Linnaeus used the name *labrusca* for this vine, since the same name had long been in use to describe wild vines in Europe and North Africa, often vineyard escapes; such vines are, in fact, viniferas. *V. labrusca* is not one of the most resistant to phylloxera, and is no longer used in breeding root-stocks. Bailey classified the cultivars of this species, some of which have grizzly-red or grizzly-white or white grapes, as *V. labruscana*.

*Vitis monticola, Buckl.*: the Sweet Mountain Grape of south-west Texas, cultivated since about 1887, and used as a rootstock or parent in breeding rootstocks; also, later, in breeding hybrid wine-vines. It is a slender vine growing to about thirty feet. The young growth is either floccose or glabrous, angled and having thin diaphragms. The leaves are reniform, up to five inches across but usually about three inches, and have a rounded or truncate basal sinus. Coarsely toothed and indistinctly three-lobed, dark and lustrous green above, usually pubescent on the under side. The short, broad panicle may be six inches across, the berries small, black or purple.

*Vitis riparia, Michx.*: Michigan, New York and Indiana. Cultivated since not later than 1828. Of the first importance in the selection, or hybridization, of root-stocks, especially in France. A vigorous, high-climbing vine with glabrous young growth and thin diaphragms. Broadly ovate or ovate leaves up to eight inches long, mostly smaller, three-lobed with short acuminate lobes, and coarsely toothed with broad, acuminate teeth. Lustrous, bright green but pubescent on the veins on both surfaces. Panicles up to eight inches, with fragrant flowers. Berries small, round, purple, bloomy. A parent of some good new hybrid wine-vines.

*Vitis rotundifolia, Michx.*: vernacular, *Muscadine*; the best-known cultivar of this species is the Scuppernong Grape. It is native to Delaware, northern Florida,

Kansas and Texas. First recorded cultivation 1806, but probably it was cultivated earlier. It is a tremendously vigorous plant growing to at least one hundred feet and widely ramified; individual plants are on record as covering two acres of ground. It has close, lenticillate bark which occasionally produces aerial roots. No diaphragms. Leaves sub-orbicular or broadly ovate two to five inches wide, acute or acuminate and with a shallow basal sinus; coarsely toothed with triangular teeth, lustrous above, yellowish and slightly pubescent on veins on the under side. Panicle small and densely packed. Fruit round and quite large, dull purple and without bloom. It does not seem to have been of much importance either as a rootstock or scion parent, possibly because of the musty taste of the fruit.

*Vitis rupestris, Sceele*: the Bush Grape. Native to southern Pennsylvania, Tennessee, Missouri, Oklahoma and south-west Texas. In cultivation since mid-nineteenth century. Of the first importance as a rootstock parent and has also been used in the breeding of new wine-grapes. It is unlike other *Vites* in being an only lightly scandent shrub, not a climber, having few or no tendrils. Rarely exceeds six feet. Diaphragms thin. Leaves reniform to orbicular-ovate and from three to four inches wide, slightly three-lobed, coarsely toothed, with a very wide basal sinus making the leaf shorter than it is wide. Lustrous and slightly glaucescent above; glabrous on the under side excepting for slight pubescence on the veins of young leaves. Panicle slender and up to four inches long. Fruit purple, somewhat glaucous, about half-inch across, of good flavour.

There are other American vines in cultivation and some are probably in use in breeding programmes. But the above are probably all the *Vites* which have, hitherto, played a part in viticulture.

# LIST OF ILLUSTRATIONS

## COLOUR PLATES

## MONOCHROME PLATES

Plates 123–6 obtained through the assistance of Mr Edward Bishop (Greenlys Public-Relations Ltd), Mr A. J. Ludbrook, the Wine and Brandy Producers' Association of New South Wales, and the Wine and Brandy Producers' Association of Victoria.

# INDEX

*Numbers in italic are plate numbers*